Critical Essays on
DONALD BARTHELME

CRITICAL ESSAYS
ON
AMERICAN LITERATURE

James Nagel, General Editor
Northeastern University

Critical Essays on
DONALD BARTHELME

edited by

RICHARD F. PATTESON

G. K. Hall & Co./New York
Maxwell Macmillan Canada/Toronto
Maxwell Macmillan International/New York Oxford Singapore Sydney

G. K. Hall & Co.   Maxwell Macmillan Canada, Inc.
Macmillan Publishing Company   1200 Eglinton Avenue East
866 Third Avenue   Suite 200
New York, NY 10022   Don Mills, Ontario M3C 3N11

Macmillan Publishing Company is part of the Maxwell Communication
Group of Companies.

Library of Congress Cataloging-in-Publication Data

Critical essays on Donald Barthelme / edited by Richard F. Patteson.
    p.   cm.—(Critical essays on American literature)
   Includes bibliographical references and index.
   ISBN 0-8161-7305-2 (alk. paper)
   1. Barthelme, Donald—Criticism and interpretation.   I. Series.
PS3552.A76Z65   1992
813'.54—dc20   91-26302
                                       CIP

---

10 9 8 7 6 5 4 3 2 1

The paper used in this publication meets the minimum requirements of
American National Standard for Information Sciences—Permanence of
Paper for Printed Library Materials, ANSI Z39.48-1984. ⊚™

Printed in the United States of America

In memory of
Donald Barthelme

Contents

◆

ESSAYS

General Editor's Note

◆

This series seeks to anthologize the most important criticism on a wide variety of topics and writers in American literature. Our readers will find in various volumes not only a generous selection of reprinted articles and reviews, but original essays, bibliographies, manuscript sections, and other materials brought to public attention for the first time. This volume, *Critical Essays on Donald Barthelme,* is the most comprehensive collection of essays ever published on this contemporary American writer. It contains both a sizeable gathering of early reviews and a broad selection of more modern scholarship as well. Among the authors of reprinted articles and reviews are John Barth, John W. Aldridge, Elizabeth Jolley, Morris Dickstein, David Gates, and Larry McCaffery. In addition to a substantial introduction by Richard F. Patteson, there are also five original essays commissioned specifically for publication in this volume, new studies by Mary Robertson, Wayne B. Stengel, Richard Walsh, Michael Trussler, and Patrick O'Donnell. We are confident that this book will make a permanent and significant contribution to the study of American literature.

JAMES NAGEL

Northeastern University

Publisher's Note

◆

Producing a volume that contains both newly commissioned and reprinted material presents the publisher with the challenge of balancing the desire to achieve stylistic consistency with the need to preserve the integrity of works first published elsewhere. In the Critical Essays series, essays commissioned especially for a particular volume are edited to be consistent with G. K. Hall's house style; reprinted essays appear in the style in which they were first published, with only typographical errors corrected. Consequently, shifts in style from one essay to another are the result of our efforts to be faithful to each text as it was originally published.

Acknowledgments

♦

I would like to thank collectively the authors of all the essays that appear in this volume as well as the editors and publishers who kindly granted permission to reprint the ones that had been previously published. In addition, particular thanks go to Linda Hutcheon, Alan Wilde, Don Graham, and Tony Tanner for steering me in the direction of people who were willing to write new essays for this collection. Lastly, I must express gratitude to Tammy Bowling for her typing and computer skills, and to Martha Irby and the interlibrary loan office of the Mississippi State University Library, without whose assistance a project like this would not have been possible.

—RICHARD F. PATTESON

Thinking Man's Minimalist:
Honoring Barthelme

John Barth

The proper work of the critic is praise, and that which cannot be praised should be surrounded with a tasteful, well-thought-out silence."

This is to praise the excellent American writer Donald Barthelme, who, in a 1981 *Paris Review* interview, cited in passing that arguable proposition (by the music critic Peter Yates).

Donald worked *hard* on that anything-but-spontaneous interview—as wise, articulate and entertaining a specimen as can be found in the *Paris Review*'s long, ongoing series of shoptalks. He worked hard on all his printed utterance, to make it worth his and our whiles. His untimely death in July at the age of 58, like the untimely death of Raymond Carver just last summer at 50, leaves our literature—leaves Literature—bereft, wham-bang, of two splendid practitioners at the peak of their powers.

Polar opposites in some obvious respects (Carver's home-grown, blue-collar realism and programmatic unsophistication, Barthelme's urbane and urban semi-Surrealism), they shared an axis of rigorous literary craftsman-ship, a preoccupation with the particulars of, shall we say, post-Eisenhower American life, and a late-modern conviction, felt to the bone, that less is more. For Carver, as for Jorge Luis Borges, the step from terse lyric poetry to terse short stories was temerity enough; neither, to my knowledge, ever attempted a novel. Barthelme was among us a bit longer than Carver and published three spare, fine specimens of that genre—all brilliant, affecting, entertaining and more deep than thick—but the short story was his long suit. Without underrating either Carver's intellectuality or Barthelme's emo-tional range, we nevertheless associate Raymond with reticent viscerality and may consider Donald the thinking man's—and woman's—Minimalist. Op-posing stars they became, in recent years, for hundreds of apprentice writers in and out of our plenteous university writing programs; one has sometimes to remind student writers that there are expansive easts and wests in their literary heritage as well as those two magnetic poles.

His writing is not the only excellent thing that Donald Barthelme

Reprinted from the *New York Times Book Review*, 3 September 1989, 9. Copyright © 1989 by *The New York Times* Company. Reprinted by permission.

leaves those who knew him personally or professionally. He was by all accounts a first-rate literary coach (most recently at the University of Houston), a conscientious literary citizen much involved with such organizations as PEN, and a gracious friend. But his fiction is our longest-lasting souvenir and the one that matters most to those of us who knew him mainly, if not only, as dedicated readers.

"We like books that have a lot of *dreck* in them," remarks one of the urban dwarfs in Barthelme's first novel, "Snow White"; and included in that novel's midpoint questionnaire for the reader is the item, "Is there too much *blague* in the narration? Not enough *blague*?" In fact the novel is *blague*-free, like all of Donald Barthelme's writing. Not enough to say that he didn't waste words; neither did extravagant Rabelais or apparently rambling Laurence Sterne. Donald barely *indulged* words—he valued them too much for that—and this rhetorical short leash makes his occasional lyric flights all the more exhilarating, like the sound of Hokie Mokie's trombone in Donald's short story, "The King of Jazz":

> You mean that sound that sounds like the cutting edge of life? That sounds like polar bears crossing Arctic ice pans? That sounds like a herd of muskox in full flight? That sounds like male walruses diving to the bottom of the sea? That sounds like fumaroles smoking on the slopes of Mt. Katmai? That sounds like the wild turkey walking through the deep, soft forest? That sounds like beavers chewing trees in an Appalachian marsh? That sounds like an oyster fungus growing on an aspen trunk? That sounds like a mule deer wandering a montane of the Sierra Nevada? That sounds like prairie dogs kissing? That sounds like witchgrass tumbling or a river meandering? That sounds like manatees munching seaweed at Cape Sable? That sounds like coatimundis moving in packs across the face of Arkansas? That sounds like—

More characteristic is the dispatch with which he ends "Snow White": a series of chapter-titles to which it would have been *de trop* to add the chapters themselves.

THE FAILURE OF SNOW WHITE'S ARSE

REVIRGINIZATION OF SNOW WHITE

APOTHEOSIS OF SNOW WHITE

SNOW WHITE RISES INTO THE SKY

THE HEROES DEPART IN SEARCH OF A NEW PRINCIPLE

HEIGH-HO

And at his tersest, with a single comma he can constrict your heart: "I visited the child's nursery school, once."

Bright as is his accomplishment in it, the genre of the novel, even the half-inch novel, must have been basically uncongenial to a narrative imagination not only agoraphobic by disposition but less inclined to dramaturgy than to the tactful elaboration of bravura ground-metaphors, such as those suggested by his novels' titles: *Snow White, The Dead Father, Paradise.* His natural narrative space was the short story, if *story* is the right word for those often plotless marvels of which he published some seven volumes over 20 years, from *Come Back, Dr. Caligari* in 1964 to *Overnight to Many Distant Cities* in 1983. (Most of the stories first appeared in the *New Yorker*; five dozen of the best are collected in *Sixty Stories,* published by Putnam in 1981.) These constitute his major literary accomplishment, and an extraordinary accomplishment it is, in quality and in consistency.

Is there really any "early Donald Barthelme"? Like Mozart and Kafka, he seems to have been born full-grown. One remarks some minor lengthening and shortening of his literary sideburns over the decades: The sportive, more or less Surreal, high-60s graphics, for example, tend to disappear after "City Life" (1970), and while he never forsook what Borges calls "that element of irrealism indispensable to art," there is a slight shift toward the realistic, even the personal, in such later stories as "Visitors" and "Affection" (in *Overnight to Many Distant Cities*). But a Donald Barthelme story from any of his too-few decades remains recognizable from its opening line:

> "Hubert gave Charles and Irene a nice baby for Christmas."
>
> "The death of God left the angels in a strange position."
>
> "When Captain Blood goes to sea, he locks the doors and windows of his house on Cow Island personally."

I have heard Donald referred to as essentially a writer of the American 1960's. It may be true that his alloy of irrealism and its opposite is more evocative of that fermentatious decade, when European formalism had its belated flowering in North American writing, than of the relatively conservative decades since. But his literary precursors antedate the century, not to mention its 60's, and are mostly non-American. "How come you write the way you do?" a Johns Hopkins apprentice writer once asked him. "Because Samuel Beckett already wrote the way *he* did," Barthelme replied. He then produced for the seminar his "short list": five books he recommended to the attention of aspiring American fiction writers. No doubt the list changed from time to time; just then it consisted of Rabelais's *Gargantua and Pantagruel,* Laurence Sterne's *Tristram Shandy,* the stories of Heinrich von Kleist, Flaubert's *Bouvard and Pecuchet* and Flann O'Brien's *At Swim-Two-Birds*—a fair sample of the kind of nonlinear narration, sportive form and cohabitation of radical fantasy with quotidian detail that mark his own fiction. He readily admired other, more "traditional" writers, but it is from the likes of these that he felt his genealogical descent.

Similarly, though he tsked at the critical tendency to group certain writers against certain others "as if we were football teams"—praising these as the true "postcontemporaries" or whatever, and consigning those to some outer darkness of the passé—he freely acknowledged his admiration for such of his "teammates," in those critics' view, as Robert Coover, Stanley Elkin, William Gaddis, William Gass, John Hawkes, Thomas Pynchon and Kurt Vonnegut, among others. A few springs ago, he and his wife, Marion, presided over a memorable Greenwich Village dinner party for most of these and their companions (together with his agent, Lynn Nesbit, whom Donald called "the mother of postmodernism"). In 1988, on the occasion of John Hawkes's academic retirement, Robert Coover impresarioed a more formal reunion of that team, complete with readings and symposia, at Brown University. Donald's throat cancer had by then already announced itself—another, elsewhere, would be the death of him—but he gave one more of his perfectly antitheatrical virtuoso readings.

How different from one another those above-mentioned teammates are! Indeed, other than their nationality and gender, their common inclination to some degree of irrealism and to the foregrounding of form and language, and the circumstance of their having appeared on the literary scene in the 1960's or thereabouts, it is not easy to see why their names should be so frequently linked (or why Grace Paley's, for example, is not regularly included in that all-male lineup). But if they constitute a team, it has no consistently brighter star than the one just lost.

Except for readers who require a new literary movement with each new network television season, the product of Donald Barthelme's imagination and artistry is an ongoing delight that we had looked forward to decades more of. Readers in the century to come (assuming etc.) will surely likewise prize that product—for its wonderful humor and wry pathos, for the cultural-historical interest its rich specificity will duly acquire, and—most of all, I hope and trust—for its superb verbal art.

Introduction

◆

RICHARD F. PATTESON

It is difficult to keep the public interested,"[1] laments the narrator of "The Flight of Pigeons from the Palace." During twenty-five years as America's most innovative creator of short fiction, Donald Barthelme found himself repeatedly reshaping fictional form, not just to interest and entertain the public (although that was a fortunate result), but to fulfill an imaginative writer's highest calling—to reinvent the world. At the time of his death in the summer of 1989, Barthelme had published eight short story collections, four novels, an award-winning children's book, and an illustrated narrative somewhat in the manner of Max Ernst.[2] Born in Philadelphia when his father was a student at the University of Pennsylvania's School of Architecture, Barthelme grew up in Houston. After attending the University of Houston and serving in the army, he worked as a reporter and later as the editor of *Location,* an avant-garde magazine produced in New York. Barthelme's long-standing preoccupation with the relationships among literature, graphic art, architecture, and music began to become more than casual at this time, and in 1963, immediately after moving to New York, he published his first story.[3] It is no coincidence that Barthelme's career parallels almost exactly his long residence in New York. His sense of the urban—the sights, sounds, gestures, words, pleasures, and anxieties of city life—is unsurpassed among writers of his generation. Barthelme's stories and novels reflect his erudition and wide-ranging interests as well as his reportorial powers of observation. There is perhaps no other body of contemporary fiction that so powerfully evokes the sheer, bewildering multiplicity of life in the late twentieth century.

I

Although Donald Barthelme is widely credited with having opened up the American short story to new formal and stylistic possibilities, it is a curious fact that for the last several years of his career, critical interest in his work declined somewhat. Despite the publication of four books on Barthelme since

1980, there have not been nearly as many evaluations of his work in scholarly journals as there were in the 1970s. This relative waning of enthusiasm is only one of several problematical elements that bedevil an attempt to put Barthelme's canon into perspective. From the beginning, his fiction has stimulated differences of opinion. There have always been those critics who feel uncomfortable with postmodernism generally or who oppose formal experimentation on principle. There have been those, as well, who fault Barthelme for not taking his experimenting seriously enough—for merely playing with narrative techniques. Even among the staunchest Barthelme partisans, dissension and lack of consensus are in evidence to an unusual degree. Some claim flatly that his early work was his best, while others (a distinct minority) find in his later stories and *Paradise* a greater warmth and more direct engagement with emotion. Similarly, while most critics sympathetic to Barthelme maintain that he is no master of longer narrative forms,[4] all of his first three novels have their ardent defenders. And, finally, there is disagreement over whether the "realistic" or "metafictional" strains in Barthelme constitute his best work.

This last issue cuts very close to the heart of the matter and is indeed a question to which Barthelme critics, both proponents and detractors, frequently return. Many agree with Larry McCaffery's view that Barthelme's strength lies in "the inward, metafictional quality of his writing, the way he uses his fiction to explore the nature of storytelling and the resources left to language and the fiction-maker."[5] Alan Wilde, on the other hand, while conceding that "elements of metafictional theory and practice are to be found throughout his work," finds Barthelme's fiction "stubbornly referential, acknowledging the pressures of the world it questions."[6] McCaffery's and Wilde's approaches are not really very far apart; their differences are largely those of emphasis. More radical are those who go beyond Wilde's conception of Barthelme as a "midfictionist" and see him as a realist writing out of a modern or even premodern tradition. These readers tend to prize *Paradise,* which is relatively conventional in terms of technique, above *Snow White* or *The Dead Father.* Their favorite stories are those like "Critique de la Vie Quotidienne" and "Bishop," which subordinate technical innovation to descriptive engagement with the familiar and the routine—what Jerome Klinkowitz calls "social mimesis."[7] Many of these stories are very good, but they do not accurately represent the main thrust of Barthelme's career, nor would they alone have earned him his legion of imitators.

It might be wise to insert a few words here on differing notions as to the nature of "realism" in Barthelme's work, since many critics (like Mary Robertson, in this volume) tend to argue that even the metafictional impulse is "realistic" in its own peculiar way. "Barthelme has managed," William Gass asserts, "to place himself in the center of modern consciousness. Nothing surrealist about him, his dislocations are real, his material quite actual."[8] Gass seems to be saying that Barthelme's dislocations are real because dislocation is a primary characteristic of reality. Richard Schickel is more specific about the link between Barthelme's technique and what Gass calls the "actual": "We perceive in fragments, live in fragments, are no doubt dying by fragments; should we not, then, write in fragments, emphasizing thereby the strange disjunctions, the even stranger juxtapositions, that are part of the everyday experience of modern life?" Schickel, referring to Barthelme's hyperbolic statement that collage is "the central principle of all art in the twentieth century in all media," finds that collage is so important "because a brain-damaged society cannot 'get things together' any more tightly, rationally than the collage implies."[9] Dislocations, as Gass says, are "real."

Richard Gilman, in one of the earliest extended treatments of Barthelme's fiction, delineates the features of that reality in some detail: "In the most summary way this new reality—which exists inextricably entangled with half a dozen others of varying ages—can be described as being open-ended, provisional, characterized by suspended judgments, by disbelief in hierarchies, by mistrust of solutions, denouements, completions. . . . It is also a reality harboring a radical mistrust of language, writing, fiction, the imagination."[10] If Gilman's is an orthodox postmodernist position, so is its corollary: as our conception of the real changes, fiction, to be truly "realistic," must change also. Two points here are particularly pertinent to Barthelme's work—the provisional or suspensive quality of life (and therefore art), and the importance of language both as an untrustworthy medium and as an object of analysis and contemplation in itself.

In a discussion of one of Barthelme's cleverest stories, "The Glass Mountain," R. E. Johnson comments upon the relationship between language and "realism" in Barthelme's fiction. While the narrator of the story climbs the glass mountain to "disenchant" an enchanted symbol on top, people on the ground below (presumably refugees from one of those earlier realities mentioned by Gilman) shout highly mimetic, down-to-earth obscenities at him. Johnson's remarks focus on the tension between the narrator's imaginative endeavor and the observers' hackneyed verbal utterances: "The narrator's materialistic acquaintances can 'be relied upon to deal with' the conventional. Realism, for the climber and his author, has nothing to do with naturalism or materialism. It is rather an insistence on the priority of the imagination as it realizes itself in language forms which are both old and new because they are at once creative and decreative."[11]

The creative and decreative uses of language by Barthelme, and his simultaneous exploitation and undermining of conventional narrative forms, arguably constitute the most fundamental source of his brand of "realism." But to speak of that realism *exclusively* in terms of semiotic systems is to slight much of the human vitality and colorful concreteness (however fragmentary) that make the inspired lunacy of his world so instantly recognizable. In the words of Francis Gillen, Barthelme's importance also lies in his "exploration of the full impact of mass-media pop culture on the consciousness of the individual who is so bombarded by canned happenings, sensations, reactions, and general noise that he can no longer distinguish the self from the surroundings."[12]

Many of the issues touched on above stamp Barthelme as a writer working in the now rather firmly established postmodernist movement, and his affinity with that movement has been recounted by a number of critics. Their frequent references to parody, borrowing, and the mixing of styles are perhaps the most obvious sign of Barthelme's postmodernism. As Robert Con Davis demonstrates in his Lacanian analysis of *The Dead Father,* the postmodernist writer has an extremely complicated relationship to his cultural past. A recent cartoon in *Harper's* depicted a breakfast cereal, "Postmodern Toasties," which advertised, "Like everything you've had before, all mixed up."[13] One of Barthelme's own characters, paraphrasing Wittgenstein, puts it this way: " 'The world is everything that was formerly the case.' "[14] Certainly the variety of narrative methods, styles, postures, voices, and genres Barthelme employs is impressive. But there are other predominantly postmodern features in Barthelme's fiction, too, including a reduction of emphasis on the growth of character, the abandonment of conventional forms of mimesis, a pronounced tendency toward playfulness, and a foregrounding of concern with creative process.

Larry McCaffery makes the point that in Barthelme, "an openness to process at the expense of finished products should lie at the center of our experience."[15] In a similar vein, John Leland observes that "Barthelme uncovers for us the play of signification rather than offering us its products for consumption."[16] And Lois Gordon concurs, citing "the shape of meaning" that Barthelme evokes, "rather than fixed or final meaning."[17] The primacy of the provisional, the processive, the incomplete, or the suspensive (as Alan Wilde calls it) over the fixed, final, whole, certain, or dogmatic is an important aspect of Barthelme's work. Thomas M. Leitch, in a persuasive essay included in this volume, suggests that it is the most important. Barthelme's fiction is antiteleological, Leitch maintains, in the "double sense of shunning commitment to any particular plot development and even to any particular informing idea of attitude."

Of course the abolition of *telos,* with the concomitant abolition of centrality, is not Donald Barthelme's invention. In *The Crying of Lot 49,* for example, Oedipa Maas is haunted by the relationship, if there is one, between her "compiled memories of clues, announcements, intimations" and "the central truth itself"[18]—if there is one; and the novel ends, if it can be said to have an end, after a mock-romantic quest, with Oedipa still waiting for an answer and the reader still held in postmodernist suspension. Gerald Graff, tracing the origins of this pervasive characteristic of postmodern literature, finds it rooted in an erosion of authority that predated even modernism. As Ortega y Gasset explained, art was expected by many in the nineteenth century to provide compensation for the decline of religion and the apparent relativism of science, but when the foundations of religion and science were shaken, art could no longer "lay claim to any final authority" either. Any "order or pattern of meaning," Graff continues, "which must be invented by human consciousness out of its own inner substance or structure . . . is necessarily uncertain of its authority."[19]

Barthelme's artistic response to this "crisis of authority"[20] is clearly a key to understanding his work. Lois Gordon insists that Barthelme "rejects centrism of any sort—character, dialogue, event. . . ."[21] Betty Flowers goes a bit further: "The reader can find neither the center of Barthelme's world nor even Barthelme himself. Not only is there no central vocabulary, no central point of view, but the fictive entity of the author himself is inconsistent. . . ."[22] Specific instances of "centerlessness" in Barthelme are not difficult to locate. There is the problem of determining the sequence of events in stories like "Will You Tell Me?" or even in *Snow White*. There is the problem of determining narrative voice in *Snow White*. Much of the story seems to be told from the perspective of the dwarfs, but the voice belongs neither to a single, identifiable dwarf nor to all of them collectively. And there is the related problem of simply determining a rhetorical center of gravity in many of the stories, as in this previously mentioned passage from "The Glass Mountain":

8. I was 200 feet up.
9. The wind was bitter.
10. My acquaintances had gathered at the bottom of the mountain to offer encouragement.
11. "Shithead."
12. "Asshole."[23]

Is the reader being let in, by an otherwise invisible implied author, on information that the narrator himself does not have (that the words of "encouragement" coming from far below are really obscenities)? Or does the narrator know what his acquaintances are saying and facetiously call it encouragement? The text offers no solution. This is a small question, but it mirrors countless others that beg vainly for answers throughout Barthelme's fiction. The stories are just *there,* dazzling in their virtuosity, but without the teleological bias or authorially imposed centralities of more traditional narratives. It is left to the reader either to establish a center and hypothesize an answer, or to accept the absence of a center and follow Barthelme's open-ended play of signification.

Charles Molesworth is right on target when he concludes that "the very absence of a central philosophical, historical, or metaphysical given . . .

makes Barthelme an important if not a major writer."[24] In many ways Barthelme's work is a fiction of absences. The absence of the kind of center that Molesworth, Gordon, Leitch, and others discuss manifests itself concretely in the stories as absent princes, fathers, husbands, heroes, and other authority figures (even bartenders), as well as systems of belief. In *Snow White* the desire for a hero is expressed a number of times. Snow White herself complains, "There is something wrong with all those people standing there, gaping and gawking. And with all those who did not come up and at least *try* to climb up. To fill the role. And with the very world itself, for not being able to supply the correct ending to the story."[25] Paul, as the questionnaire at the end of Part One helpfully informs us, is "the prince-figure,"[26] but not, as it turns out, a prince. The prince exists in the novel only as that which is anticipated. Readers of such postmodern texts as *Waiting for Godot, Jealousy,* and *The Crying of Lot 49* will recognize that in *Snow White,* too, the waiting is the important part. The narrative is a refraction of a world in suspension, with neither a beginning nor an end.[27]

At one point in the novel, Snow White sits in her room sulking, reading the very teleological Teilhard de Chardin, and wishing she were, as Chardin imagined himself to be, in a more centered universe. She reflects: "The seven of them only add up to the equivalent of about two *real men,* as we knew them from the films and from our childhood, when there were giants on the earth."[28] Barthelme's treatment of the time "when there were giants on the earth" can be rather complicated. Robert Con Davis points up many subtleties and ambiguities in Barthelme's stance toward a "paternal image" that is "always the past." If, as Davis attests, "how it deals with tradition gives post-modern fiction its identity," *The Dead Father,* with a father who "is dead only in a sense,"[29] can be seen as Barthelme's most suggestive book, the definitive meditation on the anxiety of influence. The refusal either wholly to reject or wholly to embrace tradition is one of the most encompassing aspects of postmodern suspensiveness. In "A Shower of Gold" the sculptor Peterson's dealer counsels rejection of the authority of the past: " 'You read too much in the history of art. It estranges you from those possibilities for authentic selfhood that inhere in the present century.' " Later, appearing on the quiz show *Who Am I?* Peterson seems to shun that advice, declaring, " 'My mother was a royal virgin . . . and my father a shower of gold.' " And Barthelme ends the story on a characteristically equivocal note: "Peterson went on and on and although he was, in a sense, lying, in a sense he was not."[30] In Barthelme, disenchantment of the traditional is almost always accompanied by nostalgia for it, as in the brilliantly realized story that begins, "At the Tolstoy Museum we sat and wept."[31]

The absence of the authoritative and the centripetal probably accounts for many of the problems Barthelme's detractors have with his fiction as well as for the difficulties his admirers have in agreeing about various facets of his work, but it also serves as the philosophical basis for his technique: the astonishing array of subjects, styles, and strategies that marks his originality. Barthelme's stories are filled with characters attempting to cope with that centerless world, where every manner of frustration, anxiety, and confusion seems to stand in the way of a fulfilling and creative life. Many of them, like Peterson, are artists, and nearly every Barthelme critic has remarked on the importance in his work of art and the imagination as methods of confronting a debased, seemingly purposeless reality. The powers of imagination in Barthelme's world are not as formidable, however, as they at least appeared to be in the days of Yeats and Joyce. Even Nabokov's author as omnipotent conjurer is nowhere to be found. Barthelme's magicians, as David Gates establishes in his essay on *The Slightly Irregular Fire Engine,* are only partially effective. In a world in which any authority is purely immanent and humanly constructed, not transcendent or "received," the artist's role is necessarily circumscribed; his victories, if they occur at all, are tentative and provisional. Lee Upton, in a perceptive analysis of Barthelme's artists, argues that when they fail, they do so "because their work is . . . dependent upon absences."[32]

Most of Barthelme's characters, however, are just ordinary people like the denizens of his next to last book, *Sam's Bar.* Subtitled *An American Landscape, Sam's Bar* is an illustrated narrative that takes place one night in a New York City watering hole. Sam is absent; no one knows where he is, although there is much speculation. Each of the forty regulars sits at the bar, and most speak a few lines of very funny, extraordinarily sharp dialogue. All are seated facing the assistant bartender, Chuck, who is pictured only at the beginning of the book. In nearly all of the frames the reader is placed behind the bar, looking directly at each character. Barthelme and his collaborator, illustrator Seymour Chwast, put the reader into the book—at precisely the location where Sam, the presumptive center of it all, should be, listening to the customers. This device alone says a good deal about how postmodern literature at its best is supposed to work, with the reader as an active participant in the creative process. Jerome Klinkowitz has commented that Barthelme "shows us things we may have forgotten,"[33] and one of the exchanges in *Sam's Bar* brings that notion to life. Adolf, the grounds maintenance man, mentions that he has seen Sam's picture in *People* magazine, and Hope, the secretary, asks why it was there. Adolf doesn't know, but Hope will not let the matter drop: "You didn't read what it says under the picture?" Adolf's response, "For what?," leads to the obvious reply: "It tells you what's in the picture."[34] That's it, exactly. Beneath the satire of people who read only to acquire the most peripheral, often useless, information (or who, like Adolf, skip the captions altogether), Barthelme's Hope is unwittingly telling us why we really should read, and especially why we should read writers like Donald Barthelme: to see things we may have forgotten; to look at the world as it is; to find out what's in the picture.

II

Even a summary overview of selected Barthelme criticism is made difficult by the fact that critical reaction to his work does not follow a clear trajectory: it does not evolve from one widely held set of positions or attitudes to another.[35] The most specific statement that can be safely made on the subject is that the response to Barthelme's fiction has always been strongly positive, but that there have been dissenters from the very beginning. Most of the basic stances toward Barthelme, and most of the arguments about him, have shown up in the book reviews. Marvin Mudrick, reviewing both *Come Back, Dr. Caligari* (1964) and *Snow White* (1967), calls the first book "an engaging collection of casual comic experiments, strictly from college humor" and says the second "promotes . . . self-indulgence."[36] John Aldridge, in a more thoughtful look at *Caligari* and *Unspeakable Practices, Unnatural Acts* (1968), finds that some of Barthelme's stories "demonstrate the power of sheer creative imagination to make the vital connection between satire and the social world," but that reading most of them "is like finding oneself adrift in a sea of orbiting psychic garbage." Aldridge's piece, which is included in this volume, raises the frequently recurring question of whether Barthelme constructively engages the "dreck" of contemporary culture or just wallows in it. In contrast to both Mudrick and Aldridge, William H. Gass, while not praising every story in *Unspeakable Practices*, does recognize in Barthelme's method something new and important in American literature. Barthelme at his best, Gass says, "has the art to make a treasure out of trash."[37]

The reception accorded to *City Life* (1971) was almost uniformly favorable (and that book is still regarded by many to be his best collection), but by the time *The Dead Father* appeared in 1975 the Barthelme opposition, though small in number, had gathered up a head of steam. With the publication of Hilton Kramer's review of that novel in *Commentary*, Barthelme criticism hit rock bottom. Kramer contends that Barthelme practices an aestheticism placing art above life. Governing "all" Barthelme's work, Kramer complains, is "a view that holds life itself in contempt, and seeks a redress of its grievances in the kind of literary artifice that shuts out all reference to the normal course of human feeling." After reducing *The Dead Father* to a "simple fantasy of filial revenge" and condemning the book for its presumed assault on fatherhood, adulthood, and the family, Kramer concludes his diatribe with a few less than kind words about academics, whom he sees as Barthelme's natural audience.[38] Gore Vidal, in a wide-ranging critique of the New Novel and its descendants, anticipates Kramer's attack on both "the academic bureaucracy" and Barthelme's fiction, which he sees as part of "the French pox" spread by Roland Barthes.[39] Vidal's litany of literary bugaboos—Barthes, Barthelme, Barth—begins to sound like a lexical game of some sort, but he is in earnest, and his underlying thesis, that Barthelme's fiction lacks engagement with life, is only a wittier version of Kramer's.

Much different is the assessment of Linda Kuehl, for whom Barthelme, in *Amateurs* (1976), "offers fresh surprise" and "counters grim, audacious, outrageous reality with a wry wit, warm heart, and sympathetic—if surreal—eye." Far from being the elitist implied by Kramer and Vidal, Barthelme is "a democrat by temperament" who "offers gestalts on behalf of the multitude he champions, on behalf of mechanized, betrayed Everyman."[40] Philip Stevic, reviewing the same book, calls Barthelme's work "the central exhibit of . . . the 'post-modernist' imagination." Barthelme, Stevick maintains, "has made a set of social and emotional responses for the people in his fictions that refract, in some uncanny way, the contours of our sensibility."[41] And finally, at the end of the decade, Joe David Bellamy finds even in *Great Days* (1979), which is not a particular favorite among aficionados, an artistry that liberates the imagination.

Reviews of Barthelme's books during the 1980s have been less friendly. Although *Sixty Stories* (1981) was warmly received,[42] his new work has not been. Geoffrey Stokes calls *Overnight to Many Distant Cities* (1983) "a mixed success" but praises the more recent stories in the collection for displaying a willingness "to confront and reflect . . . the world of emotion,"[43] and Robert Murray Davis, in a review reprinted in this volume, assesses one-third of the stories as "better than competent" and one-fourth of the italicized interchapters as "brilliant." Other reviews of the book have not been so kind. Joel Conarroe calls the stories in it "curiously vacuous" and the interchapters "private intrusions that communicate little beyond self-satisfaction."[44] Jonathan Penner is even more skeptical of Barthelme's achievement in *Overnight*: "The principle operating . . . through much of the book is that the further you read the less you understand. . . . Many of these pieces are designed to be not 'difficult' but impossible."[45] Barthelme's cynical message, Penner reckons, is that both life and art are meaningless.

No one reading *Paradise* (1986) could imagine Barthelme to be such a nihilist, and indeed, that novel proved to be more to the reviewers' liking. Although to Paul Stuewe "its thin story-line . . . slightly sketched characters" and "absence of . . . intellectual or emotional content" make *Paradise* "a hell of a disappointment,"[46] other readers responded to it with some enthusiasm. Elizabeth Jolley, whose review is also included here, calls the book "a collision of brilliant moments" and "a picture of human needs and wishes. . . . a fantasy of freedom in a world where there is no freedom." She adds, "Details in the novel are . . . ridiculously funny and tender as in real life." The phrase "real life," or something like it, figures in several positive evaluations of *Paradise*. Michael Feingold flatly claims that the book is good because it takes place in a world "that's believably everyday, not turned upside-down by Barthelme's usual giant balloons. . . ."[47] This is perhaps a fittingly ironic place to conclude a review of reviews—with one that praises Barthelme by implicitly condemning the work that most critics have found to be his best.

By 1971, with the publication of articles by Neil Schmitz and Robert Scholes[48] and books by Richard Gilman and Tony Tanner, serious evaluation of Barthelme's fiction was well under way. Gilman's *The Confusion of Realms* (1969) and Tanner's *City of Words* (1971)[49] set a particularly high standard for future Barthelme criticism. Gilman was the first to articulate convincingly one of Barthelme's major premises, "that princes no longer exist, in a crucial double sense. As a figure in reality . . . he has been driven out of existence precisely by contemporary life . . . and as a literary figure, the hero, he can have no stature because the reality he has been abstracted from no longer sustains the values necessary to his creation."[50] Although Gilman's subject is *Snow White,* Barthelme creatively confronts this absence throughout his career, from "The Joker's Greatest Triumph" through *The Dead Father* to *Sam's Bar* and *The King.* Tanner recognized early on the importance of collage or "assemblage" in Barthelme's art as well as the redemptive, if limited, power of the imagination.

Barthelme criticism flourished in the journals and elsewhere during the 1970s. Some critics, like John Ditsky and Sally Allen McNall, have approached his work through stylistic analysis,[51] but many, following the example of Gilman, explore the conjunction of Barthelme's fiction with contemporary life. John Gardner concedes that Barthelme "has a sharp eye for modern man's doubts and anxieties, free-floating guilt, politics, manners, turns of speech" and that "even in the most fabulous or refracted of his fictions he keeps a careful eye on how the world really works." Where Gardner finds fault, predictably, is in Barthelme's failure to propose remedies: "He knows what is wrong, but he has no clear image of, or interest in, how things ought to be." For Gardner, Barthelme's technical virtuosity is hollow, a trivial toying with literary conventions "which once helped us learn about the real."[52]

Alfred Kazin's somewhat murky paragraphs on Barthelme seem to concur with Gardner's view, at least up to a point. Kazin acknowledges Barthelme's ability to satirize a linguistic-cultural system "made up wholly of cant, clichés, stale quotations, so that words now lead a life of their own, entirely outside the powerless-feeling people who are dragged along by them." But Barthelme himself, Kazin adds, suffers "more than anyone" from complicity with that system. (How this can be true if Barthelme is "outside everything he writes about" must remain a mystery.) Kazin does, finally, call Barthelme's satire "necessary."[53] The prevailing view among critics during this period, however, is that Barthelme's fictions *do* help us "learn about the real." Most agree, in fact, that that is what they do best. Barthelme's stories, as Ihab Hassan puts it, "show fierce wit and verbal agility as well as a genuine, if totally oblique, moral perception of our collective lunacy." In them "we learn the phenomenology of a trite existence, its sludge and trash."[54]

Jerome Klinkowitz, whose work on Barthelme extends from the seventies well into the eighties, focuses on both theme and technique. Analyzing Barthelme's "art of collage," Klinkowitz argues that his fictional assemblages are not *primarily* "intellectual comments or moral judgments" at all, but *"made objects."*[55] Not all of Barthelme's stories employ the collage method, but those that do defamiliarize routine words and objects, giving them new life. Klinkowitz also discusses Barthelme's debt to both Max Ernst and Joseph Cornell and the influence in general of the graphic arts on his work. In *Literary Disruptions* (1975; revised and expanded 1980) Klinkowitz presents a broader view of Barthelme's aims and strategies. And in *The Self-Apparent Word* (1984) he makes the very important point that while much of Barthelme's fiction is "self-apparent," with language calling attention to itself *as language,* much of it is also highly referential, and "Barthelme's own preferences favor reference."[56]

The four books on Barthelme conveniently made their appearances in a pattern of generally increasing specialization. The first, Lois Gordon's *Donald Barthelme* (1981), is appropriately an introduction to Barthelme's work, and a useful one. Gordon discusses each of Barthelme's books in turn, from *Come Back, Dr. Caligari* to *Great Days.* In addition, she also provides a brief annotated bibliography, a biographical chapter, and an introduction that touches on many of the most important features of Barthelme's work: his rejection of conventional mimesis, his antiteleological bias, his use of collage, and his portrayal of a humanity "stuffed with roles, words, and expertise" but empty at the core because words and systems of belief have lost their significance. Gordon's central thesis is that Barthelme's work "reflects changes in contemporary consciousness . . . and its reinterpretations of continuing human dilemmas"[57] through an exploration of the role of language in human experience.

Charles F. Molesworth's *Donald Barthelme's Fiction: The Ironist Saved from Drowning* (1982), as the title indicates, examines Barthelme as an ironic writer. Like Gordon, Molesworth discusses in his introduction some of the dominant elements in Barthelme's fiction, but unlike her, he does not devote a chapter to each work. Instead, he investigates "Barthelme's use of the genre of the short story" which, as a genre, "recycles junk, snapping up the unconsidered trifles of our culture and civilization for a variety of different goals," and addresses the relationship of language and irony: "Barthelme is a parodist, a special sort of ironist, whose focus is less the gap between word and thing, or desire and object, but more that of the gap between word and word, or manifested desire and desired manifestation."[58]

The third book is a collaboration, Maurice Couturier and Regis Durand's *Donald Barthelme* (1982). Their study, in which chapters by Couturier alternate with chapters by Durand, is intended as a dialogue patterned after "one of the central tactics of Barthelme's fiction." The first chapter examines

Barthelme as verbal game player; the second, his sources of humor. The third chapter places Barthelme's stories in the context of postmodern absences and suspensiveness. The fourth "looks at the modicum of communication between author and reader that remains within his unstable symbolic systems," and the fifth analyzes the process by which Barthelme creates images. Their last chapter returns to the subject of artistic strategies touched on earlier in the book. Throughout their self-styled "meditation," the authors stress the effects of Barthelme's fictions on the reader.[59]

The most recent book on Barthelme is Wayne B. Stengel's *The Shape of Art in the Stories of Donald Barthelme* (1985). Stengel's approach differs from those of his predecessors in that he postulates a "typology" that encompasses most of the short fiction. "Because of Barthelme's abstract, innovative conception of art and the artist-audience relationship," Stengel explains, "any study of his short stories must find a strategy for confronting the specific problems his writing poses." For Stengel, that strategy entails surveying "the full range" of the stories and grouping them according to type: stories of identity, conflict dramatized in dialogue, society, and art. Within each of these thematic categories he identifies four approaches Barthelme takes to them: play, cognition, repetition as entrapment, and creativity as escape. A shorthand description makes this approach to Barthelme sound much more constrictive than it actually is. The method enables Stengel to develop illuminating readings of many of the stories in relation to one another, incrementally bolstering his contention that Barthelme is "a writer of consistent vision and serious intention."[60]

III

This collection offers, in addition to a selection of book reviews, critical perspectives on Barthelme's fiction from *Come Back, Dr. Caligari* to *Paradise*. The first five essays focus on his early work. Morris Dickstein's contribution, excerpted from *Gates of Eden: American Culture in the Sixties,* provides a lucid introduction to Barthelme and locates him at the forefront of American experimental writers. Barthelme, Dickstein argues, did for the short story what Barth, Pynchon, and others did for the novel. One need not agree with Morris Dickstein's assessment of the shape of Barthelme's career (with *Sadness* and *The Dead Father* heralding a decline) to appreciate the sharpness and sensitivity of his insights. William Stott also highlights the "newness" of Barthelme's fiction, which he sees as taking into account the increasing influence of nonfictional discourse in contemporary experience and the concomitant intrusion of public life into private. Thomas M. Leitch, as mentioned earlier, defines Barthelme's narratives in terms of their antiteleological bias—their failure to foreground (or often even to include) elements like development and closure that are the mainstays of traditional fiction. Alan

Wilde's essay is a lengthy but rewarding meditation on Barthelme's place in the postmodernist movement, the differences between his "presentational" and "ludic" stories, and particularly his importance as a postmodern "suspensive" (as opposed to a modern "equivocal") ironist. Mary Robertson's contribution, written expressly for this volume, exhaustively examines a single story, "Brain Damage," as a paradigm for Barthelme's work as a whole. Carefully analyzing in turn the story's narrative passages, its "headlines," and its illustrations, Robertson finds that Barthelme is in fact a realist—that in breaking up symbolic patterns, syntax, stabilizing conventions, and other types of coherence, his fiction reflects what is actually happening in contemporary discourse and culture.

Critical treatment of Barthelme's work in the early to middle 1970s is represented here by essays on *The Slightly Irregular Fire Engine* and *Amateurs.* Gates' essay, originally published some years ago and extensively revised by the author for this collection, demonstrates that *Fire Engine,* although intended and marketed as a book for children, can be usefully read in the context of the rest of the Barthelme canon. As in his other "picture" stories, Barthelme drapes the narrative elements around a seemingly miscellaneous assortment of illustrations. Gates goes on to explain how Barthelme (not surprisingly) both employs the conventions of children's literature in this work and departs from them, transforming them into something bearing his own unique stamp. Conceiving the djinn as a prototype for the artist in Barthelme, an "inept magician" whose limitations are a persistent problem but whose triumphs, however small, are significant, Gates places this book squarely among Barthelme's many other fables of imagination and creativity.[61] Wayne Stengel's essay, published here for the first time, attempts to come to terms with what some readers perceive as a loss of creative edge in Barthelme's work during the 1970s. Limiting his analysis to three stories in *Amateurs,* Stengel discovers "a large and significant fault line between early and later Barthelme," finding that, all too often, Barthelme in his later work "enters the enemy camp" and makes "totalitarianisms that wish to devour us seem all too humane, amusing, understandable, or aesthetically appealing."

Barthelme's most celebrated novels, *Snow White* and *The Dead Father,* are each represented here by two critical analyses. Larry McCaffery sees the principal subject of *Snow White* as "the relationship between man and his fictions," or more specifically, "the current condition of language and the possibilities which exist today for a writer for communicating something meaningful to his readers." McCaffery concludes that although fiction "may not be able to transcend the limits imposed by its trashy, too-familiar materials, it can accommodate itself to this condition by metafictionally incorporating this same debased condition into its very fabric." Robert A. Morace, while also recognizing the importance of language in *Snow White,* places somewhat more emphasis on the debasement of contemporary life that the novel exposes. Morace sharply disagrees with Dickstein's observation that

Snow White is "crippled by the absence of a subject," maintaining instead that the book's subject is "a crippled culture."

The two essays on *The Dead Father,* unlike McCaffery and Morace's approaches to *Snow White,* are radically different from one another in their basic premises. Richard Walsh, in a detailed exegesis of the novel written for this collection, contends that no "allegorical" reading adequately accounts "for the degree to which the literal sense generates the narrative." Walsh casts a rather cold eye on contemporary critical theory (and particularly on Lacan) as a way into Barthelme, arguing that the "literal narrative rather than its 'translation' must remain the center of attention if the exploratory process it facilitates is not to be subverted by a prejudicial allegorical framework." After a very helpful summation of much of the best criticism on the novel, Walsh turns to the text itself and stays there. His interpretation is an example of the classical close reading at its best. Robert Con Davis, on the other hand, draws richly and persuasively on Lacan to explore the nature of fatherhood in all its forms— literal, symbolic, structural. Both essays are outstanding contributions to Barthelme scholarship; together, in their complementary relationship, they strongly suggest that *The Dead Father* may well be Barthelme's most resonant single work.

The concluding essays in this volume focus on Barthelme's neglected later books, and both appear here for the first time. Michael Trussler's subtly developed analysis of Barthelme's last collection of short fiction, *Overnight to Many Distant Cities,* treats Barthelme's narrative method as "an affirmation that undermines and negates itself." The book's italicized "interchapters," Trussler explains, contribute to the text's indeterminacy rather than providing a stabilizing frame of reference. They create the "suggestion of a taxonomy" that is ultimately dismantled. The overall effect is a continuous suspension of signification[62] in which, in Trussler's clever turn of phrase, "the absence of meaning is dependent upon narrative to give it formlessness." Patrick O'Donnell sees in *Paradise* not so much a "failed attempt to write in a more traditional novelistic mode" as Barthelme's most extensive reflection on the state of art and the artist in postmodern culture. The novel's protagonist is a middle-aged architect[63] who attempts (by sharing his apartment and his bed with three young women) "to project a daytime vision where domestic order and eros commingle." The attempt ultimately fails, but O'Donnell sees in this construction and deconstruction of a contemporary male utopia an exploration of the question of form itself, shaped by "Barthelme's important, characteristic concern with 'living arrangements' in postmodern society—a concern that reveals his profound skepticism regarding the permanence of human relations matched by a desire for order and continuity in an environment where order and repression are equals." Both Trussler's and O'Donnell's essays stand as clear evidence that serious critical evaluation of Barthelme's last several books, in the context of his whole career, is long overdue.

Notes

1. Donald Barthelme, *Sadness* (New York: Farrar, Straus and Giroux, 1972), 139.

2. The definitive bibliography of Barthelme's fiction has yet to be done. Some of his work is still uncollected, and some pieces were published anonymously. The best checklist up to 1980 is in Jerome Klinkowitz's *Literary Disruptions: The Making of a Post-Contemporary American Fiction* (Urbana: University of Illinois Press, 1980), 252–62. Barthelme's major work includes the collections *Come Back, Dr. Caligari* (1964), *Unspeakable Practices, Unnatural Acts* (1968), *City Life* (1970), *Sadness* (1972), *Guilty Pleasures* (1974), *Amateurs* (1976), *Great Days* (1979), and *Overnight to Many Distant Cities* (1983); the novels *Snow White* (1967), *The Dead Father* (1975), *Paradise* (1986), and *The King,* with illustrations by Barry Moser (1990); the children's book *The Slightly Irregular Fire Engine* (1971); and the virtually unclassifiable *Sam's Bar* (1987), in collaboration with illustrator Seymour Chwast. Most of Barthelme's best short fiction, much of which originally appeared in the *New Yorker,* has also been collected in *Sixty Stories* (1981) and *Forty Stories* (1987). *Guilty Pleasures* is a collection of pastiches and parodies, along with some stories, which was marketed as nonfiction.

3. A brief biographical sketch of Barthelme can be found, among other places, in the first chapter of Lois Gordon's *Donald Barthelme* (Boston: G. K. Hall, 1981).

4. Charles Molesworth, for instance, in *Donald Barthelme's Fiction: The Ironist Saved from Drowning* (Columbia: University of Missouri Press, 1982), 82, says that *Snow White* and *The Dead Father* "are merely extensions of a style that works better in the short-story form."

5. Larry McCaffery, *The Metafictional Muse: The Works of Robert Coover, Donald Barthelme, and William H. Gass* (Pittsburgh: University of Pittsburgh Press, 1982), 100.

6. Alan Wilde, *Middle Grounds: Studies in Contemporary American Fiction* (Philadelphia: University of Pennsylvania Press, 1987), 35.

7. Jerome Klinkowitz, "Donald Barthelme's Art of Collage," in *The Practice of Fiction in America: Writers from Hawthorne to the Present* (Ames: Iowa State University Press, 1980), 110.

8. William H. Gass, "The Leading Edge of the Trash Phenomenon," *New York Review of Books,* 25 April 1968, 5. Reprinted in *Fiction and the Figures of Life* (New York: Knopf, 1970), 97–103.

9. Richard Schickel, "Freaked Out on Barthelme," *New York Times Magazine,* 16 August 1970, 14, 42. For a fuller discussion of Barthelme's use of collage, see Klinkowitz, "Donald Barthelme's Art of Collage." Several critics have seized on a line spoken by one of the characters in "See the Moon" ("Fragments are the only forms I trust") and taken it as the author's own view. Barthelme replied, in an interview with Jerome Klinkowitz, "I hope that whatever I think about aesthetics would be a shade more complicated that that." See Joe David Bellamy, *The New Fiction: Interviews with Innovative American Writers* (Urbana: University of Illinois Press, 1974), 53.

10. Richard Gilman, *The Confusion of Realms* (New York: Random House, 1969), 43. Gilman's contribution to Barthelme scholarship is represented in this volume by his review of *Snow White.* That review was largely incorporated into *The Confusion of Realms.*

11. R. E. Johnson, " 'Bees Barking in the Night': The End and Beginning of Donald Barthelme's Narrative," *Boundary 2* 5 (1976–77): 88–89. Alan Wilde, in the essay reprinted here, interprets this story somewhat differently, contrasting the "pure, disenchanted phenomenal reality" of the spectators with the enchanted symbol.

12. Francis Gillen, "Donald Barthelme's City: A Guide," *Twentieth Century Literature* 18 (1972): 37.

13. Jeff Reid, "Breakfast Theory: A Morning Methodology," *Harper's* 279 (August 1989): 27.

14. Donald Barthelme, *Amateurs* (New York: Farrar, Straus and Giroux, 1976), 128.

15. McCaffery, 123.

16. John Leland, "Remarks Re-marked: Barthelme, What Curios of Signs!" *Boundary 2* 5 (1976–77): 797.

17. Gordon, 24.

18. Thomas Pynchon, *The Crying of Lot 49* (1966; reprint, New York: Bantam, 1982), 69.

19. Gerald Graff, "The Myth of the Postmodernist Breakthrough," *TriQuarterly* 26 (1973): 388–89. It should be noted that Regis Durand (among others) does not quite agree with Graff's etiology, drawing a sharper distinction between postmodernism and what has come before. See Maurice Couturier and Regis Durand, *Donald Barthelme* (New York: Methuen, 1982), 38.

20. The phrase is Ortega y Gasset's. See Graff, 388.

21. Gordon, 24.

22. Betty Flowers, "Barthelme's *Snow White:* The Reader-Patient Relationship," *Critique* 16 (1975): 43. It should be stressed that Flowers finds no *central* point of view and no *consistent* "fictive authorial identity" in Barthelme. That is not the same as denying the existence of these elements altogether. The kind of satire and even, some would suggest, social consciousness and commentary that much of Barthelme's work displays would be impossible without any point of view at all.

23. Donald Barthelme, *City Life* (New York: Farrar, Straus and Giroux, 1970), 59.

24. Molesworth, 83. Molesworth also concedes, however, that this very phenomenon "is what makes Barthelme less than a major writer for many readers."

25. Donald Barthelme, *Snow White* (New York: Atheneum, 1967), 132.

26. Barthelme, *Snow White,* 132.

27. John Leland points out that "the novel refuses to distinguish beginnings and endings—that is, it refuses linearity," and he goes on to say, "*Snow White* refuses to form a totality. . . . To find a 'stable' meaning, a point of identity and closure, becomes then only an exercise in exhaustion." See Leland, 801, 805–6.

28. Barthelme, *Snow White,* 41–42. Snow White's location of "real men" in films and childhood fantasies does not seem nearly so ironic after the Reagan years as it did when this novel was first published.

29. Donald Barthelme, *The Dead Father* (New York: Penguin, 1986), 14. For a fuller discussion of *The Dead Father* and Barthelme's "art of absences," see Couturier and Durand, 33–41.

30. Donald Barthelme, *Come Back, Dr. Caligari* (Boston: Little, Brown, 1964), 175, 183.

31. Barthelme, *City Life,* 43.

32. Lee Upton, "Failed Artists in Donald Barthelme's *Sixty Stories,*" *Critique* 26 (Fall 1984): 11–17.

33. Klinkowitz, "Donald Barthelme's Art of Collage," 109.

34. Donald Barthelme and Seymour Chwast, *Sam's Bar: An American Landscape* (Garden City, N.Y.: Doubleday, 1987).

35. Several lists of Barthelme criticism have been assembled. Each of the four books on him includes a bibliography of secondary material. Jerome Klinkowitz's (in *Literary Disruptions*) is the most complete, although it extends only through 1979. During the 1980s, however, so few critical articles on Barthelme have appeared that an update of Klinkowitz is not yet necessary. The best essays of the 1980s are those that appear in this volume (by Robert Con Davis, Thomas M. Leitch, and Robert A. Morace), as well as Lee Upton's "Failed Artists in Donald Barthelme's *Sixty Stories.*"

36. Marvin Mudrick, "Sarraute, Duras, Burroughs, Barthelme, and a Postscript," *Hudson Review* 20 (Autumn 1967): 482, 484.

37. Gass, 6.

38. Hilton Kramer, "Barthelme's Comedy of Patricide," *Commentary* 61 (August 1976):

56–59. Kramer even traces Barthelme's shortcomings to "that hatred of the family that was a hallmark of the ideology of the counterculture of the 60's. . . ."

39. Gore Vidal, *Matters of Fact and of Fiction* (New York: Random House, 1977), 125, 102. First published in *New York Review of Books* in July 1974.

40. Linda Kuehl, "*Amateurs,*" *Saturday Review,* 11 December 1976, 69–70.

41. Philip Stevick, "The Bad-Taste Blues," *Nation,* 29 January 1977, 119–20.

42. See, for instance, John Romano, "Writing Like a Stand-Up Comic," *New York Times Book Review,* 4 October 1981, 9, 23.

43. Geoffrey Stokes, "Over Decades to Many Distant Cities," *Village Voice,* 17 January 1984, 39.

44. Joel Conarroe, "Some Tame, Some Wild," *New York Times Book Review,* 18 December 1983, 8, 22.

45. Jonathan Penner, "Donald Barthelme's Just-Not Stories," *Washington Post Book World,* 27 November 1983, 10.

46. Paul Steuwe, "A Lively Deal . . . Tubeside Companion . . . Stellar Stella," *Quill and Quire* 53 (January 1987): 33.

47. Michael Feingold, "Beautiful Schemer," *Village Voice,* 3 February 1987, 51.

48. Neil Schmitz, "Donald Barthelme and the Emergence of Modern Satire," *Minnesota Review* 1 (Fall 1971): 109–18; Robert Scholes, "Metafiction," *Iowa Review* 1 (Fall 1970): 100–115.

49. Gilman, 43–52; Tony Tanner, *City of Words: American Fiction 1950–1970* (New York: Harper and Row, 1971), 400–406.

50. Gilman, 47.

51. John Ditsky, " 'With Ingenuity and Hard Work Distracted': The Narrative Style of Donald Barthelme," *Style* 9 (1975): 388–400; Sally Allen McNall, " 'But Why Am I Troubling Myself about Cans?': Style, Reaction and Lack of Reaction in Barthelme's *Snow White,*" *Language and Style* 8 (Spring 1975): 81–94.

52. John Gardner, *On Moral Fiction* (New York: Basic Books, 1978), 79–80. Christopher Lasch tends to agree with Gardner's view that Barthelme's fiction accurately mirrors "the culture of commodities and consumerism" without offering a way out of it. See Lasch, *The Culture of Narcissism: American Life in an Age of Diminishing Expectations* (New York: Norton, 1978), 20, 151–53.

53. Alfred Kazin, *Bright Book of Life: American Novelists and Storytellers from Hemingway to Mailer* (Boston: Little, Brown, 1973), 271–74.

54. Ihab Hassan, *Contemporary American Literature: 1945–1972* (New York: Ungar, 1973), 84.

55. Klinkowitz, "Barthelme's Art of Collage," 107.

56. Jerome Klinkowitz, *The Self-Apparent Word: Fiction as Language/Language as Fiction* (Carbondale: Southern Illinois University Press, 1984), 74.

57. Gordon, 22, 213.

58. Molesworth, 8.

59. Couturier and Durand, 10.

60. Wayne B. Stengel, *The Shape of Art in the Stories of Donald Barthelme* (Baton Rouge: Louisiana State University Press, 1985), 5.

61. See also Upton, "Failed Artists in Barthelme's *Sixty Stories.*" Upton's thesis and Gates's are complementary in many ways, with Gates focusing on a single work and Upton analyzing the limited powers of the artist in a range of stories.

62. See Alan Wilde's essay in this volume for a detailed discussion of the importance of "suspensiveness" in Barthelme.

63. Both Trussler and O'Donnell make incisive observations about the importance of architecture in Barthelme's work.

BOOK REVIEWS

◆

Dance of Death

John W. Aldridge

The literary movement known as Black Humor or Dark Comedy, which achieved a certain inflated prominence in the early sixties, has lately shown signs of reaching some condition of impasse or exhaustion. The high claims of its initial publicity have not been fulfilled, and although it has attracted talents as diversely original as John Barth, Joseph Heller, Thomas Pynchon, Bruce Jay Friedman, and Donald Barthelme, these writers continue to seem notable more for their potential than for their clearly major distinction. The movement has also been compromised by the accumulation around it of a small army of camp followers, clowns, and pitchmen, who have apparently seen in it a chance to cash in on their mediocrity through emulation of their betters, and who have busied themselves perverting the styles of Black Humor into affectations, and affectations into platitudes.

From the beginning the movement has had considerably more than its share of critical attention because it appeared to be a development toward imaginative revitalization of a form that had long been moribund, the form of novelistic satire and self-parody, and because it seemed to promise some renewal of relationship between fiction and the actualities of the social world, a relationship which had grown so tenuous in the forties and fifties that vast sectors of the reading public eagerly mistook the erotic voyeurisms of John O'Hara for penetrating insights into the sociology of American life.

But it has gradually become evident that the promises which critics discovered in Black Humor were projections more of their own hopes than of creative possibilities actually present in the movement itself. For just as Black Humor has all along been characterized by a kind of fashionableness achieved without passing through any of the arduous stages of slow arrival and gradual acceptance, so it has quickly ossified into one more cliché of anti-cliché, one more casualty of the instantly assimilative and accommodative processes of our culture. As has happened with so much post-avant-garde art, there seems to have been only the briefest interval between the time when Black Humor was recognized as an important innovative gesture and the time when it was absorbed into style and decor and became nearly indistinguishable from the advertising gimmicks and promotional techniques which have so often been the rightful objects of its horror. The pose or stance of the Black Humorist soon became as familiar and predictable and as falsely provocative as the set of a *Vogue* mannequin's thighs. Suddenly, it seemed capable of registering only the histrionics of a ritual angst, a merely ornamental, because creatively unearned, absurdity, a sleek couturier note of apocalypse.

Yet it was in the nature of Black Humor to be peculiarly susceptible to this kind of debasement. Even at its best it always verged perilously on the sick joke, the nightclub wisecrack, the pop art slapstick of the comic-strip cartoon. Its characteristic humor was often more black-face than black, and the ubiquitous Catch-22 of its satire seemed too flip and feeble, and above all too *good-natured,* a mockery of the insidious workings of bureaucratic conspiracy. In fact, the most crippling weakness of Black Humor was that it cut itself off from the vital source of effective satire—the close observation of the social and political world—just because it was too easily horrified by the grotesqueness and complexity of that world, and so found it less painful to retreat into cuteness than to endure and create the true dark comedy of contemporary anguish. In its programmatic preoccupation with the sickness, the absurdity, the incomprehensibility of events, it abdicated its responsibility to deal coherently with events. The result was that, except in a very few cases, such as Barth's *The Sot-Weed Factor* and Friedman's *Stern,* the prime requirement of successful satire was never fulfilled by Black Humor writers: the living reality of the object or condition being satirized was too obliquely suggested in their work or was altogether missing from it.

It has often been argued in defense of Black Humor that fiction in our time has lost the possibility of making this social connection because the events of the social world have become themselves fictitious. Life not only imitates fiction but assimilates to itself the fiction-making functions, so that the happenings reported on any day in the newspapers will in effect out-imagine the creative mind and thus cheat it of its revelatory and prophetic powers. But this would seem to suggest that fiction is best produced in dull ages, and the history of literature indicates that just the opposite is true. Rather, it seems to be the case that contemporary experience has so anesthetized us to the impact of grotesque and appalling occurrences that we no longer believe they can have any connection with, or any power to influence, the course of individual destiny or the drama of our hermetically personal consciousness. We have suffered a paralysis or eclipse of imagination before the nightmare of history in this age. Hence, we cannot imagine a fictional rationale in which events might be interpreted meaningfully in relation to the self. Our only recourse seems to be to fantasize the feelings of dislocation which obsess the self, or project images which convey, however incoherently, our sense of moral and emotional trivialization in the face of events.

Of the Black Humor writers whose work represents some expression of, or adjustment to, this dilemma, Donald Barthelme is in many ways the most interesting because he has the talent and intelligence occasionally to overcome its worst effects. A few stories in both his first volume, *Come Back, Dr. Caligari,* and this new book [*Unspeakable Practices, Unnatural Acts*] brilliantly demonstrate the power of sheer creative imagination to make the vital connection between satire and the social world. Barthelme's recurrent theme is precisely the trivialization of contemporary life and consciousness, and in these few stories he is able to dramatize his sense of that trivialization within the context of living fact and event which created it. But there is a vast distance between the stories which succeed in this way and the many others which are victimized by the fallacy of imitative form, in which dislocation is expressed through dislocation, and trivialization through trivia, to the amusement and edification of nobody. These stories strike one as exercises in free association and automatic writing or as descriptions of bad dreams jotted down in the middle of the night for the benefit of one's analyst, and some of them sound as though they had been begun in the hope that of their own accord, through the sheer act of being written, they would eventually discover their subject and meaning.

Reading them is like finding oneself adrift in a sea of orbiting psychic garbage. Punctured beer cans, potato peelings, gnawed apple cores, squashed toothpaste tubes, stringy hanks of some dubious-looking viscous material float around and seemingly through one, always in the same fixed relation to oneself and everything else, and always somehow impenetrable because one is so completely penetrated by them. The stories are quite literally verbal immersions in dreck, the evacuated crud and muck of contemporary life, and they very effectively dramatize the sensations of being suffocated and shat upon and generally soiled and despoiled in soul and mind which accompany our daily experience of contemporary life. But they do not dramatize the cultural, political, or historical circumstances which give rise to these sensations nor do they end in a satirical or even a specific thematic formulation. Everything is offered in deadpan and with the mechanical iterativeness of items recited from a grocery list. Everything is offered, but somehow finally nothing is given.

The effect is actually very much like that of some of the New Wave films which introduce the viewer to an experience through a process of such total saturation in trivial details that it is often impossible to tell which detail or episode is supposed to be more important than some other, hence impossible to detect the thematic principle which finally binds the details together into meaning. One always suspects the artist of suggesting that he does not really know what he intends the depicted experience to mean, and so will leave it to us to decide for ourselves. In such a case, we are obliged, as Virginia Woolf once said, to do the artist's imagining for him, and while that may be a kindness to him, it is no help whatever to the cause of art.

Barthelme appears to be indictable on the same charge. Over and over in his stories he seems to be inviting us to take over the job of bringing into focus some idea which has eluded his powers of imaginative resolution. For example, in this new volume the story called "Edward and Pia" apparently has to do with an American expatriate and his Scandinavian mistress and the emptiness of their existence in Europe. The characters move apathetically through a horizontal succession of experiences, none of which is distinguished from any other in the slightest way, presumably because they are all equally without meaning and value. We learn that Edward and Pia went to Sweden, that Pia was pregnant, that in London they had seen *Marat/Sade* at the Aldwych Theater, that Edward and Pia walked the streets of Amsterdam and were hungry, that they went to the cinema to see an Eddie Constantine picture, that on Sunday Edward went to the bakery and bought bread, that Edward and Pia went to Berlin on the train, that Edward received a letter from London, that Edward looked in the window of the used-radio store and it was full of used radios, that Edward put his hands on Pia's breasts, that the nipples were the largest he had ever seen. Then he counted his money. He had two hundred and forty crowns. And so on and on and on.

All this is undoubtedly redolent of the trivialization of life in our time, and it may well be an attempt to say something about the form of spiritual death that accompanies the atrophy of all sane responses to life and all hopes of finding causal relationships within experience. But it comes through most clearly as an example of imagination succumbing to the trivia which is its material.

There may even be some justice in the thought that such benumbed recitations of detail are intended to be viewed as if they were being enacted under the outraged eye of the cosmos, and we are meant to hear rumbling behind it all the distant thunder of the archangelic armies advancing to bring down upon us the terrible wrath of God. But as Auden saw, even during such a cosmic occurrence as the crucifixion, dogs go placidly on with their doggy life, and "the expensive delicate ship that must have seen something amazing," the fall of Brueghel's Icarus into the sea, "had somewhere to get to and sailed calmly on."

It would appear that the cosmic and the apocalyptic, whether in art or in life, cannot be dramatized directly, cannot meaningfully stand alone. They can finally be understood only in terms of their simple and probably ironical relationship to the doggy life and the very real people sailing away on that ship. It is the task of fiction continually to reaffirm this relationship. Or, in an age such as ours, fiction may be obliged to reinvent it. For between the crucifixion and the doggy life, between our grandiose visions of doom and the specific creature experiences which embody them, there now lies a chasm which only the best talent and intelligence can hope to bridge. It takes little of either simply to say that the chasm is there and then to laugh at its existence. We know it is there, and the knowledge has long ago ceased to amuse.

Barthelme's Fairy Tale

RICHARD GILMAN

It is one of the peculiarities of the imagination," Wallace Stevens once said, "that it is always at the end of an era. What happens is that it is always attaching itself to a new reality and adhering to it. It is not that there is a new imagination, but that there is a new reality."

My occasion for quoting Stevens is the publication of Donald Barthelme's first novel, a work throughly recalcitrant to being discussed in the habitual language of journalistic criticism. One of a handful of American writers who are working to replenish and extend the art of fiction instead of trying to add to the stock of entertainments, visions and humanist documents that fiction keeps piling up, Barthelme has previously published a volume of short stories, *Come Back, Dr. Caligari,* of exceptional technical interest and uncategorizable élan. Like those stories, his novel may be read by ignoring Stevens' dictum, read, that is, as the work of a highly idiosyncratic imagination, a *new* imagination, popping up like a wild-crested tropical bird in our parlors. But to do that would be to truckle to the imagination in its quest for novelty, eccentric fame, autocratic rule; like any other's, Barthelme's possesses that impulse. And yet its truest accomplishment is to be representative, to adhere with consciousness, craft and potency to a new reality.

In the most summary way this new reality can be described as being open-ended, provisional, characterized by suspended judgments, by disbelief in hierarchies, by mistrust of solutions, denouements and completions, by self-consciousness issuing in tremendous earnestness but also in far-ranging mockery, by emphasis on the flesh to the anachronization of the spirit, by a wealth of possibility whose individual possibilities tend to cancel one another out, by unfreedom felt as freedom and the reverse, by cults of youth, sex, change, noise and chemically induced "truth." It is also a reality harboring a radical mistrust of language, writing, fiction, the imagination. For the literary imagination whose native land all this is, so that it has itself partly been shaped by it, the problem is to adhere (as Stevens also said) without being compliant, to resist at the same time as it stays in connection, and to find in that tension the foundation of its would-be art. All writing fails when it slips out of one of those two obligations.

Reprinted by permission from the *New Republic,* 3 June 1967, 27–30. Copyright © 1967, The New Republic, Inc.

29

Irrelevant literature is that which refuses reality, conformist that which accepts it too readily. But even that writing which appears to be taking the most daring line toward a confronted reality may actually be serving its valetudinarian interests instead of its liberation in and through the imagination.

The trouble with much so-called "black humor" or "absurd" writing or neo-surrealism (under one of whose tags *Snow White* is certain to be wrongly fixed) is that in some sense it remains subservient to the actuality from which it draws its instigations and energies. The imagination's exotic bird beating at the end of a long string, it stirs up the air but leaves it afterward as it was. Superficially, we might say thematically rebellious, it remains artistically Tory, holding on to one or another conception of beauty, to tension and development, to character, story and plot, to moral or social or psychological "significance."

There are of course great risks in trying to make fictive art without those things: you can fall into chaos or impenetrable murk, or into total sterile abstraction. Popularity isn't likely to drop into your lap. But *Snow White*'s ambitions being what they are, it runs the risk most nakedly, and suffers an immediate loss. If it weren't, for instance, for its refusal to be a "novel," a story proceeding, however wildly or wondrously, like any other, it might well become the *Catcher in the Rye* of this generation. For its "content" includes the substance of our age's newest awareness and pre-awarenesses, its behavior and bemusements, its vocabularies, costumes and stances, and especially those of the disaffiliated young, the disabused and not-again-to-be-taken-in.

But it is a double thing, as Salinger's book couldn't quite manage to be. Its structure adheres closely to the movements and pressures of our new reality, but at the same time it shapes itself into an independent object, not to be exploited for extra-literary purposes and not to be accounted for by extra-aesthetic principles. High-handed, unaccommodating, it fashions a critique of everything it seizes, refusing to become a literary myth for these things (for disaffiliation as in Salinger, for example), putting them to other uses than explanation, morale-building or the erection of new, putatively redeeming beauty.

On its most available level *Snow White* is a parodic contemporary retelling of the fairy tale. The only thing resembling a narrative is that the book does move on to fulfill in its own very special way the basic situation of the fairy tale. But Barthelme continually breaks up the progression of events, switching horses in mid-stream, turning lyricism abruptly into parody, exposition into incantation, inserting pure irrelevancies, pure indigestible fragments like bits of stucco on a smooth wall, allowing nothing to *follow* or link up in any kind of logical development. Few of the "chapters" are more than one or two pages long (some are two lines) and there are frequent chapter-heading-like passages, set in large black upper-case, with messages of surpassing inconsequence or misinformation:

> THE REVOLUTION OF THE PAST
> GENERATION IN THE RELIGIOUS
> SCIENCES HAS SCARCELY PENE-
> TRATED POPULAR CONSCIOUS-
> NESS AND HAS YET TO SIGNIFI-
> CANTLY INFLUENCE PUBLIC ATTI-
> TUDES THAT REST UPON TOTALLY
> OUTMODED CONCEPTIONS.

What emerges through the seeming chaos of styles and procedures, the irrelevancies and non sequiturs, is a set of determinable facts. In a house in an unnamed city seven men—Bill, Dan, Hubert, Kevin, Henry, Edward and Clem—live with Snow White, whom they have found in a forest before the book begins and who is now twenty-two and of course beautiful. Each day the seven go out to work ("Heigh Ho") "filling the vats and washing the buildings," while Snow White keeps house, cooks and awaits their return, whereupon sexual activity presumably takes place, although it is never more than ironically hinted at. At a later point two more "characters" complete the original dramatis personae: Jane, a young woman who is the witch figure, and Paul, the prince whom Snow White is waiting for.

From the beginning we are aware that the fairy tale is undergoing a modernization, becoming the up-to-date expression of a change in human typology and self-estimation. " 'I am princely,' Paul reflected in his eat-in kitchen." But he is not princely. It is one of Barthelme's central purposes to establish that princes no longer exist, in a crucial double sense. As a figure in reality—the strong, decisive man, the prince of good fellows—he has been driven out of existence precisely by contemporary life, with its neuroses, communal psychological tyrannies and violent self-consciousness; and as a literary figure, the hero, he can have no stature because the reality he has been abstracted from no longer sustains the values necessary to his creation.

Reality no longer sustains the values necessary to the creation of Snow White, either, or the witch or the dwarfs. There is therefore no happy ending to this *Snow White,* no denouement except one that mocks the original's, no satisfaction to be obtained from a clear, completed arc of fictional experience. Fiction, Barthelme is saying, has lost its power to transform and convince and substitute, just as reality has lost, perhaps only temporarily (but that is not the concern of the imagination), its need and capacity to sustain fictions of this kind.

Everything therefore works to undermine the données of the fairy story, to prevent it from retracing its classic parabola. Thus Snow White, the least self-conscious figure in literature, is here full of self-consciousness of an exact and tragi-comic contemporary kind. "Who am I to love?" she asks herself about her inability to requite the seven men. "Is there a Paul," she muses, "or have I only projected him in the shape of my longing, boredom and pain . . . is my richly appointed body to go down the drain at twenty-two?" As for Paul himself, he is locked in grotesque incapacity to fulfill his destiny, which is of course to *reach* Snow White, to rescue her by his prowess and fertility from her condition of potentiality. At one point he sets up an underground observation station, complete with systems of mirrors and trained dogs, so as to spy on her; at another he enters a monastery; in the end he drinks the poison intended for Snow White. He is, as she finally sighs, not a prince but "pure frog," he is incapable of being conjured into heroic form. There is an exquisite irony in the description of him as "a well-integrated personality . . . he makes contact . . . a beautiful human being."

This desperate, comic losing struggle of the characters to fulfill their classic roles—the seven men, for instance, are continually afflicted with misgivings, jealousies and strange psychosomatic ailments—is the outcome of a mocking humanization fatal to their existence as archetypes and of a dissolution of their story's clean, utilitarian, wish-fulfilling dream-logic into ambiguity, dissonance and fragmentation. In Grimm each of the major personages (the dwarfs being considered as one) is wholly and purely a representative, an incarnation: Snow White of beauty and abused innocence, the witch of envy and malice, the prince of redemptive strength and the dwarfs of selfless service. For Barthelme's imagination these exemplary careers are agencies of an acute and devastating skepticism.

But at the same time they are material for a new literary action by which literature itself is made to expose the bankruptcy of its traditional, normative procedures, so that new literature might be formed on the dead ground. Fiction, Barthelme assumes, can no longer be (if it ever wholly was) the "expression" or "interpretation" or simulacrum of life and its values. Nor can it be the reader of its secret thoughts, nor the vehicle of surrogate emotions or aspirations nor in fact of experience of any kind except an aesthetic one. There ought not be a logic of fictional event, fulfilling reality's reputed craving for a compensation for its own ill-logic; fiction cannot be the savior or map-maker of reality, nor the cicerone through its confused travels. And finally, fiction ought not be an employment of language for ends beyond itself, but language in its own right, mysteriously saturated with reality, perpetually establishing a new synthesis of reality and the imagination and doing this partly by driving out all language which has accomplished an earlier synthesis.

In one of his frequent dead-pan pseudo-scientific passages, Barthelme has the manager of a "plastic buffalo hump" factory talk about the accumulation of trash in the world. "We're in humps right now . . . from a philosophical point of view," he says, because since trash is accumulating at a rate which will soon reach 100 percent of everything there is, men will have to learn how to "dig" it, and "what in fact could be more useless or trash-like" than humps? From this he moves on to a reference to "those aspects of language that may be seen as a model of the trash phenomenon." In another passage Snow White complains: "Oh I wish there were some words in the world that were not the words I always hear!" And in still another reference to the pressure of language deadening, hardening, turning to trash, to discarded actuality, Paul says: "I would wish to retract everything if I could, so that the written world would be. . . ."

What it would be is, hopefully, here, in *Snow White*. A landscape filled with the dissolving remnants of earlier literary landscapes (there are parodies of Shakespeare, Rimbaud, Eliot and others), a battleground for old beauty and new form (which is always partially ugly since it rises in the face of sanctified notions of beauty), the book makes its way by dealing steadily with the problems of language. One "retracts" what the written world has been composed of not by ignoring it, by writing new language, but by discrediting it as the answer to one's own contemporary needs. So Barthelme retracts the fairy story by discrediting its operation now, and so Picasso, to take an example from another medium, retracted representationalism by discrediting its claims to be what art has to be.

To this end, Barthelme composes his book in a variety of styles, although if there is a predominant one it is a flat, arch, professorial tone, elevated and full of pseudo-precision, exactly suited to his mock-learned treatment of the fairy story: "Bill can't bear to be touched. . . . We speculate that he doesn't want to be involved in human situations any more. A withdrawal. Withdrawal is one of the four modes of dealing with anxiety." But he is also a minor Joyce, with a mastery over a great diversity of vocabularies— hip talk, academic cliché, pure or communal cliché, advertising jargon, novelistic "eloquence"—and he employs them for ironic purposes, releasing through their juxtapositions and their fish-out-of-water helplessness as literary instruments a comic sense of reality's lugubrious, perpetually renewed struggle to express itself. But at the same time he incorporates them into the substance of his new literary act.

Similarly, he incorporates into his work a great many data, events, names, sociological fads and intellectual fashions, using them for both satiric purposes and aesthetic manipulation. Throwing these heterogenous contemporary phenomena helter-skelter into the book, he proceeds to fashion a net full of red herrings. From Teilhard de Chardin's noosphere to Red China's People's Volunteers, from hip enterprises like "freaking out" or "blowing one's mind" to psychoanalysis, hard-edged painting, motorcycle gangs and the motion of non-events, *Snow White* is as up to the minute as *Esquire* or *Ramparts*. Yet the novel isn't about these things, not about their meaning or even the phenomenological appearance. It is about their status in the imagination. Despotically contemporary, pressing forward with their claims on our attention in actuality, they are here abstracted into comic helplessness, deprived, by being turned into *mere* language, of their tyranny as fashionable facts. The book swirls past them on its deceptively wayward and highly conscious course.

It remains to be asked whether *Snow White,* having largely accomplished what it set out to do, exists now as full, confident new literature. Our habits are such that faced with fiction of this kind we fall back on an inquisition designed for subjects eager enough to stand up to it. Any ordinary novel can answer without hesitation or guile the questions whether it is "satisfying," whether it is shapely, convincing, whether it teaches us something useful about our lives, or is beautiful, consoling or provocative. If *Snow White* is none of these things, its pleasures and conquests must be of a new, although not necessarily unprecedented kind. I have tried to indicate what they are; what I haven't tried to do is establish a critical hegemony over the book, the kind of bored superiority to new attempts at fictional art so prevalent in our fashionable journals.

Which isn't to say that I think *Snow White* has no faults. Most blatant among them is its author's occasional inability to resist the temptation of an easy score, to resist cheap incongruity or the merely bizarre. Thus Barthelme can write about "pornographic pastry" and an "electrical wastebasket" to destroy documents and people, speak of identifying someone by the "blueberry flan" on his lapel, have someone say "I am not an American citizen. I am under Panamanian registry," refer to a plan which is "packed away in the special planning humidor, constructed especially to keep the plan fresh and exciting."

Beyond this, he tends to a certain form of unseriousness which is not quite the same thing as high, conscious, daring frivolity. Bent on his purposes of retraction, on redeeming language from exhausted uses and servitude to other powers, and the novel from its anachronistic story-telling role, he falls under the sway of an ironical manner that sometimes ends by being its own hermetic justification. In wishing not to do what has been done before, he is not wholly willing to risk doing what has not been done before.

Kierkegaard wrote that "an intelligent man has the choice (*if* he has it) to be either ironical or radical." Barthelme's irony is radical, within the realm of literary process. And yet if he isn't radical outside it, if his irony precludes his being radical *towards the world,* this may be a measure less of his talent and will than of the world as it now stands. We go on expecting fiction, if we expect anything from it, to provide us with large, impregnable, vivid alternatives to, or confirmation of, our actual experience. The latter is beneath literature, the former seems at the moment beyond it. Perhaps Barthelme has no choice (as Kierkegaard left provision for) but to make his irony constitute his radicalism. In any case, *Snow White* cannot be asked to be the kind of novel that serves as myth, alternative cosmos, the imaginary re-creation or reorganization of the world. But it keeps the very possibilities of fiction alive, and by doing that shows us more of the nature of our age and ourselves than all those novels which never recognize the crisis of literature and therefore do nothing but repeat its dead forms.

Disenchanted Symbols

Peter Berek

The glass mountain stands at the corner of Thirteenth Street and Eighth Avenue," says the narrator of a story in Donald Barthelme's new collection, *City Life*. Like so much else in Barthelme's city, this sentence joins the familiar and the bizarre. "At the top of the mountain there is a castle of pure gold, and in a room in the castle tower sits . . . a beautiful enchanted symbol." The narrator is trying to climb the glass mountain. "I had strapped climbing irons to my feet," he tells us, "and each hand grasped a sturdy plumber's friend." We appear to be living in a city where landscape and events are surreal and baffling, but the peculiar surfaces of "The Glass Mountain" reveal a subject characteristic of this collection: the tension between ordinary life and the possibilities of art.

The narrator climbs from a street where Valiants and VWs line the curb near stumps of cut-down elms and "side-walks full of dogshit in brilliant colors: ocher, umber, Mars yellow, sienna, viridian, ivory black, rose madder." Observed by acquaintances, he tries to reach the top of the mountain and disenchant the symbol. His quest may seem heroic, but he warns the reader that the trappings of heroism won't help: "the best way to fail to climb the mountain is to be a knight in full armor—one whose horse's hoofs strike fiery sparks from the sides of the mountain."

The conventional route to the castle is to be borne aloft in the claws of an eagle—as Barthelme tells us in a passage quoted from *The Yellow Fairy Book*—and the narrator follows literary convention, though momentarily taken aback because he has forgotten his Bandaids. Arriving in a courtyard filled with flowers and trees, he sees his goal. "I approached the symbol, with its layers of meaning, but when I touched it, it changed into only a beautiful princess. I threw the beautiful princess head-first down the mountain to my acquaintances. Who could be relied upon to deal with her. Symbols identify what we will not obtain."

Barthelme's subject in *City Life* is the possibilities of a literature doomed to the production of symbols that pretend to clarify more than can be clearly seen. If this is the state of literature, the task of the writer is frustrat-

Reprinted by permission from the *Nation* 25 May 1970, 630–31/ The Nation Company, Inc. © 1970.

ing. "The Glass Mountain" offers us vivid emblems of that frustration: climbing irons, plumber's friends, and the impedimenta (a favorite word of Barthelme's) of the Village are unpromising materials for the creation of Keatsian nightingales. Perhaps an unnatural age demands mechanical art: in "The Glass Mountain," each of the hundred sentences is numbered. A companion story, "Sentence," compulsively refuses to pause for a period. Part of the fun of the story lies in seeing what can be done within the framework of a single, 8-page incomplete sentence, but the punning title reminds us that the writer himself is serving a sentence he cannot bring to an end.

For works like these, created by submitting inspiration to mechanical processes, Barthelme suggests the term "rationalized art." In "Paraguay," a travelogue account of a country not to be found in South America, he describes a world where microminiaturization has triumphed, leaving "big empty spaces in which men wander, trying to touch somthing." There, "each artist's product is translated into a statement in symbolic logic. . . . Foamed by a number of techniques, the art is then run through heavy steel rollers. . . . Sheet art is generally dried in smoke and is dark brown in color. Bulk art is air-dried, and changes color in particular historical epochs." Where art is rationalized into a product, and "each citizen is given as much art as his system can tolerate," how can art be more than decor? How can it serve the traditional and necessary functions of provoking and ordering man's feelings?

The charge of mechanical chicness was directed at Barthelme's earlier books, *Come Back, Dr. Caligari, Snow White,* and *Unspeakable Practices, Unnatural Acts.* Stories made by assembling ready-made trivia into parodic gags are in danger of being so ironically detached from valuable human emotions that they become a part of the landscape they claim to mock. Barthelme hasn't given up working with what, in *Snow White,* he called "trash"; but *City Life* incorporates a new dimension of self-criticism, a questioning of the relevance of trash to human emotions.

Two of his stories ask to be read in relation to those masters of feeling, the great novelists of the 19th century. "Views of My Father Weeping" uses the clichés of realistic 19th-century fiction—coachmen, great houses, public squares—to stage a modern quest for an honest account of a father's death and a true perception of the son's feelings. "At the Tolstoy Museum" teases our notions of The Great Writer and The Masterpiece by embodying them literally in a public monument. Yet what Tolstoy represents cannot be dismissed. Within this edifice, this museum of the past, emotions are powerfully and publicly expressed: "more than any other Museum, the Tolstoy Museum induces weeping." The narrator isn't sure whether or not to be glad we have had Tolstoy, but at least continues his progress through the building. "Perhaps something vivifying will happen to me there."

The enemy of what might vivify is irony, an irony as inescapable as it is deplorable. "Kierkegaard Unfair to Schlegel," perhaps the best story in this collection, is about discontinuity between an artist's irony and the possibility, once inherent in art, of creating visions translatable into modes of life. "Do you think your irony could be helpful in changing the government?" asks the questioner in this question-and-answer story. Answer: "I think the government is often in an ironic relation to itself." The government sells surplus Army uniforms, thus creating "a vast clown army in the streets parodying the real army" and destroying the credibility of military might. Surely here is an illustration of the liberating power of irony. But the answerer of questions is not satisfied. He cites Kierkegaard, who says that "the outstanding feature of irony is that it confers upon the ironist a subjective freedom. . . . Irony is a means of depriving the object of its reality so that the subject may feel free." The consequence of such irony is the disappearance of the real world and its replacement by a "poetic" world. Poetry, says Kierkegaard, is a victory over the world, "but what is wanted . . . is not a victory over the world but a reconciliation with the world." The private pleasure of irony is not enough, but the only alternatives the answerer can find are sexual fantasy and the sentimentality of an old movie.

Donald Barthelme has not solved the problem of the morality of detachment, but he has embodied that problem in a symbolic structure that does justice to its complexity. Here, then, is the real life in *City Life*—not in the verisimilitudinous representation of human actions but in the presentation of valuable and disturbing metaphors for thinking about those actions.

Barthelme's genius is not narrative at all; when he tries to tell something like a conventional story, as in the title piece of the collection, his flat and vapid characters are as dull and empty as the world they parody. More like a lyric poet than a writer of fiction, Barthelme creates brilliant emblems of intellectual quandaries without resolving those quandaries in action. Individual sentences and paragraphs are wonderfully witty; we delight in his zany use of pictures and trick typography. But his final achievement is less unconventional than his surface appearance. When at his best—as he is six or seven times in *City Life*—Donald Barthelme's creations help vivify our plight even if they do not clarify its outcome.

Review of *Sadness*

CHARLES THOMAS SAMUELS

A highly self-conscious writer, Donald Barthelme indicated in the first story of his first collection both his main artistic strategy and the crucial question it raises. In "Florence Green Is 81" (in *Come Back, Dr. Caligari*) the narrator muses, "I am free associating, brilliantly, brilliantly, to put you into the problem. Or for fear of boring you: which?"

Barthelme's stories are normally made up of fragments seemingly associated at random; the closer they come to narrative development, character portrayal or any other conventional purpose, the more overtly they signal their fragmentation. Barthelme may separate the parts of a story with numbers or blank space, or interpose graphic divisions. Earlier writers have drawn similar attention to the formal arbitrariness of fiction—one thinks of Sterne, who also favored graphic intrusions and blank space, or Thackeray, who said in "Vanity Fair" that his characters were puppets—but not even contemporary meta-fictionists like Borges go so far in insisting that the reader take the story as a made object, not a window on life.

Although Barthelme's strategies vary in significance from story to story, they all spring from a common impulse. He is very conscious that formulas achieve familiarity and that familiarity breeds inattention. Though he wishes that literature could still provide insight and inspiration as it did in the great, mercifully unself-conscious days of a writer like Tolstoy (see "At the Tolstoy Museum" in *City Life*), he is also aware that modern readers have experienced too much literature to respond freshly to the old modes, so he free-associates to "make it new." While less theoretical contemporaries resort to marginal subject matter, idiosyncratic viewpoints or shocking language, Barthelme uses formal dislocation to achieve this goal.

But making it new can become an end in itself. Barthelme's question in "Florence Green" highlights the most meaningful distinction between what is valuable in his work and what is merely catchy. He almost always exhibits not only fragmentation but brilliance—wit, terse elegance, zany inventiveness. Thus, if one wants to approach some ultimate judgment of his work, one mustn't get lost in the dazzlements of Barthelme's style or lose Barthelme (as has so often happened) in general questions of avant-garde writing

Reprinted from *New York Times Book Review*, 5 November 1972, 27–28 and 30–31. Copyright © 1972 by The New York Times Company. Reprinted by permission.

and the strangeness of the age; one must separate those works that "put you into the problem" from those that seem only to fear boredom.

Before *Sadness,* his fifth book, most of Barthelme's best stories put you into the problem of art in a world hostile to the continued vitality of imagination. Examples occur in each of his books, but *City Life* contains most of them. As a group, these stories constitute brilliant literary criticism written in fictive form. Anxious parables, they assert that literature, which was once a means of revitalizing the imagination and opposing banality, has itself become exhausted and banal.

The best stories in *Sadness* put us into a different, though related problem. Not parables so much as monologues spoken by neurasthenics, they throb with distress at what one of them calls "the present era's emphasis on emotional cost control" and "its insistent, almost annoying lucidity." Like the parables about art, they yearn for an openness whose best sign is seeing beyond life into mystery. But, like the parables about art, they show the dreadful diffusion of "knowingness."

The most straightforward story, and therefore the clearest indication of Barthelme's theme, is "The Sandman," which is cast in the form of a letter written to a psychiatrist by the boyfriend of one of his patients, a girl. She wants to buy a piano, and she finds the world "unsatisfactory," so the analyst tries to fathom the buried reason for her desire and to neutralize her distaste with "adjustment." Each of these goals is contemptible to the letter-writer. Ambivalence, which the analyst deplores, is to his opponent a sign of humanity. Despite his romantic attitudes, however, the letter-writer shows himself to be caught in the rationalism that he derides. As he worries over alternative explanations of his own assertions and writes footnotes to his arguments, he demonstrates why even innocence must now be argued for in the language of sophistication. He too was once a patient.

Barthelme's spokesmen, who admire the hopefulness of myths and fairy tales, are too modern to believe what they admire. The author's well-known juxtapositions of past and present, of fable and brand-name realism, of fiction and anti-fiction, all serve to dramatize this. It is the subject of his novel, *Snow White,* of some of the best of his previous tales (like "Hiding Man," "A Shower of Gold," and "The Glass Mountain"), and it is beautifully expressed in *Sadness* by "The Temptation of St. Anthony," which places that archetypical example of beleaguered faith into a contemporary setting that drains the contest of importance.

When St. Anthony first arrives on the modern scene, he is "underrated . . . mostly by people who didn't like things that were ineffable. . . . 'If he'd just go out and get a job, like everybody else, then he could be saintly all day long, if he wanted to'—that was a common theme." But his contemporaries soon tire of his sacred deviation and try to prove him a fake. When this fails, they tempt him—because doubt is even more insupportable to them than ineffability. Yet they cannot really test his sanctity because they don't care about the outcome. Too sophisticated to believe in sainthood, they are also too tolerant to lament its exposure. This is the cruel joke in which the narrator is trapped.

Arch anachronisms, deadpan narration and bizarre details make the story funny, but its point is baleful. Never more so than when the speaker shows how little this recognition is capable of altering things: "Doubt is maybe a reaction to a strong claim on your attention, one that has implications for your life-style, for change. And you absolutely, in many cases, *don't want* to do this. A number of great plays have demonstrated this dilemma, on the stage." Or: "There is a sort of hatred going around for people who have lifted their sights above the common run. Probably it has always been this way." The narrator styles himself not "a disciple, that would be putting it far too strongly; I was sort of like a friend." No wonder St. Anthony regards the temptations as "entertainment."

Like the apostle of feeling in "The Sandman," who spoke his opponent's language of reductive rationalism, the narrator of "The Temptation" has known and understood too much to work up a saving sweat. In a world where nothing is new or mysterious, nothing can move us. "After such knowledge, what forgiveness?" wrote T. S. Eliot, and Barthelme resembles Eliot in his disconnected narratives, his yearning after a vanished age of belief, his sense of being dwarfed by a vast, unassimilable culture.

Eliot's passionate tone and disjointed, allusive structure are evident in the book's best story, "The Party." Distilling a whole world of pain, the Prufrockian narrator unpacks the mental clutter and accommodation that preclude any definite break with his trivial life. By so doing, he also shows that his creator's casual humor is—at its best—not a pleasure offered to the reader but a critical reflection of sensibilities freezing in their own "cool."

"I went to a party and corrected a pronunciation," the recitation begins, "The man whose voice I had adjusted fell back into the kitchen. I praised a Bonnard. It was not a Bonnard. My new glasses, I explained, and I'm terribly sorry, but significant variations elude me, vodka exhausts me, I was young once, essential services are being maintained." Outside the window there is a constant pounding of drums, King Kong enters through the window, but the guests aren't frightened. Here "extraordinary efforts were routine." "Kong himself is now an adjunct professor of art history at Rutgers, co-author of a text on tomb sculpture; if he chooses to come to a party through the window he is simply trying to make himself interesting." Inside the party, two nuns watch a contest between teams named "*Osservatore Romano*" and the "Diet of Worms." The very equanimity with which the story unites these bizarre details depicts the condition that is stifling the speaker. Sated with "wonderful elegance" that is beyond being shocked, he is a Prufrock in reverse, whose problem is not contacting another person but breaking up with the girl whom he has taken to the party.

In these stories and others like "The Catechist" and "A City of

Churches," *Sadness* puts us into Barthelme's Waste Land. "These fragments I have shored against my ruins," says Eliot's seer. Barthelme's narrators, themselves both witnesses and representatives of collapse, might better say, "These fragments are my ruins."

But in several of the stories, fragments remain fragments. An example is "Departures," a piece composed of eight numbered parts, united by their common reference to the title. Part one tells of some youths who run away from home; three is an anecdote about children being bused to school; eight tells of a man whose lover is leaving him; etc. However, there is no reason for eight sections; lacking any principle of accretion, the piece could go on forever. Yet it can't be dismissed because the fifth section—a tall tale, a "departure" from realism—is both wonderfully funny and a paradigm of Barthelme's art.

Art is sometimes the subject of a story. Tricked up with intertitles, quotations, allusions and even a playful distillation of the author's critical status ("He can maunder." "Can't he maunder!" "I have not heard maundering of this quality since—" "He is a maundering fool"), "Daumier" seems to be a kind of *apologia pro arte sua*. Spoken by a man who seeks self-transcendence through the construction of fictive surrogate selves, the story ends with a heart-felt tribute to the healing effect of imagination: "The self cannot be escaped, but it can be, with ingenuity and hard work, distracted. There are always openings, if you can find them, there is always something to do." Unfortunately, the distractions provided in the story—accounts of the surrogates' adventures with Ignatius Loyola, Dumas's musketeers and other figures of doubtful relevance and obscure interrelation—are likely not so much to distract you as to drive you to distraction.

When Barthelme's fragments imply some comprehensible entity, they succeed—even when, as in "The Party" or "The Temptation of St. Anthony," the entity is a wholeness shattered before the story began. But sometimes the fragments don't portray a denial of coherence; they deny coherence. Such works show it's possible to write something resembling a story without needing anything resembling a point, and their virtuosity is impressive. But virtuosity in its own behalf seems an example of the same heartless insouciance that Barthelme is mocking elsewhere. There can be few writers whose best work is both so contradictory to their worst and so superior to it.

However, if Barthelme gives all too much evidence for those who dismiss him as a literary con man, he has also written stories that belong among the finest examples of the art in recent times. As he admits in "The Flight of Pigeons From the Palace," he has the impulse to astound a "public . . . it is difficult to keep . . . interested." But if at times he only gives this public what it "demands" ("new wonders piled on new wonders"), at other times he exposes the impoverishment of spirit that the demand implies. "The Flight of Pigeons" is wittily illustrated with engravings of "marvels" and we're amused by the writer's audaciousness in solving the problem of novelty that the tale posits. But in his best work Barthelme is more truly audacious; for he uses not gimmicks but words which have (as he says) "enough aesthetic excitement . . . to satisfy anyone but a damned fool"—to illustrate a world dead to mystery, dead to caring, dead to life.

Daddy, You're Perfectly Swell!

RICHARD TODD

The thing to be is a disturbing novelist. On the other hand, there is much to be said for being a comforting novelist. One can say things for it. Things can be said, for being comforting.

Why are you writing that way, said Belinda. Belinda looking over my shoulder.

Hostility of Belinda. Threatenedness of me.

You are writing like Donald Barthelme. In his manner. It gives offense.

Impertinent rejoinder.

Touch of Belinda's breast to the neck nape. Moment of détente. Belinda's glance. Belinda regarding *The Dead Father* (Farrar, Straus and Giroux, $7.95).

So. He has committed a novel, said Belinda.

Nod of assent.

You have drunk all of it.

Further nods.

How can you do this to yourself? Consider the brain cells you have wiped out, Belinda said.

But he is such a comfort, I said.

Well, enough of that. Or *faugh,* as a Barthelme character would say.

The Dead Father has appeared, Donald Barthelme's second novel, or his eighth book of stories, depending on how you look at it. I think novel is closer to the truth, though long passages of it might find a place anywhere in the collected works. It is full of delights, even if not all of them attach themselves to one another.

There is a way of talking about Barthelme that allies him with a distinguished modernist movement—disciple of Borges, exemplar of the ideas of Roland Barthes, and so on—but this overlooks the distinctive pleasures of his work, his gift for parody and social satire. He has an ear as deadly as a black belt's hand. He speaks dozens of the specialized dialects that make up our language, and he mocks their pretension and the pretentious surety of those who use them. If he addresses himself mainly to sufferers of contemporary spiritual malaise, he is particularly merciless on the language that is used to describe that illness. He sometimes indulges in low college humor. He cuts up, is cute. But at his best, he achieves a lunatic poise; he provides a way of listening to the cacophony around us: he gives comfort.

What is going on in *The Dead Father* is that a figure of that name is being hauled across the landscape by means of a steel cable to his final resting place. The figure resembles a human being in many respects, though it is "3200 cubits" long. The Dead Father has a wooden leg, large enough to contain confessionals. Nineteen men do the hauling, while four aristrocratic types do the existential suffering over the meaning of this event. This novel, as may be clear, takes a bit of getting into. It is heavy on symbol. Actually, The Dead Father becomes a symbol of some plasticity. He is God first of all. God as a father. And father as God. After that he's what you will: The Novel, Western Culture, Truth, Duty, Honor, Country. He is the order that we seek, and the control we seek to escape. A symbol with multiple possibilities—but still a heavy symbol, and it isn't at all clear at the start that Barthelme can bear up under the load. But he inventively does.

The party wends its way across the countryside in a parody of any number of literary quests. The party encounters the Wends. (I guess Barthelme meant the pun.) The Wends don't recognize fathers:

> We Wends are the fathers of ourselves.
> You are?
> Yes, said the Wend, that which all men have wished to be, from the very beginning, we are.
> Amazing, said Thomas, how is that accomplished?
> It is accomplished by being a Wend, the leader said. Wends have no wives, they only have mothers. Each Wend impregnates his own mother and thus fathers himself. We are all married to our mothers, in proper legal fashion.
> Thomas was counting on his fingers.
> You are skeptical, said the chief. That is because you are not a Wend.
> The mechanics of the thing elude me, said Thomas.
> Take my word for it, said the Wend, it is not more difficult than Christianity.

The party moves on.

Not every moment in this book relates neatly to Oedipal themes. Random and innovative dalliances occur. Clitoral politics are explored. Indoor gardening and vegetarianism are considered. Allusions to the writing of Erving Goffman and the music of Karlheinz Stockhausen. The need for newness in sexual sport is affirmed, culminating in a dance with the apes. But the best section of the book does in fact have to do with fathers, actual fathers. The party meets a translator "from English into English," who has prepared "A Manual for Sons." (This section appeared originally as a short story in *The New Yorker.*) It consists of meditations on the bestiality of fatherhood, inspired monologues from father to son, and it includes this touching sentence: "He is mad about being small when you were big, but no, that's not it, he is mad about being helpless when you were powerful, but no, not that either, he is mad about being contingent when you were necessary, not quite it, he is insane because when he loved you, you didn't notice."

Sentiment earns a larger place for itself in this novel than in anything Barthelme has written before. It resides, mostly, in The Dead Father himself. As perhaps I should have made plain before, The Dead Father has died only "in a sense." He is "dead but still with us, still with us, but dead." He has lost his clout. He knows he's bound for the grave. But he speaks. He occasionally breaks away from his cable and accomplishes some mayhem. He is a randy old goat, yearns for the attention of both fetching ladies in the party. Told he is too old, "The Dead Father fell down on the ground and began chewing the dirt of the road."

We are sorry to see The Dead Father go, when the bulldozers appear and begin to fill his grave. He reminds us of whatever it is that we imagine to have existed in a more coherent world. Not to put too fine a point on this, but if Barthelme continues in this direction, he might become a disturbing novelist.

Barthelme and Delights
of Mind-Travel

JOE DAVID BELLAMY

When we look back on this period, will the work of Donald Barthelme seem the forerunner of a whole new variety of consciousness or merely a particularly skilled and elegant example of decadence? *Great Days,* his most recent collection of short fiction, is another emotional and linguistic demolition derby in the characteristic manner: whimsical, elusive, and miraculously inventive.

Barthelme's aesthetic elevates the liberation of pure imagination above all other notions. Bringing novelties into being is his primary objective, and he faces the task with the sure-footedness of a tightrope walker and the precision of a clock-maker. He believes utterly in the delights of mind-travel and in the healing powers of dreams. Art, as it embodies these modes, is one of the new human activities, he seems to be saying, to save us from despair.

Despair has become one of his favorite subjects for jest. "At dusk medals are awarded those who have made it through the day," someone quips in his story, "The New Music." "The New Music" is a collage of fractured dialogues, where the characters are seen "sighing and leaning against each other, holding their silver plates"—as if to say, "If we're so rich, how come we ain't happy?" Another, more consoling voice chimes in: "Luckily we have the new music now. To give us aid and comfort." The implication is that "the new music" will save us from despair, or "sadness," as Barthelme called it in another of his books; and "The New Music" is, after all, not simply music but also the title of his own literary concoction.

Characteristically, there is always something else going on in a Barthelme story, something other than the apparent subject of content. Metaphorical traps and tricks proliferate in an apparent effort to describe emotional conditions and human situations too obvious, personal, ridiculous, difficult, embarrassing, or full of pain to confront directly. The astute reader is stimulated to speculate at length over these hidden mountain ranges of feeling-content, or else to supply his own filler. Snatches of eavesdropped conversations as matter-of-fact and believable as those overheard in the local bus station may alternate

Reprinted by permission from *Washington Post Book World,* 11 February 1979, 1, 4. Copyright © *The Washington Post.*

with subconscious voices answering implied questions the reader must seek on his own. Meanwhile, on the surface of the narrative, the laws of nature are suspended as are the laws of human probability. The improbable is common-place, and ironies abound.

In "Cortes and Montezuma," for example, we are entertained by a wealth of bizarre customs and sights: puddles of gold, crickets in cages, gods with names like Smoking Mirror and Blue Hummingbird. We are apparently the privileged observers of the historical meeting and "friendship" between the Spanish explorer Cortes and the Aztec emperor Montezuma (prior to Cortes's conquest) in ancient Mexico. It is a dreamlike landscape rife with ominous tensions and signs, cross-cultural misunderstandings and lurking paranoia, wherein the two leaders discuss, for instance, the relative merits of the Holy Trinity as it incorporates the pagan concept of human sacrifice. Each man, secretly suspicious, hires a detective to follow the other. "Visions are best," Montezuma remarks, "better than the best detective," as if to glorify his own powers of surveillance. But, ironically, Montezuma himself is stoned to death at the end, in a manner foreseen in a vision by Cortes's lover.

"The Abduction from the Seraglio" is an oddly affective tale of unre-quited love told as a comic/surreal science-fiction yarn. The characters live in enormous I-beam-constructed buildings, and the hero spends his creative energies making "welded-steel four-thousand-pound artichokes." Constanze, the girl for whom he yearns, has run off with a Plymouth dealer, who "has this mysterious power over people and events which is called ten million dollars a year, gross."

There are repeated complaints and bitter jokes throughout *Great Days* about betrayal and the impermanence and difficulty of human relationships. Barthelme's characters evidently need someone to love them forever, but they are of the opinion that such love is a romantic delusion.

More than ever before, Barthelme begins to seem, in some ways, a classic satirist, obsessed by the predominance and multiplicity of human vanities. Yet, the typical Barthelme protagonist whistles along good-naturedly in the teeth of the boredom, despair, absurdity, betrayal, moral decay, and deplorable behavior surrounding him. He has access to all the best technical information from a gamut of fields, but he is simply swamped by it. He has little sense of which bits of endless data should prove useful to him. The promise of science and technology—to make the world ultimately knowable—has backfired by overwhelming him with unclassifiable facts.

Great Days is challenging and funny—further proof, if we needed it, that Donald Barthelme deserves his reputation as a major literary phenome-non of these great days. Whatever his standing in the year 2000, I predict that other writers and anthropologists of the imagination, when searching for creative folklore, will continue to peruse his pages, like so many interior decorators combing through books of wallpaper samples.

Review of
Overnight to Many Distant Cities

ROBERT MURRAY DAVIS

For twenty years, Donald Barthelme has been literally the most accessible exemplar of avant-garde American fiction, right up front in the *New Yorker*—no need to track him through the labyrinth of the fur and jewelry ads—and in books published by major houses. Conservative reviewers may still be hostile but are no longer puzzled, and those with more advanced tastes are able to regard Barthelme as part of the establishment.

For those who study the shape of a career rather than individual stories or collections, *Overnight to Many Distant Cities* will make a statement about the directions in which Barthelme is moving or, more accurately, is failing to move after *Sixty Stories* (1981), which summarized and defined his early career. Whether one terms the process momentum or inertia, the stories in *Overnight* embody much the same themes in many of the same methods as Barthelme's earlier work. In fact, three of the twelve stories, "Wrack" (printed with illustrations in the *New Yorker* version), "The Mothball Fleet," and "The Sea of Hesitation," were published more than ten years ago and are here collected—heavily revised and augmented in the first case, less so in the second and third—for the first time. Two others, "Henrietta and Alexandra" and "Terminus," as well as nine of twelve vignettes, have apparently never before been published at all.

Whatever the history of composition, the stories have familiar characters and situations: Barthelme's recurrent, often unnamed protagonist—urban without being urbane, intelligent without being wise, able to analyze but not to change—is a bit further along in years; a husband and wife fail to make contact but live on, more or less together, not too unhappily—this a new turn; a reluctant subject is cross-examined about the ownership of various objects in Beckettian dialogue; a film character, here Captain Blood rather than the Phantom of the Opera or King Kong, appears in a problematic modern context; a major reputation—here Goethe rather than Tolstoy—is undercut; realpolitik and censorship are introduced into a fairy tale. New—at least as separate entities—are what the dust jacket calls "brief

Reprinted by permission from *Studies in Short Fiction* 21 (Summer 1984): 277–79. Copyright © *Studies in Short Fiction*, Newberry College.

visionary texts," printed in italics between the longer stories, like the interchapters of Hemingway's *In Our Time*. Some of them read like transcriptions of dreams ("I put a name in an envelope"), some like monologues undercutting current fashions or fads ("Well we all had our Willie & Wade records"). Three of them—"They called for more structure," "Financially the paper," and "The first thing the baby did wrong"—compress into a page and a half a coherent world of fantasy or obsession as brilliantly as anything Barthelme has done.

The problem with judging Barthelme's work in a given story or as a whole is that he is witty and inventive, and the humorous and surprising turns, found in anything he publishes, can disarm casual criticism. On my first reading of this volume, I was so delighted by individual sentences and paragraphs that I failed to ask questions about the quality of the stories as stories. Between first and second readings, I went through more than 1,200 pages of anonymous stories in typescript (one a very fair imitation of Barthelme) and was forced to consider not mere verbal dexterity or local effect but larger considerations of form. Made sensitive to distinctions between mannerism and style, formula and form, mere writing and the written, I came back to *Overnight* and discovered that about a third of the stories are better than competent and that a fourth of the "visionary texts" are brilliant and the rest dross.

Perhaps it is more useful—certainly it is easier—to explain why "Visitors," "The Sea of Hesitation," "Lightning," and the title story succeed than why "Captain Blood," "Affection," "Wrack," and "The Palace at Four A.M." do not. The first four have, for one thing, a single speaker or focal character who by the very act of speaking or observing or reflecting on the disparate and inconclusive fragments of his life imposes the form of the quest for Barthelme's grail-substitute, "What is wonderful?" The dilemmas and failures and momentary joys are not sociologically different from those in "Affection," but the lack of narrative focus in this story leaves it a series of fragments rather than an imaginative whole. One of his earlier characters says, "Fragments are the only forms I trust," and Barthelme selects and presents them wittily and sharply, but they cannot be trusted to themselves.

Even when a successful piece is more conventionally coherent than, say, "The Sea of Hesitation," the coherence is imposed by the characters rather than by the form. In "The first thing the baby did wrong," a father is caught in the logic of a theory of child-rearing which requires isolating his daughter for four hours every time she tears a page from a book. In reasonable, coherent, and increasingly desperate fashion he pursues his plan until he can foresee "that she wasn't going to get out of her room until 1992, if then," whereupon he changes the rules—"that is one of the satisfying things about being a parent"—and declares it is all right to tear pages from books. At this point the monologue ceases to be a parable, at least of the bad, repressive parent and the oppressed child, and becomes by the same inflexible logic an aggressive fantasy: "The baby and I sit happily on the floor, side by side, tearing pages out of books, and sometimes, just for fun, we go out on the street and smash a windshield together." In contrast, the fantasy of "The Palace at Four A.M." is externally imposed, built into the premises: an imaginary kingdom; a broken liaison between an ass-headed king and a diminutive, beautiful, and sexually adventurous semi-spirit of the race of bogles; anachronistic mixtures of armor and breathalyzer tests; fairy-tale situations undercut by the language of image-conscious official autobiography. The story is too busy for its own good, so mannered that there is no room left for matter. And the frame—a letter to the bogle from the king's secretary—remains only a frame.

On a smaller scale, Barthelme is funniest, most moving, and most effective when he begins with the individual voice, with characters attempting to explain themselves eloquently, ruefully, and with a guarded hope. He is least effective when he depends upon pure dialogue or lists, when he relies upon fanciful fantasy—the bright idea—or when he borrows a structure from Beckett or Borges or a continental philosopher, and forgets native models like Ambrose Bierce, Don Marquis, Mark Twain, and perhaps James Thurber. He transcends these models, in part because he knows a good deal about modernist and postmodernist writing, but he does best when he does not abandon them.

Is Simon in Hog Heaven?

Elizabeth Jolley

Although Donald Barthelme has written 12 previous books of fiction—containing some of the most innovative, influential stories of our day—reading *Paradise* is a shock and a revelation. It is a revelation of a known and existing world that is fresh because the approach is unique. The writer offers an energetic prose controlled at all times by a powerful restraint. It is a very funny novel; I laughed aloud, a rare thing while reading contemporary fiction. It is also a sad book. Its form is dramatic; the drama is built up in fragments of conversation. Sometimes it is not easy to be certain who is saying what, but it is important that the things are said. The impact of these conversations is enhanced by their sparseness. The great temptation is to read out passages: "Just listen to this—and to this and this and, wait listen to THIS. . . ."

But a review cannot be made up entirely of excerpts, however much they deserve to be shared. The actors in the drama are 53-year-old Simon and three tall, good-looking, temporarily homeless women who have moved in with him. The situation is vividly introduced and continued at intervals by an internal dialogue consisting of an exchange of questions and answers. A tantalizing first chapter is followed directly with the arrival and reactions ("Boy is this place empty") of the three women. His spacious New York apartment is practically unfurnished. "I said I didn't know what we were going to do for beds." The women are models who have just finished a lingerie show in a bar. That sort of thing is often sordid and tedious in real life but not in this book: "Bikini pants are burning at eye level" and "The white lacy *Büstenhalter* encompassing the golden breasts nudging your arm." Details in the novel that could be described as "sexy" are never dull and never salacious; rather, they are natural and necessary, ridiculously funny and tender as in real life.

Simon, an architect with "a tragic sense of brick," after discovering a pipe bomb wired under his Volvo, has left his job and his wife, giving himself a sabbatical, his first for 14 years. In reality he has left not because of the bomb, but because of "the prospect of listening to his wife's voice for another hour, another minute." The pipe bomb and its implication are not mentioned again.

Reprinted from *New York Times Book Review*, 26 October 1986, 7. Copyright © 1986 by The New York Times Company. Reprinted by permission.

Other characters are Simon's mother, occupied with her own life, out-spoken but only by telephone ("What fool bought brisket?"), and Simon's wife. "In bed, he was almost asleep. She came in and threw four quarts of icewater at him." Their relationship is now conducted by telephone (she calls him) and correspondence from a lawyer (hers).

And there is Simon's daughter, Sarah. "I got pregnant. Mom tell you? . . . Then I spontaneously aborted. Last month." Sarah, at whose birth Simon was present, dressed all in green paper clothes, is not the recipient of a General Electric fellowship. As a small child she rode about in a toy fire engine and "put out many exciting fires with it." His role of father seems now to be mainly one of providing, from a distance, funds. Sarah needs a typewriter. It is hinted that she needs more than money. A flashback recalls that, as a little girl, she would rush in and "climb into bed with Simon and his wife, settling in between them with soft little groans of satisfaction." Sarah calls her father Bluebeard; her presence at the other end of the tele-phone, together with Simon's few but clearly remembered scenes from her childhood, reflects sharply the frantic and broken standards of a society. The little Sarah, captured by television, screamed when he tried to turn it off. Later she is convicted of shoplifting—a tiny item, a lip gloss called Penum-bra. The author has made his comment in possibly the most moving of all ways. Other comments are made in descriptions, just in passing almost, as if for landscape and setting—of a brutal attack on a policewoman, for one, and of a man dying alone on a porch.

The three women, who have given all their money to fight hunger in Africa, emerge in compact scatterings of conversation. They have no pros-pects for the time being of further employment. They all have their individ-ual ways of walking; sometimes they bump into one another. They talk a great deal, to one another and to Simon and about Simon, even within his hearing. They have their own standard of honesty and morality and seem to live in the immediate present. Simon seems expected to respond to extraordi-nary sexual advances. Are some of these fantasies? Can you wake up with six breasts hanging over you? And can two women kiss one spot at the same time? The women enjoy food and drink, they cook and wash together mak-ing a lot of noise. They make love with Simon, sometimes singly, sometimes in pairs, turning from him to each other.

Their unfurnished and easygoing existence is punctuated by truths from the outside world. There are some splendid passages of satire. Veronica, one of Simon's roommates, is talking to him, describing her life. She tells him that in her high school the yearbook was dedicated to the young men, former students, who had been killed in Vietnam. "They had pictures, every year, of the latest bunch. Every year for four years." She describes her own marriage. She married a Roman Catholic and had to explain to the priest that she was not a Catholic. "And the priest says, 'Well, we can work with you on that.'

Then I told him I was still married to another guy, the guy I was married to before I met this guy. And the priest says, 'Well, we can work with you on that.' So I just thought I'd tell him that I was born without a vagina, that I just had this sort of marble insert where the vagina was supposed to be, to see if he would say, 'Well, we can work with you on that.' "

It is the rhythm of speech, the laconic tone, that transforms the content. There are some very specific erotic passages, but owing to their tone they do not bore, as such descriptions often do. One of the women states quite simply that Simon is not exactly perfection but she's had more orgasms with him than with anyone else. Some readers might be offended; but, in that case, the book is not for them.

Simon's marriage comes to an end. We cannot know what is wrong between Simon and his wife. Throwing ice water over a husband in bed is the action of a frustrated woman who is too angry to think of the consequences— that she will either have to set to and change the bedclothes or sleep in a wet bed. But Simon is the husband who has left the wife. "Simon's wife's lawyer's letter arrives and outlines her demands: She wants full custody of the child, the Pine Street house, both cars, sixty-five thousand dollars a year in alimony, child support at a level consonant with the child's previous style of life, fifty percent of all retirement funds . . . fifty percent of his partnership interest in the firm in perpetuity, and fifty percent of all odds and ends of stocks, bonds, cash and real property not subsumable under one of the previous rubrics. The client has been severely damaged in all ways. . . .

" 'What are you going to do?' Veronica asks.

" 'Give it to her, I guess.' " His attitude is breathtakingly and astonishingly human and reflects many such attitudes in similar circumstances.

The three women become restless and argumentative and Simon is told, "Thirty-five percent of all American women aren't allowed to talk at dinner parties. Think about that."

"How do you know?"

"It's in a book." Many authors, strident in the feminist cause, will never achieve the immensity Mr. Barthelme achieves quietly in that small exchange.

The women will be leaving and Simon accepts this. His nightmares are universal. The wisdom offered in the conversations can reach many. Anger is universal. "Each person could be angry at any given point with one, two, or three others, or angry at the self. . . . He reached forty-nine possibilities before his math expired."

Donald Barthelme is a writer to be read and admired and read again. *Paradise,* made up of the collision of brilliant moments, cannot be summed up. It is a picture of human needs and wishes and fantasies. Is Simon in hog heaven? It is a criticism without judgment on contemporary American life. Is it just America? In addition to being funny and deeply moving, *Paradise* is a disturbing book because it is a fantasy of freedom in a world where there is no freedom. Is this just America? The last lines forbid any last lines by a reviewer:

"Q: Feels like Saturday today, I don't know why . . ."

"A: It does feel a bit like Saturday . . ."

ESSAYS

Fiction at the Crossroads

Morris Dickstein

When two publishers in 1962 brought out overlapping collections of the work of the Argentine writer Jorge Luis Borges it was an important event for American readers, but few could have anticipated the impact it would have on our fiction. His work hardly fit into any traditional niche. The short story, even in the hands of Chekhov and Joyce, had always been the most conservative of all literary genres, the most tied to nineteenth-century conventions of incident and character, the least given to formal or technical innovation. Borges' stories hardly seemed to be stories at all; some of the best masqueraded as essays, laborious researches about nonexistent countries, ingenious commentaries on nonexistent books, mingled fantastically with the most out-of-the-way knowledge of real countries and real books. Where the traditional story took for granted the difference between the solid world out there and the imaginary world that tried to imitate it, Borges willfully confounded them. His stories were "fictions," original creations, less reflections than subversive interrogations of reality. They were also "labyrinths" which, like Kafka's writing, dressed out their mystery in a guise of earnest lucidity and matter-of-factness.

Today there is not much life in the old kind of story, though some good ones and many bad ones continue to be written. This sort of well-crafted object, which used to be the staple of dozens of now-defunct magazines, became so moribund in the sixties that it will now probably experience a mild resurgence, since changes in culture often proceed like swings of the pendulum. But the publication in 1975 of anthologies like *Superfiction* by Joe David Bellamy and *Statements* by members of the Fiction Collective confirms that our younger and more talented fiction writers have by no means abandoned the experimental impulse, though it may sometimes take them in wayward and even fruitless directions. Like so much of what emerged from the sixties, fiction today is a lesson in the uses of liberation. Whatever the results (and I intend to stress their current limitations), they remain inherently superior to a return to the old stringent molds, which conservative pundits are always ready to reimpose.

The progress of American fiction in the 1960s conjoined two different but related insurgencies against the constraints of traditional form, and against the cautious realism and psychological inwardness that had been dominant since the second world war. The first rebellion gave rise to big, eclectic books like John Barth's *The Sot-Weed Factor*, Heller's *Catch-22*, and Pynchon's *V.*, as well as ribald free-form tirades like Mailer's *Why Are We In Vietnam?* and Roth's *Portnoy's Complaint*. In all these books the grand raw materials of history, politics, literary tradition, and personal identity were transposed into fantasy, black or obscene humor, and apocalyptic personal expression. . . .

These writers did not so much cease to be realists as seek grotesque or hilarious (but accurate) equivalents for realities that were themselves fantastic. *Catch-22* not only did not lie about war, it scarcely even exaggerated. Portnoy is not fair to his mother but he is true to her, even as he caricatures and mythicizes her. These writers took advantage of the decline of censorship and of the constricting demands of formal neatness and realistic verisimilitude to broaden the range of fictional possibility, to discover new literary ancestors— Céline, Henry Miller, Nabokov, Genet—and to claim their legacy.

In the last three years of the sixties, however, culminating in the publication of Donald Barthelme's *City Life* (1970), but to some extent continuing right to the present day, a second insurgency came to the fore. Between 1967 and 1970 American fiction, following its Latin American counterpart, entered a new and more unexpected phase, which was also a more deliberately experimental one. For convenience we can call this the Borgesian phase, though Borges has not been the only model for the short, sometimes dazzlingly short, and multi-layered fiction that is involved. (Interestingly, Borges' example served to release the influence of others, including his own master, Kafka, and even such different writers as Beckett and Robbe-Grillet.)

In just these three years there were many significant collections of this new short fiction, including Barthelme's *Unspeakable Practices, Unnatural Acts* (the mock melodrama of the title is typical of him), Barth's *Lost in the Funhouse* (Barth's funhouse is the original American equivalent of Borges' labyrinth), William H. Gass's *In the Heart of the Heart of the Country*, Robert Coover's *Pricksongs & Descants* (subtitled "Fictions"), plus many of the impacted, truncated melodramas in Leonard Michaels' *Going Places* and some of the stories in Vonnegut's *Welcome to the Monkey House* (his novels were even more to the point). But the last of them, Barthelme's *City Life*, was more audacious and more successful than any of the other volumes, a book that went beyond experimental ingenuity to find new ways of connecting fiction with feeling. I'd like to use it as my positive pole in examining the uses of liberation in fiction, and I'll play it off against a larger number of other works, including some by Barthelme, which (to my mind) take experiment and liberation down less rewarding paths.

The collections I've listed all had a great deal in common, yet no two are alike. All tended to eliminate (or use ironically) the realistic matrix in which most works of fiction are embedded—the life-like quality that gives them credibility and coherence, the thematic explicitness that gives them the gratifying feel of significance. "We like books," Barthelme once wrote, "that have a lot of *dreck* in them, matter which presents itself as not wholly relevant (or indeed, at all relevant) but which, carefully attended to, can supply a kind of 'sense' of what is going on."[1] But these writers sometimes pay a heavy price for excising or satirizing this dross, which is rarely dross in good fiction anyway. They fall into inaccessibility, abstraction, or mere cleverness, substituting the *dreck* of literary self-consciousness for that of popular realism.

Coover and Barth, for example, seem overwhelmed by their own freedom, by the writer's power to invent a scene, a character, a world, to choose which word and which sentence he will set down next. Take Coover's maniacally brilliant and finally oppressive story "The Babysitter" (in *Pricksongs & Descants*), an elaborate set of variations on a few deliberately banal and melodramatic characters and plot possibilities, all merging into one another, all going off at once—a fiction-making machine run amok with its own powers, threatening to blow up in our faces, or blow our minds.

Several of Barth's stories in *Lost in the Funhouse* do comparable things in a more playful and self-ironical way. The title piece, for example, interweaves a sharp-minded yet pedantic commentary on fictional technique between the lines of a story that can't quite get itself written. In "Title" and "Life-Story," Barth can already subject this very manner of formal self-consciousness to a weary and ambivalent parody, which in turn gives the stories another layer of the same self-consciousness they criticize. Barth's fictions make the case against themselves neatly: "Another story about writing a story! Another regressus in infinitum! Who doesn't prefer art that at least overtly imitates something other than its own processes? That doesn't continually proclaim 'Don't forget I'm an artifice!'?"[2] At times the formalism and literary preciosity that were routed from the novel during the sixties seem to have returned with a vengeance in the new short fiction.

Self-consciousness has always been a key element in modern art, however, and in fiction (as Robert Alter has demonstrated anew in *Partial Magic*) it has a long ancestry that goes back beyond modernism to Diderot, Sterne, and Cervantes, a tradition that sometimes makes nineteenth-century realism look like a mere episode. (Fortunately we also have Erich Auerbach's book *Mimesis* to demonstrate the long and complex history of the realist method.) E. M. Forster once said that it's intrinsic to the artist to experiment with his medium, but in the twentieth century we've often seen how the spiral of self-consciousness can reach a point of diminishing returns. This happens when artists mimic other artists without fully appropriating them, or when they make their concerns as artists their exclusive subject. We need to hold fast to the distinction, often hard to apply, between experiment for its own sake, out of touch with any lived reality, and experiments that create genuinely new ways of seeing. The fiction of the sixties shows how the once-subversive gestures of modernism can themselves become tiresome conventions (as Barth suggests but can't seem to evade); but it also indicates, quite to the contrary, that only now that the towering first generation of modernists has been safely interred in literary history have our young writers been willing to resume the risks of the modernist program, which is nothing if not experimental and avant-garde.

I'd like to examine Barthelme's achievement in *City Life* and elsewhere to show what experimental writing has only recently been able to do without becoming self-indulgent or imitative. . . . Barthelme's earlier books, which were as intransigently original as *City Life,* were mostly notable for what they did *not* do, for the kinds of coherence they refused to supply, for their discontinuities and even incongruities, which mixed abstract ideas with pop allusions, political figures with fairy-tale characters, pedantically precise facts with wild generalities and exaggerations, and so on. They aimed to cut the reader off, to keep him guessing and thinking, to make him angry. His novel *Snow White* (1967) was a book that adamantly refused to go anywhere at all. Without benefit of plot, characters, or even much of the sober-zany humor of the stories in his first book, *Come Back, Dr. Caligari* (1964), the novel mainly limited itself to fragmentary take-offs on a huge variety of rhetorical styles and verbal trash. It was a minor-league version of what Ezra Pound saw in *Ulysses,* a species of encyclopedic satire; the book was all language, and at least on first acquaintance it seemed certain that the language was just not good enough to carry it.

Subsequent readings of *Snow White* have given me much more pleasure; though the book doesn't work as a whole, it has grown with time. It's still too detached, too satirical and fragmentary, but the author's really dry and wicked wit has worn surprisingly well. But it's finally too much of a book about itself and crippled by the absence of a subject. Its detachment is deliberate, but it leaves a void that language and satire can't entirely fill. By the book's whimsical discontinuities, by a certain deadpan mechanical quality, by a whole range of Brechtian alienation devices, Barthelme was deliberately blocking the debased and facile kinds of identification that we readers make in traditional fiction, yet he found little to substitute. . . . Taking a cue, I suspect, from Godard's films, Barthelme eliminated most of the dross of primitive storytelling so that the *dreck* of contemporary culture could more devastatingly display itself. He tried to remain, as he said, "on the leading edge of this trash phenomenon,"[3] but the project was too plainly negative, and despite his wit he nearly foundered in the swill.

In his next book, *Unspeakable Practices, Unnatural Acts,* Barthelme still proclaimed that "fragments are the only forms I trust," but the fragments began insidiously to cohere, into point fables like "The Balloon" and "The Police Band," into surreal and indirect political commentary, such as "The

President" and "Robert Kennedy Saved from Drowning." Like Vonnegut and Pynchon, whom he somewhat resembles—indeed, like Dickens and Kafka—Barthelme discovered that fantasy and caricature could serve maliciously to heighten reality as well to block it out, that fiction could, by symbolism and indirection, recover the world that it had long since abandoned to the journalists and historians.

"The President" is part Swift, part Kafka, part surrealist playlet; its hero is "only forty-eight inches high at the shoulder," a graduate of City College, a "tiny, strange, and brilliant man."[4] He is like no president we've ever had, but his spooky presence tells us something about all of them. (In a similar way, when Pynchon and Vonnegut take on the Southern California scene, or the Eichmann case, or the Dresden bombings, they refract these topical subjects through a very personal imaginative medium, but without losing touch.)

In the Kennedy story Barthelme tried neither to explain Kennedy nor to give a credible portrait of him, but rather to thicken him into an enigma— he is called K. throughout—to find symbolic equivalents for his image, and for our fascination. Authentic facts—how he frequently changed shirts each day—mingle with astonishing inventions, such as Kennedy's capable discourse as [to] the literary criticism of Georges Poulet. The result is neither "about" Kennedy nor an excercise in Barthelme's technique, but a weird mélange of the two. The example of Borges may have made such an interrogation of reality possible, but Barthelme's handling of it is wholly original.

In *City Life* Barthelme for better or worse abjured topical occasions for literary and personal ones. The public immediacies of politics and war give way to Borgesian meditation on books, writers, and ideas. Barthelme was exploring his loyalties as an artist, and even his stylistic virtuosity, though toned down, served him well. There were a few stretches of mere verbal display or experiment for experiment's sake (an unreadable piece of Joycean gobbledygook called "Bone Bubbles" was the main offender).

Most of the stories move in an entirely different direction. At a time when some of Barthelme's contemporaries were trying hard to leave personal experience behind in hot pursuit of technical innovation, the pleasure of *City Life* came from seeing Barthelme break through to new areas of feeling with no loss of rhetorical verve. Without falling back to direct emotional statement or personal psychology, he learned to write fables whose ironies, far from blocking our emotions, make more complex demands upon them.

"Views of My Father Weeping" at once mimics a style of personal narrative, pays tribute to a whole body of literature in which such narrative abounds—it's written in the style of 1910 translations from the Russian— and interweaves two strands of action more successfully than Barthelme had ever done before. The speaker's father has been run down and killed by an aristocrat, but it is his father whom he repeatedly sees weeping: these alternating actions create between them a field of significance, an atmosphere rich in implicit emotion, while the author himself remains cool, detached, tantaliz-ingly elusive. (The story concludes, staggeringly, on the word "etc.," as if to say, you've heard all this before, fill in the blanks. The text of *Snow White* included an actual questionnaire addressed to the reader.)

Following Borges (and Cervantes, for that matter), Barthelme discov-ered anew how crucially books mediate our access to our deepest experience, and he brings to his "discussions" of literature his own large reserves of fervor and ambiguity. Few passages in the book are more vivid than the retelling of a Tolstoy story in "At the Tolstoy Museum" or the paraphrase of Kierke-gaard's theory of irony in "Kierkegaard Unfair to Schlegel." In each story the narrator, who may or may not be Barthelme, feels fascinated and alarmed by the strange, imposing figure he is confronting, by the book he is bringing to life. Tolstoy's story, he says, "is written in a very simple style. It is said to originate in a folk tale. There is a version of it in St. Augustine. I was incredibly depressed by reading this story. Its beauty. Distance."[5]

Most of Barthelme's story, however, is not about Tolstoy's work but about a museum full of huge pictures, clothing, and other supposed effects of Tolstoy—the book provides large illustrations of them—all of which are the absurdly displaced objects of the speaker's ambivalence toward Tolstoy, his nostalgia for Tolstoy's kind of writing. (The story begins with an echo of Psalm 137, a poem of exile and loss.) Tolstoy is after all the greatest of the realists, and his work is the immense anti-type to Barthelme's own mode of fantasy and irony. Yet the story that Barthelme chooses to retell, "The Three Holy Men," is a small religious parable about three hermits and the strange but authentic way that they too pray. Moreover, his account of its atmosphere is eerily exact: "Its beauty. Distance."[6] Though most realistic in detail, the parable as a whole is cool in tone, integral, moving but untouchable—in short, very much like Barthelme's own tone. Tolstoy and Barthelme, oppo-sites, rearrange themselves, and our conventional expectations are disori-ented. Traditional parable and contemporary fable meet, as if to arrange a joint subversion of realism in the cause of reality.

One could give a comparable account of the Kierkegaard story, which raises different issues, or of "The Phantom of the Opera's Friend," which, besides being wonderfully funny, further develops Barthelme's rich involve-ment with melodrama, conventional realism, and kitsch, his longing, like Barth's, to be a more traditional kind of writer. (The book's illustrations, half absurdly old-fashioned, half surreal, betray the same secret wish.)

Should the Phantom of the Opera leave his sumptuous underground quarters to take up a respectable life in the "real" world? Will the "hot meat of romance" be "cooled by the dull gravy of common sense"? Does the narrator deserve a more conventional friend, from the world of Henry James perhaps, "with whom one could be seen abroad. With whom one could exchange country weekends, on our respective estates!"?[7] Will the angels in "On Angels" recover from the death of God and find new employment to replace their lapsed duties of adoration? Tuning in next week will not answer any of these questions, but Barthelme raises them in a way that gives a new wrinkle to the possible uses of pop material for serious purposes in fiction (mingled, in his case, with flotsam and jetsam of of the most arcane intellectuality). Along with so many other of our new writers, Barthelme relegates the cultural hierarchies of the fifties to a memory. Learning to appreciate his best stories, we also learn to read in a new way, savoring them for their mock-serious humor, their imaginative weight, and their profound urbanity.

I've hardly done justice to the great variousness of *City Life,* or to the design of the book, which beautifully complements its substance. One story that must be mentioned is "Brain Damage," which has no story at all but is a superb justification of Barthelme's fragmentary and surrealist method—he brings to mind the painter Magritte as much as he does any writer. It is one of the best pieces of non-sequential fictional prose I've ever read, a series of brilliant but unrelated narrative fragments—Barthelme could have been a fine conventional novelist—that finally cohere around the single inspired metaphor of the title.

The quality and character of Barthelme's work in the late sixties, and its frequent appearance in a glossy, above-ground periodical like *The New Yorker,* helped experimental fiction come of age in this country and released a flood that has continued to swell, though aside from *Gravity's Rainbow* it has yet to roar. In this, his best book, there's very little about city life but much that adds to our imaginative life and the life of our feelings. . . . *Snow White* and a later collection called *Sadness* have shown that Barthelme is not always strong in this way. More than fiction must have been involved when a character in *Snow White* made the following speech: "After a life rich in emotional defeats, I have looked around for other modes of misery, other roads to destruction. Now I limit myself to listening to what people say, and thinking what pamby it is, what they say. My nourishment is refined from the ongoing circus of the mind in motion. Give me the odd linguistic trip, stutter and fall, and I will be content."[8]

Barthelme comes out of all his books as a complex and enigmatic person, one who has seen many things, but *Snow White* was a book of personal withdrawal, dour satire, "the odd linguistic trip." I hope I've been able to indicate how *City Life,* with its new risks and new emotional defeats, represents a quite different sort of fictional victory.

The relative failure of *Chimera*[9] underlines the limitations of nostalgia as a solution to the dilemmas of experimental fiction. Nostalgia really does take the writer backward rather than forward. Traditional stories, however conscious they may make us of the writer's "creative contradictions," in themselves provide no instrument of creative breakthrough unless the writer experiences them in a new way. Barthelme's *Snow White,* though circumscribed by its linguistic and satirical rigor, was a much more successful book, for in its purity of intention it breaks more drastically with its traditional source. Where Barth's style is mock-dainty, or chatty and low, a lesson in the art of sinking in fiction, Barthelme's language is a model of planned incongruity. Like some of the New York poets, whose playfully surreal styles have similar roots, Barthelme has a background in the visual arts; he edited art journals, did the design for *Fiction* magazine, and illustrated many of his own stories, including a children's book. All his books are attractive objects, informed by an easy elegance and urbanity, and his fictional method is similar to his visual one. Barthelme the designer is principally a collector, who does bizarre collages of nineteenth-century engravings, the effect of which is neither wholly satiric, antiquarian, nor camp, but poised in a vacant eerie zone between nostalgia and irony, mad and mod. Barthelme the writer is also a connoisseur of other people's styles, not so much literary as sub-literary ones—the punishment corner of language, where curious things happen—from Victorian kitsch to modern pop, from professional jargon and journalistic formula to the capacious regions of contemporary cliché. His puckish feeling for other people's oddities of style is what makes *Guilty Pleasures,* his 1974 collection of fables and parodies, such an engaging book. The trash of inert language is his meat and drink. *Snow White* is a book about language, a collage of styles bleached and truncated into one pure and rigorous style of its own. Its fairy-tale subject is a hollow sham, the eye of a word-storm, the common theme of an anthology of ways of not saying anything. Its purity of purpose is cold and bracing: a good book for writers to read, like a verbal purge; or like ordinary-language philosophy, always sharpening the tools. But the book suits the theory of the new fiction a little too well: its surface is rarely ruffled, let alone subverted, by any actuality.

Snow White is an extreme case. Dominated by an austere, bookish wit and a negative appetite for verbal trash, it is a work of severe ironic distance. The perfection of Barthelme's method, now so widely and ineptly imitated, comes in half a dozen stories of *Unspeakable Practices, Unnatural Acts* and nearly everything in its successor, *City Life,* still the most brilliant collection of experimental fiction these last years have produced. In stories like "Brain Damage," "At the Tolstoy Museum," and "Robert Kennedy Saved from Drowning," as I tried to show earlier, the cool mode heats up electrically, and experimental writing proceeds from critique to creation. Where *Snow White* is a clearing of the ground, these stories construct a new fictional reality. They show what even *Snow White* made clear; that Barthelme is no mere collector, but a writer who juxtaposes strange forms and fragments in a way that creates new form and releases new meanings. Where *Snow White* is mainly an ironic book, *City Life* is also an impassioned one. *Snow White* is more sophisticated and condescending but it is experientially vacuous; *City Life* gives free play to that other side of Barthelme's temperament, the melancholy nostalgia for traditional art and old-fashioned feelings, unlike Barth's a nostalgia that animates rather than inhibits him. The longing is hopeless of course—he can't try to be Tolstoy. But he can plumb his ambivalence and make that contribute to the enigma, adding thick shadows to his subject. The Barthian writer escapes from personality; though he babbles about himself incessantly he discovers very little and achieve no deep subjectivity; his self-consciousness tells him that no art, no imagination, is still possible, and the prophecy is self-fulfilling. The Barthelmian writer is scarcely ever present; he loses himself in the oddest, most unpromising subjects—Kierkegaard, Robert Kennedy, angels, the Phantom of the Opera—but the space between passion and irony is filled with new preceptions and connections, self-discoveries, as in all the best fiction. The art is not confessional but it is hauntingly personal, full of mood and mystery, and the author is arrestingly present. Where writers like Wurlitzer, proclaiming the death of feeling, merely betray their own emotional poverty, Barthelme finds new imaginative life in the heart of the contemporary wasteland, in the land of "brain damage," where art shacks up with kitsch and tradition lies down with the New. This art of incongruity brings Barthelme's stories closer to the work of the comic-apocalyptic writers of the early sixties, such as Pynchon, Heller, and Vonnegut—who meet reality halfway, and strike a Faustian bargain—than to the verbal austerities of, say, Gass's fiction, or of his own younger admirers.

Unfortunately Barthelme was unable fully to maintain his creative élan in the early seventies, and his difficulties are symptomatic of the problems of experimental writing during this period. Fiction is one of the few areas of our cultural life where the breakthroughs of the sixties have been sustained, if not carried forward. By the fall of 1973 *Newsweek* could inform its readers that Barthelme had become the greatest influence on our newer writers, but by then it seemed clear that neither the established nor the younger talents had delivered the body of innovative work the late sixties had seemed to promise. Other writers imitated Barthelme's manner rather than his inventive rigor, while he himself fell frequently into shallowness, decadence, and self-imitation. On both sides this resulted not in the kinds of stunning collage and fable that made *City Life* fresh and important but in an epidemic of easy-to-write pastiche or put-on which would have been at home in a college humor magazine of the 1950s.

It was to the credit of Barthelme's next (but weakest) collection of stories, *Sadness* (1972), that he became very conscious of the perils of repetition and self-parody. His main sadness is the fear that he's already said what he has to say: "When one has spoken a lot one has already used up all of the ideas one has. You must change the people you are speaking to so that you appear, to yourself, to be still alive."[10]

It is difficult to keep the public interested. "The public demands new wonders piled on new wonders. Often we don't know where our next marvel is coming from. The supply of strange ideas is not endless. . . . The new volcano we have just placed under contract seems very promising. . . ."[11] The realistic writer, who may take his form for granted, in principle need only find another corner of reality to portray, another "subject" for a novel. If he has the energy he can write a *Comédie Humaine;* this may be why writers like Updike and Joyce Carol Oates are so prolific. But the writer who interrogates and subverts his form at every turn has no such luck. He can run out of new wonders very easily, or stick to a manner that quickly degenerates into mannerisms.

Though it contains a few good stories, *Sadness* is a sad case in point, for it exposes the underside of all the writer's virtues. It shows who the collage method fails when the fragments remains disjunctive, unillumined. It shows how the fascination with cultural trash can devolve into a taste for trivia, lovingly collected but barely transformed. It exposes the merely campy side of Barthelme's interest in melodrama, kitsch, and old-fashioned iconography, or the snobbish side, in which the artist flaunts his cultural status while slumming and loving it. The book even betrays the limitations of Barthelme's most basic virtue, his purity of language and narrative technique, which cleans up too much—psychology, description, interaction—leaving only plastic figures with curious names, leaving elegant surfaces that mesh too well with *The New Yorker's* waning cult of style.

Barthelme is at his worst where the realistic writer is best: in describing the relations between men and women. Here he retreats entirely into the satiric and ironic mode of *Snow White* but without that book's freshness and wit. (I suspect this accounts for some of the difficulties he had in writing a second novel.) *Sadness* is much too full of the trivial and the inconsequential, the merely decorative or the merely enigmatic. I have no idea why Barthelme regressed in *Sadness* from the passionate fabulistic manner of his two previous books, except for the reasons he himself suggests, but the lesson for experimental fiction is clear enough. The "cool" mode has its limitations, especially in a period of disengagement and disintegration like our own. When "Robert Kennedy Saved from Drowning" (arguably Barthelme's best story) appeared in book form in the late sixties, an otherwise admiring William Gass dismissed it, no doubt in alarm over its topicality. But the story is both fervently engaged and formally daring. Barthelme needs a great subject, an immediate subject, to draw him at least halfway out of his irony and aesthetic detachment. The feverish immediacy of life in the late sixties, the energy and pressure and swirl, which affected all of us, worked their way into his fiction with a fascinating indirection, just as it ruined some writers who tried to devour it too directly. Without that stimulus, without the pull of social ferment and spiritual possibility, Barthelme's work in *Sadness* looks the same but feels listless and remote, sketched rather than imagined.[12]

Notes

1. Donald Barthelme, *Snow White* (New York: Atheneum, 1967), 106.
2. John Barth, *Lost in the Funhouse* (Garden City, N.Y.: Doubleday, 1968), 117.
3. Barthelme, *Snow White,* 97.
4. Donald Barthelme, *Unspeakable Practices, Unnatural Acts* (New York: Farrar, Straus and Giroux, 1968), 147, 150.
5. Donald Barthelme, *City Life* (New York: Farrar, Straus and Giroux, 1970), 47.
6. Barthelme, *City Life,* 47.
7. Barthelme, *City Life,* 103.
8. Barthelme, *Snow White,* 139.
9. [*Ed. note:* In its original form, this section was preceded by a discussion of John Barth.}
10. Donald Barthelme, *Sadness* (New York: Farrar, Straus and Giroux, 1972), 61.
11. Barthelme, *Sadness,* 139.
12. *The Dead Father* (1975), his second novel, is better but not much better. It abandons the satiric language of *Snow White* for the gusto of Rabelaisian catalogues and word-heaps. Only one segment shows Barthelme at his best: an utterly brilliant but entirely tangential text-within-a-text called "A Manual for Sons," which once appeared separately in *The New Yorker.*

Donald Barthelme and the Death of Fiction

WILLIAM STOTT

QUESTION: Is the novel dead?

ANSWER: Oh yes. Very much so.

QUESTION: What replaces it?

ANSWER: I should think that it is replaced by what existed before it was invented.

That illuminating exchange occurs in "The Explanation," a short story in Donald Barthelme's *City Life* (1970). I put it at the beginning of this paper because I hope by the end to have explained it.

A great many critics—Mary McCarthy chief among them—believe that the novel as we have known it is dying in America. I agree and, in the next pages, throw a few clods on its coffin. But while I think that fiction *as we have known it* is dying, I think fiction itself is being reborn in unlooked-for ways. This paper contends that Donald Barthelme's works—particularly his early works, the short story collections *Come Back, Doctor Caligari* (1964), and *Unspeakable Practices, Unnatural Acts* (1968), and the minimalist novel *Snow White* (1967)—analyze the older fiction's failure to come to grips with reality in America as we now experience it and offer us a new kind of fiction. [1]

Eighteenth- and nineteenth-century readers, Benjamin DeMott has said, "possessed an inexhaustible range of ignorance"; "they were grateful for information of any sort." Consequently, an important function of fiction then, perhaps the most important for most readers, was to give the facts of real life. The facts DeMott offers as examples have an eighteenth-century European flavor—"plagues, princesses . . . postilions"—but one can easily find instances a lot nearer home. [2] Browse through the endpapers of trade books published in America in the late nineteenth century, and you find the publisher advertising other books his company had for sale. Most often the books are separated into two categories: Religion and Fiction. The religious books are mainly collections of sermons, a best-selling genre of the time. Under Fiction, there are subcategories like "Social" or "Economic" or "Reformative," and the novels offered treat such "Present-Day Problems" as "Alcoholism," "Poverty," "The Latest Social Vision" (trying to cash in on the popularity of Edward Bellamy's *Looking Backward*), "The Role of the Woman

Reprinted from *Prospects: An Annual of American Cultural Studies* 1 (1975): 369–88, by permission of the author and of Cambridge University Press.

in the Modern World," "The Double Standard of Morals," "The Education of the Child."[3] The way to explore such real-life matters then was generally in a fiction.

Mary McCarthy's spirited essay "The Fact in Fiction" (1960) champions this older view of prose fiction.[4] She insists that the novel is obliged "to be true, not only true to itself like a poem or a statue, but true to actual life"; for "we not only make believe we believe a novel, we do substantially believe it, as being continuous with real life, made of the same stuff." She delights in Balzac's "explanations of the way institutions and industries work, how art is collected, political office is bought, . . . the way paper is made." She praises the historical and philosophical interludes in *War and Peace*—"the Battle of Borodino, the capture and firing of Moscow, the analysis of the character of Napoleon, the analysis of the causes of war, the great chapter on Freedom and Necessity—all of which are nonfiction and which constitute the very terrain of the novel." With its insatiable "passion for fact in the raw state," the facts of life public and life private, the "real novel," the "true novel," which she fears can no longer be written, "has or *had* many of the functions of the newspaper." It told what was actually going on in the great world.

McCarthy argues that this view of prose fiction, and hence fiction itself, has come upon hard days for two reasons. First, the contemporary novelist and his audience are "embarrassed by the insignificance (or lack of 'significance') of [the] finite world" he images. Indeed:

> he cannot quite believe in it. That is, the existence of Highbury or the Province of O——is rendered improbable, unveracious, by Buchenwald and Auschwitz, the population curve of China, and the hydrogen bomb. Improbable when "you stop to think"; this is the experience of everybody and not only of the novelist; if we stop to think for one second, arrested by some newspaper story or general reflection, our daily life becomes incredible to us. I remember reading the news of Hiroshima in a little general store on Cape Cod in Massachusetts and saying to myself as I moved up to the counter, "What am I doing buying a loaf of bread?" The coexistence of the great world and us, when contemplated, appears impossible.

The artist cannot treat "the great world" directly: he must make a concrete metaphor for it, a little finite fictive world.[5] But no metaphor, no fiction, seems to have weight alongside the public catastrophes of the day.

The second reason why McCarthy thinks fiction in jeopardy is the reverse of the first. For although the novelist and his audience no longer believe in the veracity of his fictive world, his metaphor for life, neither do they believe in Auschwitz and Hiroshima and the "infamous Ilse Koch" who "made lampshades of human skin." It is the "special quality" of such horrors to "stagger belief" and "kill . . . even curiosity." The great real world, like the novelist's little world, has become incredible, unreal. One hundred years ago, George Eliot argued in *Middlemarch* that the individual was no longer able to perform historical acts; in our time it would seem that the individual has also lost the capacity to assimilate historical events. Our century's social upheavals, in one sense the most *real* experiences of the generations that underwent them, are not, it appears, reducible to human scale: they are best treated in the abstractions of nonfiction. What about unhistorical social life? We remember that Eliot herself, though she couldn't *cause* historical change, could thoroughly *describe* small town England at a certain moment in history. For a portrait of American life today comparable to *Middlemarch's,* where would one turn? To fiction? Some people would; I confess I do, all the while knowing I won't find a novel capable of Eliot's broad comprehension because our society is not so simple as hers. For most people, though, the *Middlemarch* of our time would certainly be *Middletown,* or some other nonfiction.

Nonfiction increasingly appeases our hunger for the facts of real life. This is a recent, and perhaps a revolutionary, change in taste. Why it happened would take a book to answer—and the answer, like most important answers, would be only speculative. That it happened, though, is hard to doubt. According to John Fischer, former managing editor of *Harper's* and head of trade books at Harper and Brothers, "fiction has been losing ground to nonfiction for at least forty years. Back in the twenties, readers bought roughly two novels in their original editions for every one nonfiction book; today the reverse is true." Fischer wrote this in 1963; the trend has since accelerated: today Dan A. Lacy, senior vice president at McGraw-Hill, says the figures would be nearly four nonfiction books for every fiction. A bookseller spelling out the "ABC's of Stocking a Bookstore" in 1969 advised that nonfiction should be 50 percent of inventory, fiction 10 percent, reflecting normal sales. In paperbacks the same trend is clear. In 1956, early in the paperback revolution, only 14 percent of such books were nonfiction. By 1967 this figure had risen to above 80 percent, and more than half of the twenty best-selling paperbacks for the year were nonfiction. Magazines show the same trend. As late as 1940, magazines publishing both fiction and nonfiction ran 70 percent fiction to 30 percent nonfiction; by the mid-fifties the ration was reversed.[6]

These days it is through nonfiction that we get the facts of real life. If we want to know how to raise a child, what to do about poverty, alcoholism, and the economy, what Napoleon was like, how Americans make paper or love or money or presidents, we turn not to a book of fiction, but to one of fact: a *nonfiction.* We may even get a trifle impatient when fiction tries to speak to us directly about actual social conditions. We read Disraeli's *Sybil, or the Two Nations,* Zola's *Germinal,* Sinclair's *The Jungle,* Steinbeck's *Grapes of Wrath* or virtually any of the "social conscious" novels of the thirties, and we find ourselves saying, "But if things are really that bad, why bother to make a fiction of them? Just give us the facts so we know what to do, whom to blame."

Today we rely on nonfiction to explain our world to us, and Donald Barthelme examines what this change from fiction to nonfiction means for our lives and values. Essentially, his stories are about what happens to fiction in a nonfiction world, or—to put the same thing another way—what happens to private values when all facts are treated as public. At the end of her essay, Mary McCarthy tries to believe that the novel as we know it is not dead: "Someone, somewhere, even now may be dictating into a dictaphone: 'At five o'clock in the afternoon, in the capital of the Province of Y——, a tall man with an umbrella was knocking at the door of the governor's residence.' In short, someone may be able to believe again in the reality, the factuality of the world"—and of the small world he imagines. In "The Dolt," a story in *Unspeakable Practices,* Barthelme shows us just such a writer, a young man named Edgar who has written the beginning of a tale that "does not contradict what is known" "historically" about the world in which it is set. In spite of its factual accuracy to the great world, the story lays the groundwork of a persuasive fictional world that will examine human motives and relations. It begins: "In the town of A——, in the district of Y——, there lived a certain Madame A——, wife of that Baron A——who was in the service of the young Friedrich II of Prussia. The Baron, a man of uncommon ability, is chiefly remembered for his notorious and inexplicable blunder at the Battle of Kolin." Which blunder the story will undertake to explain through a fiction portraying the Baron's relation to his wife, "the lovely Inge, Madame A——," and Giacomo Orsini, who "was her lover, and . . . was not." Thus the small fictive world of private human interaction will serve, as fiction immemorially has, to explain the inexplicable in the great public world: Friedrich II's severe defeat, "which resulted in a loss, on the Prussian side, of 13,000 out of 33,000 men." Only it won't, because Edgar can't write the story. He has the beginning and the tag end but, as he realizes, "I don't have the middle." He can't lay bare the mystery of human relations; he can't move beyond the public facts—the Baron's "alleged suicide," Inge and Orsini's suspected adultery—into the private reality from which these confused facts grow.

Why can't he? Until the story's last page, we don't know; the reason seems to be that Edgar is a dolt, as the title suggests. In the fourth paragraph from the end, all unexpectedly, however, a new character appears. "At that moment the son manqué entered the room. The son manqué was eight feet tall and wore a serape woven out of two hundred transistor radios, all turned on and tuned to different stations. Just by looking at him you could hear Portland and Nogales, Mexico" The son *manqué* clearly represents the great world we cannot shut out of our private lives, the world the media bombards us with, Marshall McLuhan's global village perpetually turned on and tuned in. Edgar "trie[s] to think" with "this immense son leaning over him like a blaring building. But he couldn't think of anything. Thinking of anything was beyond him." Edgar's little fictive world will have no content, then, because of the overwhelming, shrill immediacy of the great world. The blaring facts of real life spell the end of the old kind of fiction. Public actuality defeats private imagination.[7]

This is what Barthelme's fiction is about, if we generalize its theme. But the specific implications of his stories are richer than these platitudes suggest. What he is up to in *Snow White,* for example, could not be plainer, yet it is quite intricate; though it happens on every page, it rarely fails to surprise. Consider: "At the horror show Hubert put his hand in Snow White's lap. A shy and tentative gesture. She let it lay there. It was warm there; that is where the vulva is." The word that jars in these sentences is, needless to say, *vulva.* Why does it? Quite simply, because it is a different kind of word from those preceding. *Shy, tentative,* and *warm* express subjective states of feeling; they are words used in everyday conversation to speak about personal experience. The nouns *lap* and *gesture* share the intimate imprecision of these adjectives. We all know what a lap is, and any technical definition of it—as *Webster's Third International's* "the front part of the lower trunk and thighs of a seated person"—strikes us as absurdly heavyhanded. *Webster's* definition only makes sense, significantly, when it gives an example of how we use the word in everyday life: "to sit on grandpa's lap." *Lap* is a private word, one spoken by relatives ("Come sit on grandpa's lap"), by friends, and—as here in Barthelme—by lovers. *Vulva,* in contrast, is exactly *not* a private word; it has no emotive value (which is why, here, it makes us grin and shudder); the lover would never whisper it to his lady. *Vulva* is a technical word, an anatomical term of precise meaning: "the external portion of the female genital organ," says *Webster's.* "The Vulva" might be a chapter in Masters and Johnson's *Human Sexual Response* (1966), along with "The Scrotum and the Testes," "The Penis," and "The Uterus." It is a *public* word belonging to scientific literature and professional consultation like that between doctor and patient.

Warm lap, and *shy and tentative gesture* are phrases expressive of human perception and emotion; as such, they fit perfectly into a fiction. *Vulva* is a scientific term that properly appears only in nonfiction. That it occurs here, out of context, tearing apart the values of the fiction that surrounds it, is precisely Barthelme's point. In *Snow White* he gives us a fictional world so riddled with nonfiction public definitions that private values can no longer be maintained.

In part, but only in part, Barthelme is doing what Saul Bellow does in his best work. Barthelme too suggests that public values have so intruded upon private life as to collapse it, make it public also; he would agree with Moses Herzog's true, cruel parody of Gresham's law: "Public life drives out private life."[8] Thus, Snow White finds Clem's lovemaking "downright anti-erotic" because his "idea of sexual congress" exhibits the "Western confusion between the concept, 'pleasure,' and the concept, 'increasing the size of the herd.' " Clem's values are public—increase the herd—so he bullishly ignores the delicacies of "approach" and "technique" which would give Snow White pleasure. Accordingly, his lovemaking is described as "sexual congress," a term of pastors and clinicians.

The difference between Bellow and Barthelme is that whereas in, say, *Seize the Day* (1956) Bellow shows a public value, the success ethic, eroding private life, Barthelme treats less public values than public *information,* expertise. Consider Snow White's habitual gesture of "let[ting] down her hair black as ebony from the window." She herself is well aware of the sexual implications that anthropologists have taught us to read into women's hairstyles, covered in puritanical cultures (as the Arab), uncovered, long, and free-falling among more promiscuous groups. As she dangles her hair, she thinks, "This motif, the long hair streaming from the high window, is a very ancient one I believe, found in many cultures, in various forms. Now I recapitulate it, for the astonishment of the vulgar and the refreshment of my venereal life." She is wholly conscious of the public meaning; indeed, she acts to "recapitulate" it in the eyes of the world, makes of herself an object for public delectation, hoping thereby to attract her prince.

Even more obviously does she see herself with public eyes, and hence objectify herself, when "in her chamber [she] removed her coat, and then her skirt, and then her slip, and then her bra. The bare breasts remained." Already it is as though the breasts didn't quite belong to her: she doesn't take them off, but one almost fears that she might, like a woman in a Pynchon novel. She thinks: "What is there to think about them. . . . Let us take stock. These breasts, my own, still stand delicately away from the trunk, as they are supposed to do. And the trunk itself is not unappealing." Examining herself in a rococo mirror, she suddenly gets emotional, almost personal, over her body, and in a significant gesture she refuses the technical word she has just used: "In fact *trunk* is a rather mean word for the main part of this assemblage of felicities. The cream-of-wheat belly! The stunning arse, in the rococo mirror! And then the especially good legs, including the important knees. I have nothing but praise for this delicious assortment!" Rather than accept the dry, medical word *trunk,* rarely seen outside *Webster's* definitions (see above) and coroner's reports ("the deceased's head had been severed from the trunk"), Snow White begins writing a poem to herself. It isn't much of a poem, to be sure, but the inestimable thing about it is that for a moment we hear some feeling and something like the kind of talk that should go on between lovers. In Snow White's world there is no prince forthcoming, so she must do her own praising. Nevertheless, however diminished, this is the language of love—the "delicious assortment" comes from a sweetheart's candy box, and the "cream-of-wheat belly" echoes Solomon's great line celebrating his beloved in the Song of Songs: "Thy belly is like a heap of wheat." Thus we feel it a defeat of something human when, at the end of the scene, Snow white reverts to a hard-eyed, unemotional stocktaking of her "nice-looking breasts": "Not the best I've ever seen. But not the worst."

Throughout *Snow White,* consciousness of public opinion, particularly expert's opinion, perverts private expression. The seven dwarfs buy a new shower curtain in hopes of enticing Snow White back to her games in the bath. They think the curtain "adequate . . . nice," or even somewhat better. But when a visiting expert, an "esthetician," pronounces it "the best-looking shower curtain in town," they are struck with a sudden frenzy to prove him right. The wish to obtain public verification for his statement makes them lose sight entirely of their private goal. Paul—the prince-figure turned Peeping Tom—remembers:

> I was fond of stick dancing at one time. There was some joy in that. But then a man came and said I was using the wrong kind of stick. He was a stick-dancing critic, he said, and no one used that kind of stick any more. The stick of choice, he said, was more brutal than the one I was using, or less brutal, I forget which. Brutalism had something to do with it. I said, fuck off, buddy, leave me alone with my old stick, the stick of my youth. He fucked off, then. But I became dissatisfied with that stick, subjected as it had been for the first time to the scrutiny of a first-rate intelligence. I sublet the stick. And that is why I have become everything I have become since, including what I now am, a voyeur.

Knowledge of the world's way stopped his dancing. Public advice perverts family expression, too: mothers bring up their children according to "page 331" of a book which recommends "batting the baby": " 'Spare the bat and the child rots,' said the mothers." They have learned the encapsulated cant in which expertise always finds popular expression; by such means do the great masters of literature shrink to meaningless pellets of critical pique:

PUSHKIN DISPLAYED VERBAL FACILITY. GOGOL WAS A REFORMER. AS A STYLIST DOSTOEVSKY HAD MANY SHORTCOMINGS. TOLSTOY. . . .[9]

When characters seek to express their private selves, they do it in the style and vocabulary to which the media and experts have accustomed them. The dwarfs' "fantasy of anger and malevolence" is lifted from a classic film: "We cooked Snow White over the big fire, in the dream. You remember the burning scene in Dreyer's *The Burning of Joan of Arc.* It was like that, only where Dreyer was vertical, we were horizontal." At Bill's trial, everyone tries so hard to mimic the inane circumlocutions they have learned from trials in films and television that the individual entirely evaporates: Shield 333, a policeman, asked "Are you Shield 333?" replies, "I are." Paul, before he becomes a voyeur, is a painter, "sure of myself and my image"; he shows Snow White a painting that both find "sublimely" and satisfyingly "poor." Yet, when she tries to praise this quality, she can do it only in the cant of art reviewers:

"I find it extremely interesting as a social phenomenon," Snow White said, "to note that during the height of what is variously called, abstract expressionism, action painting and so forth, when most artists are grouped together in a school, you have persisted in an image alone. That, I find—and I think it has been described as hard-edge painting, is an apt description, although it leaves out a lot, but I find it very interesting that in the last few years there is a tremendous new surge of work being done in the hard-edge image. I don't know if you want to comment on that,[10] but I find it extremely interesting that you . . . were one of the earliest, almost founders of that school, if you can even call it a school."

What is pitiable and almost touching here is Snow White's hesitant fear of choosing a word not consecrated by the experts in the art media, or of misapplying their jargon. She can't say what she feels because she must express herself in the way she has been taught is right.

A final instance: the dwarf's theft of Paul's typewriter. To sneak the "fine Olivetti 22" from Paul's apartment house, the "typewriter girls" accompanying the dwarfs' put it under their skirts. An absurd act, of course: just the opposite of inconspicuous. As so often, though, Barthelme's characters are mimicking a fact that is public knowledge, in this case a gesture from recent history. During the destruction of the Warsaw ghetto, certain heroic Jewish women came forward to the German lines with grenades hidden under their skirts. Once in the soldiers' hands, they pulled the pins and blew up themselves and their captors. Needless to say, the typewriter girls are in no way comparable to these women of the Warsaw ghetto; the theft they so ludicrously abet is a prank to get back at Paul in whom Snow White has expressed an interest. (Significantly, the dwarfs believe Paul's private self will be diminished if they steal his public assets: 'We have his typewriter. That much of him is ours, now.") The typewriter girls appropriate the women of the Warsaw ghetto's gesture when it is not only meaningless but defeating of their real end (to sneak the typewriter unnoticed from the building). And yet they *do* appropriate it; they make an analogy between themselves and the Jewish women. That they are able so to cheapen a heroic gesture is downright obscene—and very much Barthelme's point. For he is saying that people will cheapen anything, however noble, singular, private it be, if they have access to it. What gives the typewriter girls access to the Jewish women's gesture? An indiscriminating publicity of knowledge.

Here we approach the heart of Barthelme's complaint. The "knowledge" or "information explosion" has brought us too many facts without the emotional values that would give these facts, and our lives, meaning. Many too many of our ideas, like Snow White's "sulky notion" that "what is, is insufficient," come to us from the "rental library," the public world of the media which is not, never can be, and certainly never should be our real life. "Thanks to the democratization of education in our country," everyone learns immensely more than he can assimilate. Knowledge, values, experience, art, language are thus degraded: Dan foresees all human production becoming " 'filling' . . . 'stuffing' . . . an 'endless . . . sludge.' " In Barthelme's world this has already happened.

Or almost. Behind the scenes, through her secret poem and (to public view) gibberish thoughts, Snow White moves beyond the dwarfs' embrace into some new private value which the narrator, himself of the dwarfs' party, cannot explain. She transcends them while they keep to their old "principle": "HEIGH-HO." The reader isn't convinced by Snow White's change of heart, her "apotheosis," but again this is part of the point: in her world (a world disconcertingly like our own) privacy isn't plausible, has no way to defend itself, appears just gibberish. Barthelme offers more persuasive examples of the private self in two stories we will examine in a moment, "A Shower of Gold" and "Robert Kennedy Saved From Drowning." But in *Snow White,* his basic thought is plain enough: there is a public world and a private world and the twain must never meet.

For when they do, the private, the truest value, loses. Why does it? Barthelme nowhere says why directly, though his every page implies the reason. It is a mark of how corrupted we are that the question doesn't trouble us first thing. The public wins because it is the way of knowing we have been taught, and taught ourselves, to respect. America has no philosophy but pragmatism, we like to say; we value only what works. What works for us— because we are egalitarians and materialists—is what works in the world: what most people say works. To understand what works, and how, we create experts (Max Weber once observed that Americans could not have greater contempt for teachers nor greater respect for experts); and experts create expertise, and expertise creates the public language which Barthelme transplants into fiction. We Americans let the public prevail without even wondering why; the need to criticize this perversity in us drives Barthelme's fiction, and is what is essential to us in it.

Snow White is a confrontation of private and public, individual and expert, fiction and nonfiction. The private loses.[11] Public ways of thought subvert private values because we do not respect them enough to sustain them. Our lives, Barthelme is saying, are so infiltrated by the public information of mass media and mass education that, unless we are strong, we cannot fail to be changed in our personal relations and innermost selves. Families used to spend dinner in conversation; now, if the experts can be trusted, each weeknight a third of America eats in front of the television—watching the parade of horrors on the six o'clock news.[12] Our selves, too, like those of Barthelme's characters, have become vulnerable to public inspection and analysis, if only because we adopt these ways of thought. Our personalities, he implies, can be reduced to a neat formula as readily as Paul's or Jane's:

Have you understood, in reading to this point, that Paul is the prince-figure?
Yes ( ) No ( )

That Jane is the wicked stepmother-figure? Yes ( ) No ( )

Barthelme's questionnaire encourages us to do to his fictive world what public information does to our private life: shrink it to cant and cliché:

Has the work, for you, a metaphysical dimension? Yes ( ) No ( ) What is it (t w e n t y - f i v e   w o r d s   o r   l e s s)? _____

_____

_____

Indeed, Barthelme cunningly suggests that the public world into which his fiction is offered can modify the fiction; he will change his little world, he implies, to please the great:

In the further development of the story, would you like more emotion ( ) less emotion ( )?

Is there too much *blague* in the narration? ( ) Not enough *blague*? ( )

Most simply put, Barthelme's point is that the public world has nowadays far too much influence on the private. Great heavens, even the President of the United States worries "about Bill, Hubert, Henry, Kevin, Edward, Clem, Dan and their lover, Snow White. I sense that all is not well with them. . . . I am concerned . . . because I am the President. Finally. The President of the whole fucking country. And they are Americans . . . my Americans." Such an attitude leads to a well-meant but ruinous intervention of society in private life. The book's most terrifying passage casually introduces "the President's war on poetry": "The root causes of poetry have been studied and studied. And now that we know that pockets of poetry still exist in our great country, expecially in the large urban centers, we ought to be able to wash it out totally in one generation, if we put our backs into it." In the novel, as in life, poetry is the number one enemy of the public: the only secret Snow White keeps from the dwarfs is her poem. These days, as Barthelme imagines things, the public will organize, if necessary, to stamp out that poem before it is written.

It is characteristic of Barthelme to make art his symbol for private life. In his amazing little story "The Balloon," a sort of allegorical poem in sociologist prose, an artist creates out of the private "unease" and "sexual deprivation" caused by his beloved's absence a "concrete particular" world, a gigantic balloon that covers all Manhattan. The "meaning" of what he has made teases and perplexes the public; his creation—only a "rough draft," he insists—upsets the old ways of thinking. If the balloon had some obvious public purpose, he knows no one would have thought twice about it: "Had we painted, in great letters, 'LABORATORY TESTS PROVE' or '18% MORE

EFFECTIVE' on the sides of the balloon," had he made it an advertisement, everyone would have known how to act toward it. But it isn't an ad; it is a gratuitous gesture done for private reasons, "a spontaneous autobiographical disclosure" of frustration and love. Only the beloved knows why it was made. When she returns, the balloon, "no longer necessary or appropriate" to the artist's mood, is dismantled and "stored in West Virginia, awaiting some other time of unhappiness, sometime, perhaps, when we are angry with one another."

Similarly, in *Come Back, Doctor Caligari,* the character who most consciously and completely resists public violation of his self is an artist, the sculptor Hank Peterson in "A Shower of Gold." Because he needs money, Peterson agrees to go on a television quiz program, *Who Am I?,* which tries "to discover . . . in a root radical way . . . what people *really are.*" The program's method is to connect its contestants with a polygraph and then see if they lie in answering personal questions. The first contestant is found to be "lying! lying! lying!" when he says he loves his mother; when his real feelings are exposed, "the tote board spell[s] out, in huge, glowing white letters, the words BAD FAITH!" The second contestant confesses to a "lifelong and intolerable itch" for airplane stewardessess, which itch ruined his career. When Peterson's turn comes, he defends his real, private self by talking before a question is asked—and refusing to shut up. In his monologue he uses, because he must, the meaningless facts of the public world—"coming home I passed a sign that said in ten-foot letters COWARD SHOES"—and its jargon—"In this kind of world . . . absurd if you will, possibilities nevertheless proliferate and escalate all around us." He tells who he is, frankly but without demeaning himself, and then pleads with the audience to become private selves once more. "I am a minor artist and my dealer won't even display my work if he can help it but minor is as minor does and lightning may strike even yet. Don't be reconciled. Turn off your television sets, cash in your life insurance, indulge in mindless optimism. Visit girls at dusk. Play the guitar. How can you be alienated without first having been connected? Think back and remember how it was." His message given, Peterson continues to talk despite the threatening of the television people. His apology for the private self leads him naturally into an earlier and nobler vision of who he, as man, is: " 'My mother was a royal virgin,' Peterson said, 'and my father a shower of gold. My childhood was pastoral and energetic and rich in experiences which developed my character. As a young man I was noble in reason, infinite in faculty, in form express and admirable, and in apprehension. . . .' Peterson went on and on and although he was, in a sense, lying, in a sense he was not."

The only answer to the pressures of publicity is to reassert harder the private. Peterson would have gotten money, celebrity, for laying himself bare—an interesting comment on success in our time. But he knew what he would lose.

Barthelme's essential theme is the human cost of a society that values publicity more than privacy. He shows us, quite simply, the danger in what we Americans are doing to ourselves with our faith in other people's values, our collectivist pleasures, our encounter groups and gropings, our lust for self-exposure. The madness Barthelme satirizes, *our* madness, is real and urgent, no doubt about it. Yet I want to conclude by suggesting that in his richest stories Barthelme discovers a curiously renewed privacy, a deep implicit selfhood, in publicity.

We have already seen that the balloon that covered Manhattan arose from the psychic needs of one man. More interesting than the metaphor itself is the social-science prose in which Barthelme casts it:

> The balloon, for the twenty-two days of its existence, offered the possibility, in its randomness, of mislocation of the self, in contradistinction to the grid of precise, rectangular pathways under our feet. The amount of specialized training currently needed, and the consequent desirability of long-term commitments, has been occasioned by the steadily growing importance of complex machinery, in virtually all kinds of operations; as this tendency increases, more and more people will turn, in bewildered inadequacy, to solutions for which the balloon may stand as a prototype.

The story demonstrates that even this kind of public talk can sustain—keep aloft—the balloon of private vision. An individual's most personal needs—as here, to tell one's darling one misses her—can be expressed with tools the experts built for other purposes.

Barthelme's most original story, "Robert Kennedy Saved from Drowning," suggests much the same thing. This story, written before Robert Kennedy's assassination, is a collection of notes to be the background for a *Newsweek* profile—or a Jim Bishop *Day in the Life of*———book—about a public personality. This man, called "K." throughout the story, is described by friends and intimates; by what he does, what he eats, how he dresses; by his opinions on public matters; by his relations with his family; by his personal philosophy; by his response in a moment of peril when he nearly drowns. And at the end of this detailed public analysis, do we understand him? No. K. turns out to be multiple and various—as unpredictable as a real person always is. "He is both abrupt and kind." He ignores his staff, then overwhelms them with attention. "His reactions are impossible to catalogue": he may laugh at the amusing and get depressed at the tragic, or "these two kinds of responses may be, on a given day, inexplicably reversed." Sometimes he works hard, sometimes he can't bring himself to do anything. As a friend comments, "He's very hard to get to know, and a lot of people who think they know him rather well don't really know him at all. He says something or does something that surprises you, and you realize that all along you really didn't know him at all." A former teacher praises K. for his "unusual . . . compassion," yet he hurts a painter's feelings with a casual nasty crack and, on a certain day, fails to stop his children's tears. He gives his business close attention, yet is able to "shrug and forget about it." In short, as Karsh of Ottawa recognizes, K. just can't be predicted: it is impossible to guess how much time his portrait will take.

In fact, the story suggests that no amount of exposure would take a complete portrait. Even when, alone and at his ease, K. goes swimming, "he retains his mask." Though he is a public figure under constant scrutiny, he is infinitely a private man, radically unknowable as all people are. He will use, because he must, the empty public ways of saying things:

Urban Transportation
"The transportation problems of our cities and their rapidly expanding suburbs are the most urgent and neglected transportation problems confronting the country."

But this does not mean that he won't have untranslatably private dreams:

Orange trees.
Overhead, a steady stream of strange aircraft which resemble kitchen implements, bread boards, cookie sheets, colanders.

He will speak the drivel of public men, but he will make it say what he wants:

K. Explains a Technique
"It's an expedient in terms of how not to destroy a situation which has been a long time gestating, or, again, how *to* break it up if it appears that the situation has changed, during the gestation period. . . . In this business things are constantly altering (usually for the worse) and usually you want to give the impression that you're not watching this particular situation particularly closely, that you're paying no special attention to it, until you're ready to make your move. That is, it's best to be sudden, if you can manage it. Of course you can't do that all the time. Sometimes you're just completely wiped out, cleaned out, totaled, and then the only thing to do is shrug and forget about it."

Finally, though he may need the clichés of other, better thinkers to do it, he can explain himself and the way his private being feeds his public image, his charisma: "The Maricaudian being is, according to Poulet, a pastless futureless man, born anew at every instant. . . . The Marivaudian being has in a sense no history. Nothing follows from what has gone before. He is constantly surprised. He cannot predict his own reaction to events. He is constantly being *overtaken* by events. A condition of breathlessness and dazzlement surrounds him. In consequence he exists in a certain freshness which seems, if I may say so, very desirable."

The public press, whose reporting techniques Barthelme imitates, can only describe K. in a public way. But this way, we find, doesn't begin to unriddle the mystery of his real self. Instead, "Robert Kennedy Saved from Drowning" suggests that the public way, in failing, actually verifies and reinforces the dominion of the private. K. can't be explained in a news magazine: his public aspect has too little coherence. K.'s self is exactly what the mock notes and the article that will come from them must leave out— what they can't touch, treat, predict. But what the article leaves out is the only thing that matters, the true center of a man's life from which he moves all before him.

This curious and brilliant story shows, then, that even nonfiction ways of knowing and speech offer a home, albeit outside their gates, to the private reality that is fiction's province: fiction can be made of nonfiction. Barthelme's is. And Barthelme has saved K.—the K. whom Kafka taught us to recognize as Everyman—and Robert Kennedy and similar public figures, from drowning in the sea of publicity by simply insisting that the sea, though it has K.'s body, his acts, his words, even certain of his past dreams and thoughts, doesn't have the real man. Barthelme sees that nonfiction's numberless facts and numbing jargon, though apparently reductive of experience, may in fact serve to point us back to the great real world in which men are not finally explicable and life unanswerably happens.

If we *want* explanations and answers, this fiction proves that articles of the sort it parodies won't help: we need a fiction. For although nonfiction can give us the facts of real life, only fiction gives us glimpses at life's real facts.

Is the novel dead? As we have known it, maybe so. What replaces it, then? It is replaced by what existed before it was invented. Stories. Stories like Barthelme's. Stories about the inner life.

Notes

1. To be sure, these themes occur in Barthelme's later writings—a fact of which he is uneasily aware: in "The Flight of Pigeons from the Palace" and "The Party," two stories in *Sadness* (1972), he complains that "The supply of strange ideas is not endless" and "When one has spoken a lot one has already used up all the ideas one has." But the themes are no longer so insistent. Whereas the early Barthelme, like most American artists in the 1960s, had spasms of social concern (see, for example, his allegories "Report" and "The Police Band" in *Unspeakable Practices*), the Barthelme of the 1970s does not. For him, in *Guilty Pleasures* (1974), the Watergate Nixon is fun, not an outrage. The later Barthelme seems resigned to continual pastiche and cultivated multiplicity as the only tolerable responses to the world.

2. Benjamin DeMott, "The New World of the Novel," *Hells & Benefits* (New York: Basic Books, 1962), pp. 43, 44.

3. Many of the fiction categories come from the endpapers of the Arena Publishing Company's 1891 edition of Hamlin Garland's *Main-Travelled Roads* (Boston).

4. In Mary McCarthy, *On the Contrary* (New York: Farrar, 1961), pp. 249–70.

5. This point, a commonplace of the New Criticism, is superbly made in W. K. Wimsatt's "The Concrete Universal," *The Verbal Icon* (Lexington, Ky.: Univ. of Kentucky Press, 1967), pp. 69–83.

6. John Fischer, *The Stupidity Problem, and Other Harassments* (New York: Harper, 1964), p. 107. Fischer and Dan A. Lacy, personal communication. H. Joseph Houlihan, "ABC's of Stocking a Bookstore," p.35, and Eliot Leonard, "Paperbacks in the General Bookstore," p. 87, in *A Manual on Bookselling,* ed. Charles B. Anderson and others (New York: American Booksellers Association, 1969). Merle Miller, "Novel Writing as a Career," in *Writing in America,* ed. John Fischer and Robert B. Silvers (New Brunswick, N.J.: Rutgers Univ. Press, 1960), p. 174.

7. "The American reality," Philip Roth has said, "is . . . a kind of embarrassment to one's own meager imagination. The actuality is continually outdoing our talents." "Writing American Fiction," in *The American Novel since World War II,* ed. Marcus Klein (Greenwich, Conn.: Fawcett, 1969), p. 144.

8. Saul Bellow, *Herzog* (1964; rpt. Greenwich, Conn.: Fawcett, 1965), p. 201.

9. The ellipsis is Barthelme's: he admires Tolstoy too much to squeeze him into a phrase. The mass media is not so reticent; here is *Time* (October 19, 1970); ellipsis mine): "Tolstoy protected peasants against religious persecution, and Pushkin nurtured democratic ideals that inspired the 1925 Decembrist uprising. Gorky sought to restrain the more brutal urges of the Bolsheviks, and Pasternak remained a symbol of moral values. Solzhenitsyn . . ."

10. The gambit of a broadcast interviewer.

11. Fiction loses too: as a Barthelme hero puts it, "What an artist does, is fail" ("The Sandman," *Sadness*). But Barthelme's stories prove that fiction can be made of fiction's failure. His work belongs to the school of "The Literature of Exhaustion," as John Barth has defined it. The school's headmaster, according to Barth, is Jorge Luis Borges, whose "artistic victory . . . is that he confronts an intellectual dead end and employs it against itself to accomplish new human work" (*The American Novel since World War II,* p. 272).

12. The experts are the A. C. Nielsen Company, which estimates that "the combined audience for the three network evening news shows usually runs about 35% of the U. S. television households" (this information is from James B. Poteat of the Television Information Office). The 1970 census found that 96 percent of American "households" had TV; a 1973 estimate, by *Merchanising Week,* suggested that an incredible 99.9 percent of America's "homes" had black-and-white TV (67.1 percent had color). See the Bureau of the Census, *Statistical Abstract of the United States: 1974* (Washington, D.C.: GPO, 1974), pp. 504, 705.

Donald Barthelme and the End of the End

Thomas M. Leitch

Perhaps the most striking feature of Donald Barthelme's fiction is the number of things it gets along without. In Barthelme's fictive world, there appear to be no governing or shaping beliefs, no transcendent ideals or intimations, no very significant physical experience, no sense of place or community, no awareness on the part of his characters of any personal history or context of profession or family or, for the most part, personal relationships, no psychology of character, indeed no characters at all in the usual sense of the term, no guarantee, at the level of incident, of verisimilitude or of rational causality or of plot itself, no thickness of circumstantial detail which might make his world seem more densely realistic, and no considerable exploration of such themes as love, idealism, initiation, or death.

Of course, there are exceptions, or apparent exceptions, to each of these rules. "110 West Sixty-First Street" (in *Amateurs*[1]) concerns a precisely defined location. "Robert Kennedy Saved from Drowning" (*Unspeakable Practices, Unnatural Acts*) is a collection of episodes ostensibly intended to provide insight into the character of a politician named Robert Kennedy. "Florence Green Is 81" (*Come Back, Dr. Caligari*), like most of Barthelme's work, is full of sharply realistic, indeed photographic, detail. And *The Dead Father* is all about families, physical experience, and death. Each of these exceptions, however—and there are many others—is peculiarly suspect. We know from his title that Barthelme is writing about Robert Kennedy or 110 West Sixty-First Street, and to a certain degree these stories depend on these identifications: "Abraham Lincoln Saved from Drowning" would be a profoundly different story, and the title "61 West 110th Street," changing only the neighborhood of New York, would make that story nonsense. But these identifications, however central, are curiously disengaged. "110 West Sixty-First Street" projects a contemporary urban consciousness without committing itself to any assertions about that particular address. Barthelme's Robert Kennedy is not only unrecognizable as the brother of the late President but made more remote rather than more accessible by Barthelme's brief episodes ("K. at His Desk," "Described by Secretaries," "Behind the Bar," and so on). Even *The Dead Father* is characterized by this sort of disengagement with its

Modern Fiction Studies 28, no. 1 (1982–83):129–43. Copyright © 1982 by Purdue Research Foundation, West Lafayette, IN 47907. Reprinted with permission.

presumed subjects. The Dead Father speaks about his family: "Without children I would not be the Father. No Fatherhood without childhood. I never wanted it, it was thrust upon me" (p. 17). Barthelme describes a sexual rendezvous in similarly schematic terms:

> Cockalorum standing almost straight up but a bit of wavering.
> Julie licks.
> Pleasure of Thomas. Movement of Thomas's hips.
> Julie lights cigarette.
> Thomas remains in Position A. (p. 159)

The laconic presentation indicates or designates an experience but pointedly declines to engage that experience as experience. In Barthelme, love, death, fatherhood, and Robert Kennedy are always ideas or objects, never experiences which engage emotional commitment.

For this reason it might be more accurate to say, not that Barthelme's stories are never about passion, idealism, and death, but that the word *about* has a special, narrowly focused meaning in Barthelme that makes his fiction unusually difficult to summarize. A summary of a story, say in a review article, normally describes the subject of the story. To describe Barthelme's stories by reference to their professed subjects, the things they are about, is possible but thoroughly misleading. "The Glass Mountain" (*City Life*) is about a man trying to climb the side of a glass mountain. "Cortés and Montezuma" (*Great Days*) is about the subjugation of the Mexican ruler by the Spanish conquistador. "The Temptation of St. Anthony" (*Sadness*) has a subject accurately defined by its title. In each case, however, an accurate summary is inadequate or misleading or simply irrelevant because it fails to describe the important ways in which Barthelme's stories elude the genres his subjects imply. "The Glass Mountain" is not, despite its subject, a fairy tale: it diverges at too many points from the rules for fairy tales. "Cortés and Montezuma" is not a historical anecdote, "The Temptation of St. Anthony" an exercise in hagiography, "Robert Kennedy Saved from Drowning" a political or personal profile. These stories could more aptly be described as parodies of the genres their subjects imply; the point is simply that the subjects themselves would give anyone who did not already know Barthelme's stories a false impression of them.

It might be objected here that summary gives a false impression of any story whatsoever, and to a certain extent this is no doubt true. But the summary of most fiction is likely to be a plot summary: in saying what a given story is about, we tend to recapitulate, or at least to suggest, the plot. "Young Goodman Brown" is about a man who has an intense experience of evil at a real or imagined witches' sabbath. "The Beast in the Jungle" is about a man who spends his entire life waiting for an experience to which he feels doomed. "A Good Man Is Hard to Find" is about the confrontation between a

Georgia family, especially the grandmother of the family, and an escaped convict. Each of these situations implies a plot that is itself expressive of the author's view of the world. Even on a higher plane of generalization, the respective situations—the equivocal role of the imagination in the perception of evil, the perils of well-bred but implacable egoism, the offering of grace in a moment of supreme physical and spiritual danger—each implies a plot, and, as Aristotle says of tragedy, "the incidents and the plot are the end [*telos*]" of the whole work. Aristotle contends that "the end is the chief thing of all,"[2] and this dictum holds for many dramatists and novelists, but not for Barthelme, whose fictive situations characteristically fail to imply any *telos* in the sense of coherent plot development. Barthelme's stories are organized around situations (or suppositions or hypotheses) that commit him to no particular line of narrative development, or indeed to the very conception of development. Having created in "Daumier" a character who escapes from his "insatiable" self by postulating or daydreaming "surrogates" who are "in principle satiable," Barthelme writes: "Now in his mind's eye which was open for business at all times . . . Daumier saw a situation" (*Sadness,* pp. 163, 164–65). The situation Daumier envisions—a surrogate Daumier acting as a scout for an expedition of *au pair* girls, threatened with capture by Jesuits, across "the plains and pampas of consciousness" (p. 164)—implies no particular line of development, and when the Jesuits eventually do capture the girls and lead them off to a convent, Daumier merely switches gears to another, "second person" (p. 178) surrogate.

"Daumier" provides an unusually full exposition of Barthelme's situational or suppositional narrative method, which might be described as the examination of manifold aspects of a given situation. All of Barthelme's stories might well have begun with *Suppose.* Suppose a thirty-five-year-old man were inadvertently placed in a sixth-grade class ("Me and Miss Mandible," *Come Back, Dr. Caligari*). Suppose a giant balloon appeared one night over Manhattan ("The Balloon," *Unspeakable Practices, Unnatural Acts*). Suppose a dog fell from a third- (or fourth-) floor window and landed on an artist passing below ("The Falling Dog," *City Life*). Suppose Edward Lear, foreseeing his death, turned it into a public event ("The Death of Edward Lear," *Great Days*). In nearly every case, the hypothetical situation, instead of being subjected to a single chosen line of development, is revolved or considered under different aspects, so that Barthelme's stories often seem to assume the form of meditations. Writers such as Hawthorne, James, and O'Connor tend to choose characteristic subjects: their stories are generally variations on a typical situation or theme. But thematic analysis is largely irrelevant to Barthelme's work because his situations are themselves arbitrary and haphazard: what is characteristic, instead of thematic development, is the tone of Barthelme's handling. However illogical, disruptive, or outrageous the situations are, they are always treated circumstantially, in the same deadpan tone. Stories such as "I Bought a Little City" and "The Captured Woman" (both in

Amateurs) might have been titled "Some of the Unexpected Problems I Faced After Buying Galveston, Texas" or "Situations and Adventures That Arose Between Me and the Woman I Had Captured." In each case the premise is gratuitous: the town is already purchased, the woman captured, when the story begins, and no explanation is ever given why anyone would want (or how he would be able) to buy towns or capture women, or why towns or women would stand for such treatment. Even when a line of narrative development is pursued—will Cecelia, in "A City of Churches," be forced to operate a car-rental agency in a city whose inhabitants all live in churches and would never rent a car "in a hundred years" (*Sadness,* p. 53)? will the Dean, in "Porcupines at the University" (*Amateurs*), be able to prevent the threatened invasion of porcupines?—the development, like the characters' thoughts, is completely logistical. What are the effects of laying out plots of land to resemble pieces of a giant jigsaw puzzle? Can a Gatling gun repel a wave of porcupines? Barthelme's landscapes are without shadows or narrative past: each story begins with a premise which, like the rules of a game, is simply given. The action of the characters, when they act at all, is to come to terms with the given situation by adapting their normal habits to its requirements, however bizarre. When the captured woman offers her husband "the chance to rescue me on a white horse—one of the truly great moments his life affords," he writes back to tell her "how well he and the kid are doing together. How she hardly ever cries now. How *calm* the house is" (*Amateurs,* p. 97).

The discordance between the fantastic situation and the determination to cope with it logistically, more than any summary or catalogue of situations, gives the flavor of Barthelme's world. In this respect, at least, his work seems less kindred to that of other short story writers than to that of other figures associated with *The New Yorker,* in which most of Barthelme's stories first appeared—figures such as S. J. Perelman, James Thurber, Saul Steinberg, and Woody Allen, whose humorous effects arise from a contrast between outrageous premises and deadpan presentation. "I can't get in touch with your uncle," a Thurber medium tells her dismayed client, "but there's a horse here that wants to say hello."[3] The trick is to intimate and deflate metaphysical or teleological pretenses as economically as possible, as in Woody Allen's aphorism: "Not only is there no God, but try getting a plumber on weekends."[4] The fictional form most dependent on this rhythm of presentation is of course the cartoon, itself an essential avatar of *The New Yorker*'s sensibility, and Barthelme's stories might themselves be considered cartoons that resemble those not only of *New Yorker* artists like Thurber and Steinberg but also of such recent figures as B. Kliban and Monty Python. Kliban's straightforward acceptance of outrageous premises—his cartoons include "Gondolier Attacked by Rabbis" and "Never Give a Gun to Ducks"—rivals Barthelme's own; the graphic work of the British comic troupe Monty Python, which freely adapts, juxtaposes, and animates stolid

Victorian graphic designs, undercuts its targets very much as Barthelme's work does, and looks a good deal like Barthelme's own graphic work in "At the Tolstoy Museum" and "Brain Damage" (*City Life*), "The Flight of Pigeons from the Palace" (*Sadness*), "The Expedition" and "A Nation of Wheels" (*Guilty Pleasures*).

Barthelme's fiction, like the graphic work of Kliban and Monty Python, produces its effects by combining materials calling for different responses which are undercut by the process of juxtapostion. A print of a wheel and another of a hastily barricaded city are perfectly serious; but when they are put in the same frame in different scales, they imply a situation whose patent absurdity (America becomes a nation of wheels in the sense that wheels take over the country) suggests in turn the perfect deadpan caption: "All defenses were found to be penetrable" (*Guilty Pleasures,* p. 138). Barthelme has called this structural procedure "the principle of collage . . . the central principle of all art in the twentieth century in all media," and explained: "New York City is or can be regarded as a collage, as opposed to, say, a tribal village in which all the huts . . . are the same hut, duplicated. The point of collage is that unlike things are stuck together to make, in the best case, a new reality. This new reality, in the best case, may be or imply a comment on the other reality from which it came, and may be also much else. It's an *itself,* if it's successful: [an] . . . 'anxious object,' which does not know whether it's a work of art or a pile of junk."[5]

Barthelme's observation that any collage, including his own fiction, is "an *itself*" suggests a dimension, not only of his work, but of all fiction, which critics are often unable to appreciate or discuss systematically. Short stories and novels, like ritual tragedy, normally have a teleological dimension, an end toward which the events of the plot are moving. Aristotle uses *telos* in the double sense of unity of plot (as the plot of *Oedipus* or *Macbeth,* for example, rushes forward to an end) and unity of thought, conception, or purpose. S. H. Butcher, in his commentary on the *Poetics,* has concluded that for Aristotle, poetic unity is manifested not only "in the causal connection that binds together the several parts of a play," but also "in the fact that the whole series of events, with all the moral forces that are brought into collision, are directed to a single end. . . . The end is linked to the beginning with inevitable certainty, and in the end we discern the meaning of the whole."[6] The end or *telos* implies both a line of development for the plot and a rationale which allows a literary or dramatic work to be apprehended as a unitary whole and for which, in an ultimate sense, the work was written.

This comprehensively end-oriented or teleological quality, however, is neither exhaustive nor always primary. In musical comedies such as *Swing Time* and *On the Town,* the plot provides a teleological interest (will Fred Astaire throw over Betty Furness for Ginger Rogers? will the three sailors on leave in New York find excitement and romance with the proper women?), but no one watches musicals for the plot. Here spectacle, despite Aristotle, takes precedence over plot, whose essential function is to supply a pretext for Astaire's Bojangles number or Gene Kelly's dancing through the Empire State Building. A narrative situation normally implies not only a plot and rationale—or numerous rationales, of which a given writer can be expected to choose one—but myriad possibilities for spectacles, situations, or effects to be enjoyed for their own sake, on their own terms, purely as display. To the degree that a story such as "The Captured Woman" or "Daumier," instead of developing its situation in terms of a given *telos,* chooses to display the situation as such, the story becomes, in Barthelme's terms, "an *itself.*"

Although the example of films such as *Swing Time* and *On the Town* is drawn from outside literature, Barthelme's emphasis on situational display does not simply make him a pariah or sport among short story writers, because the short story is itself a preeminently situational or suppositional literary form. Lyric poets characteristically explore the nuances of a mental state or the musical resources of language; dramatists show how men in their actions are happy or the reverse; novelists create an extensive fictional world. What short story writers mainly do is suppose, or elaborate on a given hypothetical situation. Short stories relate anecdotes, point morals, illuminate character, or provide examples, emphasizing in every case the situational basis of their conception. When Poe spends the first half of "The Murders in the Rue Morgue" developing an argumentative proposition that the detective story is designed to support, he is only making plainer the tacit beginning of every short story: "Put case that . . ." or "Suppose . . ." In most short stories this suppositional quality is complemented by the teleology a situation implies, either a *telos* of action (as in the stories of Poe, Maupassant, Conrad, Hemingway, and O'Connor) or of revelation (as in Hawthorne, Turgenev, James, Chekhov, and Joyce). Suppose this situation arose: what would these people do about it? or: what would it all mean?

By defining the end or *telos* of fiction in the double sense of characters' decisive action and readers' comprehensive perception, recent critics have undertaken to describe all fiction in structural terms. Michael McCanles, beginning with the observations that "the ultimate principle of a work's organization of its parts, of its mythos or plot, is the informing idea [what McCanles calls the dianoia] which is, as it were, present everywhere and therefore visible nowhere as itself one of its parts" and that, from the viewpoint of the agent, "the mythos he generates—the action of a narrative or drama, the sequence of words in a lyric—results rather from his resistance to the total vision of his system which is summed up in the dianoia," has contended that "the drive toward univocal and static resolution which is the *telos* of plot in . . . [narrative and dramatic] modes is consummated only at the end of the discursive sequence."[7] Tzvetan Todorov has argued along similar lines: "An 'ideal' narrative begins with a stable situation which is disturbed by some power or force. There results a state of disequilibrium; by the action of a force directed in the opposite direction, the equilibrium is re-established; the second equilibrium is similar to the first, but never identical."[8]

These models work well for what Todorov calls "classical" narrative (his example is *The Decameron*), but distinctly less well for more recent fiction. Consider the work of Kurt Vonnegut, Jr., who, like his character Kilgore Trout, is fundamentally an idea man. Despite occasional exceptions (*God Bless You, Mr. Rosewater*), the endings of Vonnegut's novels neither pose nor intend to pose as teleologically definitive. Indeed, in the terms McCanles and Todorov establish, Vonnegut's endings are manifest failures, the weakest parts of his books, which typically elaborate situations that have narrative implications but no narrative teleology. The difference between Vonnegut's conception of fiction and those of structural analysts is the difference between open and closed conceptions of narrative, the difference between *what if?* and *if . . . then.* Suppose someone invented a chemical reagent that could bring life on earth to an end and, by a series of mishaps, it did. What then? This suppositional account of *Cat's Cradle* suggests how Vonnegut could have accomplished the remarkable feat of writing an apocalyptic novel without committing himself to any particular teleology—without even being able to bring the novel to a satisfactory conclusion on its own terms, for its terms (intelligible plot, purposive agents, and so on) are those of classical narrative which readers expect to imply a *telos.*

Like Vonnegut, Barthelme is primarily an idea man, but one whose forms more successfully display his lack of commitment to any teleology. Instead of using a classical narrative form and declining to provide an ending, Barthelme prefers forms that do not commit him even to the idea of an ending. The first part of *Snow White* ends with a series of self-reflexive multiple-choice questions addressed to the reader. "The Agreement" (*Amateurs*) and "Concerning the Bodyguard" (*Great Days*) consist almost entirely of questions about their nominal subjects. Nearly half the stories in *Great Days* take the form of dialogues—a most useful form for Barthelme, because, like the question, it posits a situation without committing itself to any assertions about it. Even a story such as "On Angels," in which a number of propositions are advanced, is described as "impure speculation" on the implications of its opening sentence: "The death of God left the angels in a strange position" (*City Life,* pp. 129, 127). The death of God, by depriving angels of any possible meaning, reduces (or purifies) them to the status of pure phenomenon: a narrative premise which by its very nature can imply no teleology and indeed no significance. The persistence of information about angels—the story cites accounts by Swedenborg, Gustav Davidson, and Joseph Lyons—in a world that has largely fallen away from belief in God is a perfect situation for Barthelme, for the host of angels, unable now to mean or do anything, can be considered simply as an *itself.* Barthelme's fiction is antiteleological in the double sense of shunning commitment to any particular plot development and even to any particular informing idea or attitude. In McCanles' terms, Barthelme's stories seek to exclude both mythos and dianoia; and these omissions, underlying all of Barthelme's other characteristic omissions, are the most important of all. It is not the case, as in the novels of Vonnegut (or, say, in those of Alain Robbe-Grillet), of a fictional form that undercuts the expectations it encourages about an intelligible plot and revelation; the possibility of such development simply does not arise.

Why does Barthelme employ a narrative form which makes no commitments to an end in the sense of either plot (mythos) or informing idea (dianoia)? He hints at one possible explanation in "Kierkegaard Unfair to Schlegel," the second of two linked dialogues between Q and A in *City Life*. A illustrates how useful it is to be an ironist by telling a story about finding an enormous number of toys and games in a house he was renting: devices, though designed to offer an escape from boredom, which were themselves boring and embarrassing. By making an ironical comment on the situation, A says, he can "annihilate the situation of being uncomfortable in this house. The shuffleboard sticks, the barbells, balls of all kinds—my joke has, in effect, thrown them out of the world" (p. 87). Irony, says A (borrowing at this point from Kierkegaard's *Concept of Irony*), by establishing a relation between a statement and its object that is not a relation of truth or identity, frees the speaker, negatively speaking, from the object by "depriving the object of its reality," so that the speaker "is not bound by what he has said" (p. 88). A next asks Q to "consider an irony directed not against a given object but against the whole of existence": such a comprehensive irony frees the speaker absolutely from the limitations, imperfections, and embarrassments of the world and, in Kierkegaard's terms, "opens up a higher actuality, expands and transfigures the imperfect into the perfect" (pp. 88, 89). Kierkegaard observes that Schlegel's novel *Lucinde* so uses irony that it achieves "a victory over the world"; but "what is wanted, Kierkegaard says, is not a victory over the world but a reconciliation with the world. . . . The true task is reconciliation with actuality and the true reconciliation, Kierkegaard says, is religion" (p. 89). A contends that Kierkegaard is unfair to Schlegel because, for example, he "fastens upon Schlegel's novel in its prescriptive aspect—in which it presents itself as a text telling us how to live—and neglects other aspects, its objecthood for one," but adds: "My reasons are not so interesting. What is interesting is my making the statement that I think Kierkegaard is unfair to Schlegel. And that the whole thing is nothing else but a damned shame and crime!" (p. 90). Next follows a picture of a large black square, the last of several such squares in the two dialogues, and then A concludes: "Because that is not what I think at all. We have to do here with my own irony. Because of course Kierkegaard was 'fair' to Schlegel. In making a statement to the contrary I am attempting to . . . I might have several purposes—simply being provocative, for example. But mostly I am trying to annihilate Kierkegaard in order to deal with his disapproval" (p. 90).

As A's last remarks suggest, this passage is both a rationale and an exemplary illustration of Barthelme's narrative procedure. His decision to minimize any teleological commitment, like Schlegel's irony, gives him a vertiginous but exhilarating freedom from an unsatisfactory world. A's arguments against Kierkegaard, as he admits, are not intended as a logical refutation but as an interesting, provocative act whose value lies not in its "prescriptive aspect" but in its "objecthood." By displaying narrative situations as objects with no necessary direction or meaning, Barthelme emphasizes the objective dimension of his fiction, a dimension implicit in all fiction. His method is itself displayed most simply and economically in "Nothing: A Preliminary Account," which sets out to define nothing by making an exhaustive catalogue of things nothing is not: "It's not the yellow curtains. Nor curtain rings. Nor is it bran in a bucket, not bran, nor is it the large, reddish farm animal eating the bran from the bucket, the man who placed the bran in the bucket, his wife, or the raisin-faced farmer who's about to foreclose on the farm . . ." (*Guilty Pleasures*, p. 161). Despite the undoubted accuracy of such observations and the pleasure they may arouse, what they assert about their subject is precisely nothing.

"Nothing," like the other pieces collected in *Guilty Pleasures*, feels even less like a short story than the work in Barthelme's other collections. The miscellaneous quality of the pieces in *Guilty Pleasures* reveals how Barthelme's stories are based on, and tend to elide into, forms outside prose fiction: New Journalism, book reviews, interviews, political satire. Despite the satires in the second part of *Guilty Pleasures*, Barthelme is not primarily a satirist arguing from a well-defined corrective viewpoint like Horace or Molière nor a romantic ironist like Schlegel but rather a parodist, again like S. J. Perelman or Woody Allen. A satire like *Tartuffe* operates according to rules prescribing the inflation of a satiric butt to a certain climactic point at which his pretensions are deflated: satire thus implies both a moral belief and a structural principle. In a more broadly conceived satire like *Joseph Andrews*, in which Lady Booby, Mrs. Slipslop, Parson Adams, and numerous strangers all come in for satiric deflation, the moral belief remains constant—pretension and vanity are always bad, even in so admirable a character as Adams—but the deflation or reversal serves as a smaller and less definitive structural unit; if it did not, the novel would end with Fielding's first satiric thrust. A parodist like Woody Allen commits himself to no moral belief at all, because he adopts a voice only to display its potential for contradiction and absurdity. The structural unit of parody is the joke ("Not only is there no God, but try getting a plumber on weekends"), which serves as a deflation in miniature. In all of Allen's early films—*Bananas*, for example, or *Love and Death*—a situation is maintained or developed only for the purpose of setting up a series of jokes, and the audience is asked to accept the convention allowing Woody Allen to deliver one punch line after the next, revealing each time more knowledge than the character he is portraying, without ever stepping decisively out of the character that makes all his jokes possible. Reversals and deflations are structurally incessant in parodies of this sort, and equally incessant in Barthelme: instead of a single, definitive deflation, we are presented with an unremitting and inveterate reduction of everything described.

Barthelme's own characters suggest why he should prefer a narrative form so inveterately reductive. Just as the comic mode has always sought to deflate hypocrisy and pretension, the forms of prose fiction, by their very emphasis on circumstantial reality, have always tended to chasten or undermine any idealism that sought to escape the requirements of circumstance. Don Quixote, Julien Sorel, Anna Karenina, Isabel Archer—all are idealistic figures compromised or thwarted by the particular circumstances of their world. In each case, the rhythm of the novel is to show the heroic possibilities of idealism and to dramatize its defeat. Barthelme finds this rhythm inappropriate because the distortions of the modern world are so severe that statistically normal behavior is absurd. As the title character in "The Reference" says: "Some people like to bang their heads against stone walls, don't they? Some people like to sleep with their sisters. Some people like to put on suits and ties and go sit in a concert hall and listen to the New York Philharmonic *Orchestra* for God's sake" (*Amateurs,* p. 152). In a world so inveterately absurd, it is impossible to take idealism seriously long enough to make it worth undercutting: "Goals incapable of attainment have driven many a man to despair, but despair is easier to get to than that—one need merely look out the window, for example" ("And Then," *Amateurs,* p. 109). A story like "On Angels" does not itself deprive angels of their actual meaning: it comically reveals the absurdity of a given situation, the persistence of a vast store of information about angels in a world which, for the most part, has already deprived them of meaning.

"On Angels" might almost have been written by Woody Allen, who has treated the death of God with a similar lack of teleological commitment (see "Mr. Big," the closing selection in *Getting Even*). In general, however, there is an important structural difference between Allen's work and Barthelme's. In Allen's parodies and films, the basic compositional unit is the joke, implying a rising and falling rhythm from exposition to deflation of a given situation, repeated indefinitely. In Barthelme's best stories—for example, "Daumier," "The Indian Uprising" (*Unspeakable Practices, Unnatural Acts*), and "Views of My Father Weeping" (*City Life*)—the reductive or parodistic impulse has become so inveterate that there are no punch lines and so no stable and discrete compositional units whatever. Allen's parodistic stance commits him, if not to a moral belief, at least to a given series of effects: anyone who failed to find the jokes in *Love and Death* funny could justly claim to have been cheated. Barthelme, who escapes this commitment, incurs another one far more difficult to fulfill: his situations must be worth display-ing on their own terms, despite their lack of purpose or implied *telos*. His stories succeed as anxious objects or not at all, because there is nothing else for them to be.

It is excessively difficult to establish a critical vocabulary for a fiction that so resolutely resists structural closure. Some problems of analysis might be resolved by classifying Barthelme's stories as anatomies, to use the word by which Northrop Frye designates certain works by such writers as Petronius, Apuleius, Rabelais, Erasmus, Swift, Voltaire, and Peacock. The anatomy, according to Frye, "deals less with people as such than with mental attitudes" and "presents people as mouthpieces of the ideas they represent." In such works, Frye observes, "the intellectual structure built up from the story makes for violent dislocations in the customary logic of narrative." Although "a magpie instinct to collect facts" is a hallmark of the anatomist, short anatomies have been written in the form of "a dialogue or colloquy, in which dramatic interest is in a conflict of ideas rather than of character."[9] In Frye's terms, Barthelme would be an anatomist, not of manners or ideas, but of objects, artifacts of human culture, junk. Such a conclusion could be supported by passages like the following paragraph from "The Indian Uprising":

> Red men in waves like people scattering in a square startled by something tragic or a sudden, loud noise accumulated against the barricades we had made of window dummies, silk, thoughtfully planned job descriptions (including scales for the orderly progress of other colors), wine in demijohns, and robes. I analyzed the composition of the barricade nearest me and found two ashtrays, ceramic, one dark brown and one dark brown with an orange blur at the lip; a tin frying pan; two-litre bottles of red wine; three-quarter-litre bottles of Black & White, aquavit, cognac, vodka, gin, Fad #6 sherry; a hollow-core door in birch veneer on black wrought-iron legs; a blanket, red-orange with faint blue stripes; a red pillow and a blue pillow; a woven straw wastebasket; two glass jars for flowers; corkscrews and can openers; two plates and two cups, ceramic, dark brown; a yellow-and-purple poster; a Yugoslavian carved flute, wood, dark brown; and other items. I decided I knew nothing. (*Unspeakable Practices, Unnatural Acts,* pp. 4–5)

This painstaking catalogue of cultural debris achieves its eerie and dazzling effect by removing each object from the context that would give it meaning: as William H. Gass has shrewdly remarked of Barthelme, "Any-thing dropped in the dreck *is* dreck, at once, as an uneaten porkchop mislaid in the garbage."[10] The fear of objects losing their meanings, as when they are sold at an auction that deprives them of the context they had for their owners, underlies a good deal of recent American fiction, including Gass's *Omensetter's Luck,* which begins with an auction, and Thomas Pynchon's *Crying of Lot 49,* which ends with one. Such anxiety accords well with what Frye calls the "highly intellectualized" temper of the anatomy. Unlike Gass and Pynchon (and, for example, John Barth), however, Barthelme does not present lists of objects in order to assimilate them into a coherent intellectual structure. The form of the anatomy implies, if not a teleology of plot, certainly an intellectual *telos* or rationale. But Barthelme's work makes neither of these teleological commitments because it projects neither an order for the situations, facts, and objects it presents nor an intelligible attitude toward them. Barthelme is more truly a magpie than the writers Frye considers because he has a magpie's interest in his material, displaying it not because it implies a *telos* but because it is bright and eye-catching. The "trash phenomenon," which one of his characters describes as having "(1) an 'endless' quality and (2) a 'sludge' quality" (*Snow White,* pp. 97, 96), is not threatening or lamentable in Barthelme; it is just there, like a pile of Christmas gifts waiting to be unwrapped, thrown together for the moment in a context that emphasizes their objecthood at the expense of their meaning.

Barthelme's preference for displaying his material rather than anatomizing it suggests that his fiction involves a compositional principle other than the intellectual rationale described by Frye or the different but similarly structural principles of Todorov and McCanles. In Barthelme's work, as in musical comedy, a situation need imply no *telos,* neither an intelligible plot nor a coherent rationale, if it is worth displaying for its own sake. The limitation of structuralist criticism, preeminently a reader's criticism, is that it presupposes a given structure to be filled in, whereas, from the writer's point of view, fiction often involves a situation to be filled out. The two perspectives are complementary, not contradictory, but Barthelme's work places unusual stress on the second.

Barthelme's narrative situations are less often teleological than tellable, to use the term Mary Louise Pratt has borrowed from the linguist William Labov and applied to literary texts. Tellable assertions, explains Pratt, "must represent states of affairs that are held to be unusual, contrary to expectations, or otherwise problematic." Although Pratt uses "interesting" as a synonym for "tellable" and notes that "information does not have to be new to be tellable," she emphasizes the teleological dimension that makes most narratives tellable in contending that the speaker of a tellable utterance is seeking "an *interpretation* of the problematic event, an assignment of meaning and value," so that spoken narratives commonly fail, if they do fail, in teleological terms: "The experience was trivial, the teller longwinded, or we 'missed the point.' "[11] Stories can be repeated over and over, however, even to an audience already familiar with their point. Children, as every parent knows, have the greatest tolerance for unvaried narrative repetition, and indeed are suspicious of variation; but the tolerance persists in adults' fondness for familiar anecdotes: "I love to hear you tell the story of how you got the wedding guests to move those pianos."

Adults have more appetite than children for narrative elaboration. Pratt points out that because "what literary works chiefly do is elaborate on the states of affairs they posit," fictive narration can be "exceedingly redundant"; an author, like an oral storyteller, "can pile detail upon detail, and can even be blatantly repetitive, because he is understood to be enabling his audience to imagine and comprehend the state of affairs more fully and to savor it for a longer time."[12] Tellable narratives are to a great extent both retellable and capable of practically endless elaboration; indeed, the better an audience already knows a narrative, the less concerned it is that the narrator get to the point.

An important implication of Pratt's discussion, though one she does not make explicit, is that often the process of elaboration itself can make a narrative tellable: that is, insofar as the point of a narrative is display rather than *telos*, elaboration, repetition, and discursiveness are precisely what make the narrative tellable. The difference between most novels and their plot summaries is that the summaries retain narrative *telos* without tellability. Imagine a summary of the sentence describing a barricade in "The Indian Uprising": "I examined the barricade nearest me and found it was made up of many objects, miscellaneous, recherché, absurd." The point of Barthelme's sentence, insofar as it has a point, is the plenitude or exuberance of particularization that makes it, unlike its summary, tellable.

This way of establishing tellability is characteristic of a great deal of fiction besides Barthelme's. To the extent that any fiction elaborates a given situation without implying a *telos*, or without altering the *telos* the situation itself implies, it seeks to make that situation more tellable. Sometimes, as often in Barthelme, the main point of the elaboration is its pointlessness—a point by which audiences are understandably bewildered. One of Monty Python's most notorious sketches is called "The Death of Mary Queen of Scots." Two members of the troupe sit next to a window in a room, and from offstage, presumably through the window, comes the exchange, "Are you Mary Queen of Scots?"—"Aye." There follow perhaps thirty seconds of mayhem offstage: beating, thumping, ripping, pummeling, intermingled with bloodcurdling shrieks. Finally, a voice from outside says quietly: "There, she's dead," to which another voice replies, "No I ain't!" During the first five seconds or so of pounding and screeching, the mayhem is certainly, in Pratt's terms, unusual or problematic, but it soon thereafter becomes pointless and tedious, until, when it has gone on too long to be accidentally pointless, the audience gradually realizes that the pointlessness is intentional. Once the sketch has established this new convention of pure discursiveness, so that pounding and screeching can be considered as normal behavior, an audience often finds it amusing to a degree this summary will hardly suggest. The principle of display here might be described by the maxim *too much is enough* or by the compositional principle, most notably exemplified by Tristram Shandy, of getting carried away.

The designedly pointless repetitiveness of much of Monty Python's material has attracted a large, but not universal, audience. Television viewers are so accustomed to a simplified (and radically foreshortened) teleology in situation comedies and comic sketches that their initial reaction to Monty Python is often bored or bemused: "This is just silly." Most readers of Sterne and Dickens, however, accept their narratives as tellable precisely because of the conventions of elaboration, repetition, and discursiveness. A character like Mr. Micawber, who has no psychology to speak of, is far less provocative or sympathetic than any of George Eliot's characters, and students first approaching Dickens often consider Micawber simply unpromising or shallow. But Dickens' theatrical or histrionic conception of Micawber, which prescribes for him always the same gestures and speeches, gives him a magical or incantatory vitality. Just as all Dickens' grotesques have a tellability based on the conviction established by the unvarying repetition with which they are displayed, Shandy's disgressions have a tellability based always on their antitelelogical irrelevance, their resistance to development, closure, or informing rationale.

Although writers like Barthelme, Dickens, and Sterne are unusually discursive, narrative fiction in general is shaped by both a structural imperative, an impulse in the broadest sense teleological, and a discursive or elaborative impulse. Narrative tellability can be based on either teleology or elaboration—circumstantial detail, for example, establishes a sense of verisimilitude and an elaborative range that can both make a narrative more tellable—and no narrative, not even Barthelme's, works absolutely in isolation from either impulse, though their relative importance may vary widely from one narrative to the next. Barthelme's resolute emphasis on narrative elaboration, which reduces the importance of *telos* to a minimum, is significant principally as a challenge to the limitations of thematic and structural analysis and as a reminder that the first requisite of a narrative, the merit on which all other merits depend, is that it be worth telling.

Notes

1. Parenthetical references throughout are to the Little, Brown edition of *Come Back, Dr. Caligari* (Boston, 1964) and the Farrar, Straus and Giroux editions of *Snow White* (New York, 1967), *Unspeakable Practices, Unnatural Acts* (1968), *City Life* (1970), *Sadness* (1972), *Guilty Pleasures* (1974), *The Dead Father* (1975), *Amateurs* (1976), and *Great Days* (1979).

2. *Aristotle's Theory of Poetry and Fine Art,* trans. S. H. Butcher, 4th ed. (1911; rpt. New York: Dover, 1951), Ch. 6, p. 27.

3. *Men, Women and Dogs,* new ed. (New York: Dodd, Mead, 1975), p. 50.

4. "My Philosophy," in *Getting Even* (New York: Random House, 1971), p. 33.

5. Joe David Bellamy, *The New Fiction: Interviews with Innovative American Writers* (Urbana: University of Illinois Press, 1974), pp. 51–52.

6. *Aristotle's Theory of Poetry and Fine Art,* pp. 284–85.

7. "Mythos and Dianoia: A Dialectical Methodology of Literary Form," in *Literary Monographs,* vol. 4, ed. Eric Rothstein (Madison: University of Wisconsin Press, 1971), pp. 4, 25.

8. "The Grammar of Narrative," in *The Poetics of Prose,* trans. Richard Howard (Ithaca, N. Y.: Cornell University Press, 1977), p. 111.

9. *Anatomy of Criticism: Four Essays* (Princeton, N. J.: Princeton University Press, 1957), pp. 309–311.

10. "The Leading Edge of the Trash Phenomenon," in *Fiction and the Figures of Life* (1971; rpt. New York: Vintage, 1972), p. 101.

11. *Toward a Speech Act Theory of Literary Discourse* (Bloomington: Indiana University Press, 1977), pp. 136–38, 51.

12. *Toward a Speech Act Theory of Literary Discourse,* pp. 148, 146.

Barthelme Unfair to Kierkegaard: Some Thoughts on Modern and Postmodern Irony

ALAN WILDE

Irony has taken some hard knocks from critics lately, a victim of its association with modernist strategies and theories. The reaction is understandable enough, given the urgent desire in recent years to proclaim the emergence of a new sensibility. When the mood is for manifestoes and declarations of independence, oedipal impulses typically direct themselves against the central assumptions of the previous generation or, alternately, push forward claims of radical historical discontinuity. But anyone surveying recent literature (as opposed to criticism of it) is unlikely to find reasons for either celebrating or mourning the death of irony. Whether or not one agrees with Geoffrey Thurley, for example, "that a preoccupation with irony and self-knowledge has secured a dislocation of sensibility exactly the reverse of the synthesis Richards, Eliot, and Leavis intended to guarantee,"[1] the fact is that his argument works to discredit not irony in general but what particular writers did with it. Of course, irony has undergone significant transformations since Thurley's "intellectualist critics" annexed it, but that is precisely the point. Somehow irony manages again and again to escape its association with this or that school and to recast itself into constantly new modes. With all the resilience and tenacity of some allotropic element, it contrives both to declare its flexibility, its openness to change, and to retain its essential identity as a characteristic response to the polysemic world we necessarily inhabit. This being the case, what we require today are not recriminations against ancestral specters—the ghosts of irony past—but a more neutral discrimination of ironies: a taxonomy of specific forms, which, even as they proliferate and continue to coexist in various states of imbalance, assert their family resemblance.

My aim, however, is somewhat more limited. It is possible by now, I think, to take for granted the modulation of irony over the last two centuries from satiric technique to autonomous vision: a vision, that is, not simply of incongruities or disparities mediated by the satirist's normative presence but

Reprinted from *Boundary 2* 5, no. 1 (1976–77): 45–70.

of life itself as inherently fractured and discordant.[2] I want, therefore (accepting the distinction between modern and postmodern as a rough approximation to the undoubted fact, if not at all to a fixed moment or even period, of change), to consider here only those ironies that lie on either side of the current juncture of generational conflict, and particularly to attend to the type of irony now in the process of defining itself, which the fiction of Donald Barthelme will serve to exemplify.

At its more typical (in Gide or Pirandello, for example, or better still, in *A Passage to India*), modernist irony assumes and responds to the disjunctive plurality of the observed world. But so too, in their different ways, do the fictional ironies of Flaubert, Dickens, or Barthelme. What distinguishes Forster's novel is not simply its perception of fragmentation but the fact that the moral and epistemological possibilities it envisions are conceived of as equally and simultaneously valid. However discontinuous, however cut across by the gulfs, abysses, and voids that are omnipresent in modern literature, the data and values of Forster's world present themselves, in the final analysis, as symmetrically opposed, obstinately ranged along the horns of an irresolvable dilemma. Irony becomes, then, both equivocal and absolute—or absolute because equivocal.[3] Further, given the form, as well as the excess, of its awareness, consciousness generates an immobility (the "paralysed force" of Eliot's hollow men) in the face of activity and choice. Confronted by a world he understands too well to change, the ironist locates (or finds) himself at a distance from that world: the cosmic counterpart of the characteristically modern spectator of life, who reenacts within the fiction or poetry he inhabits his author's incapacities and dreams.

The word cosmic, however, to the degree that it retains its associations with the concept of order, needs to be qualified. Certainly the modern ironic work of art is, as such, the image of order; which is to say that, at its extreme point, modernist irony doubles back on itself, converting the dilemma that is its subject into the very form by which it expresses and stabilizes itself—thereby validating Forster's contention that "works of art . . . are the only objects in the material universe to possess internal order."[4] But even in a novel as near-perfect as *A Passage to India,* the subordination of the referential to the aesthetic can never be complete. Literature is a window as well as a mirror, and through the window Forster and other modernists provide, one glimpses a shift in cosmological assumptions, which threatens the integrity of even the symmetrically fragmented world I've described. For more fundamental than the disorders to which Forster and Woolf or Yeats and Eliot constantly allude is the perspective from which they view them. And that, in the case of all these writers, at least in their earlier works, is based on the model of the fixed observer viewing an essentially ordered, three-dimensional world. The gradual breakdown of this model, or, what comes to the same thing, the infinite extension of its boundaries, transforms depth into a void and the sensible world, paradoxically, into a flattened-out map—to borrow

John Vernon's useful metaphor.[5] The ironist as primary and irreducible subject confronts, across an unbridgeable gulf, an increasingly static, conceptualized, and objective surface, while into the vestigial depth, now become empty space, the novel or poem inserts itself: the last trace of order and connection.

Art as order serves, then, to guarantee the ironist's distance and detachment. But it functions too as a paradigm of that willed movement of transcendence by means of which most of the modernists express their desire to leave behind altogether self-consciousness and discontinuity. Whether the path chosen is one of discovery—the need, like Rhoda's in *The Waves,* to find "the thing that lies beneath the semblance of the thing"—or of creation—Yeat's "Translunar Paradise"—modern literature confesses a longing to overcome the ironic vision with the countervision of an "anironic," resolving unity. And it is precisely that concept of a heterocosm, the image of a perfectly ordered world, which in its autonomous perfection becomes both moral and referential, that postmodern literature rejects (or attempts to reject), even as it carries on and redefines the problem of the artist's relation to the reality that surrounds him.

"Surrounds" is the operative word here, as we move closer to the present. The point is hardly that postmodern irony displays a greater awareness of life's fragmentation and disconnections than its predecessor (one thinks inevitably of Eliot's "heap of broken images" and still more of the Rhine maiden's barren comment: "I can connect / Nothing with nothing"). It is, rather, that in the process of its transformation—within, it should be noted, the works of authors rightly thought of as modern: in Virginia Woolf's late novels, for example, or Forster's recently published *The Life to Come,* or even Isherwood's *The Berlin Stories*—irony positions itself differently vis-à-vis the objects of its perceptions. No longer poised juridically above the world he surveys, the postmodern ironist is, typically, involved *in,* though not necessarily *with,* that world: a part of, even though he may be apart from the other objects in, his own perceptual field. Moreover, and as one would expect, with a change in the angle of vision there comes a change in the vision itself.[6] The symmetry of modernist disorder gives way to the apparent randomness of simple contiguity; omniscience of understanding to an indecision about the very meanings and relations of things; Woolf's anguished cry—"Why is life so tragic; so like a little strip of pavement over an abyss"[7]—to an attitude that takes for granted, more, naturalizes, the abyss as one constituent among others of the new, prolific, and dumb reality.

Predicated, then, on the assumption of the ironist's immanence in the world he describes, contemporary literature substitutes for the equivocal irony of the modernists one that can be more accurately described as *suspensive.* More alert, perhaps, but otherwise undistinguishable from his fellow browsers milling about in the technological clutter and confusion of the world-as-shopping-mall, the ironist today keeps his eyes and his options open. Not paralyzed but stupefied, he staggers from store to store, counter to counter, his attitude one of slightly dazed and sometimes dazzled acceptance. So Paul, the victim of Coover's "A Pedestrian Accident," who is literally flattened to physical and mental numbness by a truck marked "MAGIC KISS LIPSTICK IN 14 DIFFERENT SHADES," scans the surrounding scene, collapsed, like him, to "Stuff and Tickle," with fascination and occasional aesthetic bemusement, and "[lets] himself be absorbed by it; there was, after all nothing else to do."[8] It is this kind of acceptance (in the sense that—to take a less dramatic example—one accepts the inevitability of his bad back going out from time to time) which both expresses and creates the shape of recent ironic fiction.

The notion of acceptance, at least during the last hundred years or so, inevitably conjures up a more or less bleak sense of the ordinary. From Laforgue's "Ah! que la vie est quotidienne" to Barthelme's "Critique de la Vie Quotidienne,"[9] by way of Neruda's "Walking Around," with its surrealist image of dailiness as random laundry on a line, weeping "lentas lágrimas sucias," the obstinate triviality of life increasingly impinges on the literary consciousness. But here again some discriminations need to be made. The modernist sensibility, haunted by a vision of pervasive grayness and (as in *Howards End*) of a creeping red rust, finds ultimate expression in one of Forster's comments in *A Passage to India:* "Most of life is so dull that there is nothing to be said about it . . . and a perfectly adjusted organism would be silent." But for all its flat and bitter finality, the remark heralds not silence but a dramatic exploration of metaphysical extremes, first in the chaotic negations of the cave and then in the all-embracing oneness of the Hindu festival; and if Forster fails in his quest for a redeeming order, it is not because of complacence or a willingness to accede to the dailiness of life. Barthelme's "Critique," on the other hand (reminiscent of Laforgue in its elegance and archness, though its bitterness is certainly more pedestrian and low-keyed), accommodates itself more easily to the banal horrors of *la vie quotidienne*. Not that the story is without incident (there is, notably, the moment when the narrator's former wife tries to "ventilate" him with a horse pistol [S, 12], but if it is true, as Philip Stevick notes in his introduction to *Anti-Story,* that "to allow the middle range of experience to co-exist, in a single work, with the extremities of contemporary experience is to do strange things to that ordinariness, to deny it its solidity,"[10] it is equally the case that that coexistence may, as it does in Barthelme's fiction, serve to render extremity more ordinary—to deny *it,* and not the middle range of experience, a solidity of specification and response.

In any case, the "Critique," though it manages, characteristically to combine the hilarious and the dismal, provides a rather too facile treatment of its subject, and its value is more representative than particular, supplying as it does a pattern for more successful examples (the Edward and Pia stories of *Unspeakable Practices,* among others) of Barthelme's relentless investigation of the humdrum. Of these, the best is probably the title story of *City Life*. More eccentric in incident and development, it expresses in a number of ways Barthelme's relation to *la vie quotidienne*. Speculating in the final section of the tale on "the most exquisite mysterious muck," which is the city she lives in and "which is itself the creation of that muck of mucks, human consciousness" (CL, 178–79), Ramona goes on to contemplate the possible explanation of the virgin birth of her child: "Upon me, their glance has fallen," she thinks, reflecting on various of the men in her life. "The engendering force was, perhaps, the fused glance of all of them. From the millions of units crawling about on the surface of the city, their wavering desirous eye selected me. . . . *I accepted. What was the alternative?*" (CL, 179–80; my italics). Ramona's last words sum up, *mutatis mutandis,* that is, allowing for a different level of awareness and for the artist's privileged sense of control, Barthelme's attitude as well. Implicated in the world he describes, Barthelme accepts—at least in this group of stories—not only the material that world offers him but the ironically suspensive mood resignation entails. How else to react to "brain damage," when, as the narrator of the story by that name admits: "*I could describe it better if I weren't afflicted with it . . .*" (CL, 156)? Or, as Dan announces, in a much quoted passage from *Snow White,* apropos of the linguistic "trash phenomenon": "I hazard that we may very well soon reach a point where it's 100 percent. Now at such a point, you will agree, the question turns from a question of disposing of this 'trash' to a question of appreciating its qualities, because, after all, it's 100 percent, right?" (SW, 97).

There is a danger, however, of equating appreciation or even acceptance with the presence in these stories of a significative void—especially if one attempts to bring to bear on them the same analytic techniques regularly applied to the classics of modern literature. But the lack of an easily paraphrasable theme or an extractable moral or, on the other hand, of a pattern of search and, if not resolution, then closure doesn't necessarily imply the absence of human reference of one kind or another. Nevertheless, a number of recent critics seem bent on developing a good deal further than Forster would have accepted his definition of art as a "self-contained harmony" (TC, 59). So Ronald Sukenick, describing a particular elaboration of "the new tradition," writes, playfully perhaps but I think seriously: "Needless to say the Bossa Nova has no plot, no story, no character, no chronological sequence, no verisimilitude, no imitation, no allegory, no symbolism, no subject matter, no 'meaning.' It resists interpretation. . . . The Bossa Nova is non-representational—it represents itself."[11] The main lines of Sukenick's argument are familiar enough to readers of Robbe-Grillet's *Pour un nouveau roman,* but it is worth quoting further his remarks on "abstraction, improvisation, and opacity," which are the essential features of the bossanova style:

> As abstraction frees fiction from the representational and the need to imitate some version of reality other than its own, so improvisation liberates it from

any *a priori* order and allows it to discover new sequences and interconnections in the flow of experience. . . . Opacity implies that we should direct our attention to the surface of a work, and such techniques as graphics and typographical variations, in calling the reader's attention to the technological reality of the book, are useful in keeping his mind on that surface instead of undermining it with profundities. (pp. 44–45)

Although Barthelme provides Sukenick with one of his major examples, it isn't clear which exactly of his stories Sukenick has in mind, but the explorations of *la vie quotidienne* will serve as an initial test of whether or how fully Barthelme conforms to the ideal, bossanova pattern. The major problem Sukenick raises has to do with "meaning," and it is one Barthelme deals with directly from time to time as well. So, in "Kierkegaard Unfair to Schlegel," the narrator notes disapprovingly that the philosopher "fastens upon Schlegel's novel [*Lucinde*] in its prescriptive aspect—in which it presents itself as a text telling us how to live—and neglects other aspects, its objecthood for one" (CL, 96). But Barthelme seems, generally, less dogmatic than Sukenick, and in a recent interview, elaborating on an earlier remark about collage, he hedges his bet on the question: "This new reality," he says, apropos of what is produced by the collage, "in the best case, may be or imply a comment on the other reality from which it came, and may be also much else. It's an *itself,* if it's successful."[12] In any case, if, in his emphasis on the self-referential quality of art, Sukenick means to suggest that the principal intention of contemporary literature is not to re-present a stable, objective reality or if the suggestion is simply that the formal (even when disguised as the anti-formal) takes precedence over the mimetic, there is no need to quarrel. But more is surely implied in the praise of Barthelme as "very bossanova"; and in the face of this denial of meaning, it is necessary to assert that the stories of daily life do "refer," that they refer most directly to the kind of inner life Barthelme (or his narrators) frequently deny their "characters." In other words, the stories are, in Susanne Langer's sense of the term, "presentational": the knowledge they provide is of the forms of feeling. Not to recognize this fact is to miss what may be most distinctive about Barthelme's work—the articulation not of the larger, more dramatic emotions to which modernist fiction is keyed but of an extraordinary range of minor, banal dissatisfactions. "Yours is not a modern problem," one character tells another in "*City Life.*" "The problem today is no angst but lack of angst" (CL, 176). Barthelme's stories express not anomie or accidie or dread but a muted series of irritations, frustrations, and bafflements. The title of his fifth volume is exactly right. Even at its most funny or absurd, Barthelme's is a world of *Sadness,* sadness occasionally moderated by snatches after sexual satisfaction, by a persistent intellectual curiosity, and by the inventive pleasures of art—but never, especially in the stories of acceptance, cancelled by any of them.

The question of art brings us back to Sukenick's description and to another group of stories, which, to be fair, are probably more the kind of thing he had in mind in choosing Barthelme as one of his exemplars. The distinction between the two kinds of fiction is apparent in a piece called "The Balloon." The story ends (somewhat contradictorily, given its initial assertions) with the narrator's admission that the balloon "is a spontaneous autobiographical disclosure, having to do with the unease I felt at your absence, and with sexual deprivation . . ." (UP, 21). It is, in other words, in its fantastic way, an expression of the forms of feeling; and the story as a whole can be taken as one of Barthelme's most inventive descriptions of the presentational mode. Without its explanatory ending, however, the story suggests something different. Or at any rate the responses and reactions of the characters *within it* to the gigantic balloon that covers their city for some forty-five blocks points to less discursive meanings. (I emphasize for its paradigmatic value the anecdotal aspect of the story—quite simply what happens in it— because in the final analysis "The Balloon" is an exercise not *in* but *about* play, that is, a highly ideated, conceptualized work; but of that aspect of Barthelme's fiction, more later.) What is important for the moment are the narrator's assertions, first, that "it is wrong to speak of 'situations,' implying sets of circumstances leading to some resolution, some escape of tension; there were no situations, simply the balloon hanging there" (UP, 15–16), and, then, that "we have learned not to insist on meanings, and they are rarely even looked for now, except in cases involving the simplest, safest phenomena" (UP, 16). In brief, the story tells how various New Yorkers respond to this curious presence that is "not limited, or defined" (UP, 20)— how they manage (or don't manage) to accept the "unmeaning" particularity of the balloon: its *thereness*.

Finally, then, "The Balloon" can be seen as a parable of reactions to reality as in irreducibly mysterious, varied, and changing surface; and as such, the story serves as prototype for those of Barthelme's fictions in which he and his narrators perceive the world as a kind of haphazard, endlessly organizable and reorganizable playground. Thus, whereas the presentational stories take as their recurrent starting point the inevitable flaws of human relations, the ludic ones (to borrow a word from Barthelme out of Huizinga) deal with the odd relationship between the individual mind and the humanized world of things and objects on which that mind has, collectively and precariously, left its imprint.

Predictably, the ludic fictions most obviously inspire Barthelme's technical innovations. The use of collage, of fragments,[13] of pictures and black spaces; the sudden irruption of large, capitalized remarks, which may or may not comment on the surrounding text; the reliance on what one critic (referring to his own "rhythms") calls "interval (with abrupt interface) & repeat/ repeat of cliché (with slight variation)"[14]; the constant experimentation with styles, ranging from the severly paratactic to the most involutedly suborinative: all function, of course, to call attention to the fact of writing (or écriture, as we are learning to say), to the medium in which Barthelme and his perceptual field intersect. Indeed, Sukenick's animus against depth makes a good deal of sense in connection with stories like "Sentence": one nine-page long, remarkably resourceful experiment in syntax. The emphasis on surface has, of course, spatial, moral, and psychological implications, but the force of Sukenick's argument and of Barthelme's practice suggests that the question is, in the first instance, an aesthetic one; and we may start with that in coming again at the problem of meaning.

It's difficult to avoid the inference that a good deal of contemporary literature represents a belated response to the by-now familiar imperatives of modern painting. So Clement Greenberg writes: "Realistic, illusionist art had dissembled the medium, using art to conceal art. Modernism used art to call attention to art. The limitations that constitute the medium of painting—the flat surface, the shape of the support, the properties of pigment—were treated by the Old Masters as negative factors that could be acknowledged only implicitly or indirectly. Modernist painting has come to regard these same limitations as positive factors that are to be acknowledged openly."[15] Translation of Greenberg's "limitations" into literary terms—the flat page, the technological shape of the book, the physical properties of words—provides the foundation on which ultra-formalists, advocates of the non-referential, and anti-mimetic critics construct their minimalist or purely aesthetic theories. No doubt, Barthelme's most experimental fictions, do, at their best, give something of the sense of art as gratuitous play (at their worst, they suggest "attempts to make complex the simple, so that we will not be bored" [UP, 133]); but whether even play is without meaning is another matter.

The apotheosis of play sounds in fact suspiciously like yet another affirmation of art for art's sake; and it should seem clear by now that that phrase, unsupported by some clarifying or defining context, is among the most perversely empty literary slogans ever invented. Not that there is any difficulty in understanding Woolf's animus against books that require that "the reader should finish them, actively and practically, for himself";[16] or Clive Bell's against paintings pandering to a taste for the anecdotal; or, in a different way, Forster's counterpointing of the order of art and the disorder of life. But what is invariably at issue in these and other cases is a refusal of the didactic and tendentious, an unwillingness to convert art into an instrument of immediate utility. There is, however, nothing contradictory between the services of art and the attribution to it of semantic or even moral force, provided one keeps one's terms of reference large and flexible. Surely, confronted with even the most homogeneously colored, unpainterly painting, one can argue (Barthelme is summarizing Huizinga) "that the play element in culture serves a civilizing function" (GP, 130), or, in a formulation I prefer, one can follow Merleau-Ponty: "What will be transmitted to the canvas," he writes, "will no longer be only a vital or sensual value. . . .

There will also be the emblem of a way of inhabiting the world, of handling it, and of interpreting it . . . in short, the emblem of a certain relationship to being."[17]

The problems that accrue as one moves from pigments to words are familiar enough. And even if one chooses to regard words as being as devoid of fixed, inherent meaning as pigments; even if one maintains that the relation between signifiers and signifieds is arbitrary, that meaning is generated diacritically, that, above all, signifieds are overdetermined in relation to signifiers so that ambiguity is not only potential but inevitable; even if, finally, as one of Barthelme's narrator's maintains, "signs are signs, and . . . some of them are lies" (CB, 109), still the difficulties remain. But what the semiotic vocabulary does suggest is that, if Barthelme's fictions are to be compared with painting, the comparison ought more properly to take as its point of reference not modernist but Pop art. A number of reviewers have drawn the analogy casually, but it is worth pursuing further, especially in relation to picture stories like "The Expedition." In his admirable study, Lawrence Alloway describes Pop art as "essentially, an art about signs and sign systems":[18] The attitude of the Pop artists toward the signs and objects they use," he writes, "is neither one of simple acclaim, celebrating consumer goods, nor of satirical condemnation of the system in favor of some humanistic norm of conduct. On the contrary, they use the objects of the man-made environment with a sense of meaning in process" (p. 47). The last phrase is particularly to the point, as are Alloway's comments on "the provisional nature of all communication," on "the mobility of signs" (p. 47), and on "the significative doubt of Pop art" (p. 21). Stories such as "The Joker's Greatest Triumph," which tackles the problem of reusing the cultural detritus of our times, or "A Nation of Wheels," with (to use another of Alloway's phrases) its combination of "high style and low subjects" (p. 19), express perfectly the ways in which supposedly self-referential play and an adherence to surface work not to deny but to create meaning. To be sure, the meanings are neither altogether stable nor completely clear. In fact, it is precisely the referential ambiguity that generates the suspensiveness of Barthelme's irony, as it does Warhol's or Lichtenstein's or John's.

Like the Pop artists, Barthelme puts aside the central modernist preoccupation with epistemology, and it may well be the absence of questions about how we know that has operated most strongly to "defamiliarize" his (and their) work. Barthelme's concerns are, rather, ontological in their acceptance of a world that is, willy-nilly, a given of experience. Here, one can speak legitimately of surface in that there is not for Barthelme, as there is for Clive Bell, a potential awareness of "essential reality, of the God in everything, of the universal in the particular, of the all-pervading rhythm . . . that which lies behind the appearance of all things—that which gives to all things their individual significance, the thing in itself, the ultimate reality."[19] But the absence of depth implies the lack not of meaning but of certainties. Life has become, for better or for worse, less mysterious but more puzzling, and beside Bell's cadenced, assured phrases one needs to juxtapose Ramona's laconic "I accepted. What was the alternative?" Not for Ramona—and not for Barthelme—the ultimate reality." Over the past several decades the quest has become a futile, indeed an unreal, one. "We must not . . . wonder," Merleau-Ponty writes, "whether we really perceive a world, we must instead say: the world is what we perceive" (PhP, xvi). The question, then, is how exactly to live in that world (a largely humanized world in Barthelme's fiction), and Ramona's answer—a kind of grim-lipped hilarity in the face of the provisional—is emblematic of her author's in many ways as well. "The world in the evening seems fraught with the absence of promise" (S, 3–4), the narrator of "Critique de la Vie Quotidienne" remarks; and so too do the days. The simpletons of Barthelme's fictions are those like Perpetua, who, having left her husband, imagines that she sees a "new life . . . spread out before her like a red velvet map" (S, 37). Wisdom, so it seems, lies in a stoicism of sorts. At the end of "The Policemen's Ball," the unspecified "horrors" that have waited for Horace throughout his evening-long seduction of Margot "had moved outside Horace's apartment. Not even policemen and their ladies are safe, the horrors thought. No one is safe. Safety does not exist. Ha ha ha ha ha ha ha ha ha ha!" (CL, 62). Barthelme is one up on Horace, being an intimate of the horrors and the chronicler of their laugh. But by the same token, his is the more difficult position to maintain. To be conscious and even to value, as he obviously does, that "muck of mucks" called consciousness and at the same time to acquiesce completely in an attitude of suspensiveness toward things as they are, exacts a difficult balance. So it is hardly surprising that from time to time, and increasingly, Barthelme's acceptance moves beyond Ramona's resignation to explore alternatives both more affirmative and more complex, creating in the process a more comprehensive and flexible irony as well.

In one of the stories of *Guilty Pleasures,* Barthelme returns to the problem of the quotidian in a baroque exhibition of play about play. The fascination of the piece—apart from its pyrotechnical inventiveness—lies in the fact that as Hector, an almost frighteningly prodigious game-freak, and Amanda, his ever more weary and unconvinced protegée, play and discuss games and game-theory, we become aware of the various impulses that underlie Barthelme's different kinds of fictions. Amanda's briefly enthusiastic response to Hector's inventions (" 'These games are marvellous,' Amanda said. 'I like them especially because they are so meaningless and boring, and trivial' " [GP, 133] underscores the presentational element in the stories: the link between fictional form and the forms of feeling; while Hector's final creation, "Ennui . . . the absence of games . . . the modern world at its most vulnerable" (GP, 134), expresses the Beckettian source and rationale for the ludic pieces. But another of Amanda's comments, which supplies the story's title—"Games Are the Enemies of Beauty, Truth, and Sleep, Amanda Said"—is more interesting still and different in kind from the others. For what the comment does is to embody a persistent reactive strain in Barthelme's work, which belies still further the programmatic rejections of meaning in much postmodern criticism. Not that Amanda is to be regarded transparently as a *porte-parole*. One can hardly imagine Barthelme using in his own person, even with the ironic qualification of "and Sleep," such high-flown words as beauty and truth. Nonetheless, Amanda's rejection, as compared with Ramona's acceptance, marks a difference: a refusal simply to acquiesce in cultural givens, which defines a number of Barthelme's stories too.

I don't want to make too much of poor, besotted Amanda. The point is simply that in her refusal of life as a game and of games as an adequate representation of life she gestures toward a more conceptual mode of apprehending and defining her situation; and this generalizing, reflective response to the experiential, to the immediately perceived, works better in some ways for Barthelme also, whose most successful, if not always his most obviously and dramatically innovative, fictions are of this kind. Furthermore, if Amanda's gesture is, despite its vocabulary, essentially negative, the same can be said of the force behind much of Barthelme's conceptual work. So much then for Amanda. Barthelme's rejections are the more interesting, and they are very much of a piece. Except in some of the more feeble parodies, however, they are *not,* as one might expect, rejections of the daily (though they do in fact lead ultimately to a reassessment of attitudes toward it) but of those who seek to stabilize and rationalize that world. In other words, Barthelme is, at his best, an anti-conceptual conceptualizer, working inductively toward an understanding of the necessity but also of the limits of acceptance.

In a general way, what Barthelme takes his stand against are pretensions to certainty and the insistence on perfection; large demands and great expectations; dogmatisms and theories of all kinds. In "Kierkegaard Unfair to Schlegel," the enemy is religion, as it is in "The Rise of Capitalism," where the saints deliver "the same old message" (S, 146) of hope in the other-worldly; in "The Sandman," it is prescriptive, specifically psychological, change; in "Report," the technocratic mentality; in "Engineer-Private Paul Klee," war. "Me and Miss Mandible" takes on education and the reliability of signs, "Marie, Marie, Hold on Tight" (if I read that curious story correctly), the pedantically theoretical questioning of the pedantic. Two of the stories deserve closer attention. In "The Photographs," two English scientists, or a Bob and Ray version of them, discuss, against the background of one's revelation of his affair with the other's wife, what they are to do with the photographs the practical-minded Reggie has inadvertently taken of the human soul. Their central exchange on the subject goes as follows:

"It seems to me to boil down to this: Are we better off *with* souls, or just possibly *without* them?"

"Yes. I see what you mean. You prefer the uncertainty."

"Exactly. It's more creative. Take for example, my, ah, arrangement with your wife, Dorothea. Stippled with uncertainty. . . . The humdrum is defeated. Momentarily, of course."

"Yes, I can understand that. Gives the thing a bit of zest."

"Yes. You'd be taking away people's zest. They'd all have to go around being good and all that." (GP, 158–59)

And so they decide to burn the photographs, proving in two senses that, as Barthelme says in his introduction: "Guilty pleasures are the best."

The attack on certainty, hidden meanings, and depth is carried still further in one of the most subtle and funny of the fictions, "The Glass Mountain." Divided neatly and parodically into a hundred sections, so as to subvert the fairytale or romance form it reductively imitates, the story describes the narrator's successful ascent of the mountain, with its "sparkling blue-white depths" (CL, 66), and his discovery at the top of "the beautiful enchanted symbol." "I approached the symbol, with its layers of meaning," he writes in section 97, "but when I touched it, it changed into only a beautiful princess," whom he disposes of in the next section by throwing her "headfirst down the mountain to my acquaintances" (CL, 71). The motive for the quest is explained earlier on:

57. A few questions thronged into my mind.
58. Does one climb a glass mountain, at considerable personal discomfort, simply to disenchant a symbol?
59. Do today's stronger egos still *need* symbols?
60. I decided that the answer to these questions was "yes." (CL, 68)

The project of the story, and of others like it, is in fact precisely one of demythifying, of disenchanting—not, as among English writers of the thirties, language and the world[20] but the cultural imperatives (scientific, religious, psychological, governmental, and aesthetic) of the present and the past: of everything, in short, from Batman to the American Dream. As compared with the enchanted symbol, the narrator's acquaintances, shouting throughout the climb a volley of obscene discouragements and standing on the sidewalks below—which the narrator sees with a curiously radiant intensity as "full of dogshit in brilliant colors: ocher, umber, Mars yellow, sienna, viridian, ivory black, rose madder" (CL, 66)—are pure, disenchanted, phenomenal reality, and, so the story implies, all the better for that.

Barthelme's irony becomes in these stories, or—an important reservation—in those aspects of them I've isolated, something more, or less, than suspensive. (Part of the total effect of "The Glass Mountain" derives, certainly, from the narrator's blandly accepting, mountain's eye view of such sights as "hundreds of young people shooting up in doorways, behind parked cars" [CL, 66].) The rejection of certainty, even if the ostensible goal is no more definite than an uncommitted openness to experience, implies a less provisional attitude than that discussed earlier in this essay. Indeed, the ability to sustain indefinitely an attitude of total acceptance—unless one effectively neutralizes reality by genuinely and intransigently pursuing the high aesthetic road, as some practitioners of the *nouveau nouveau roman* purport to do—requires something like the bemusement of one of Barthelme's city dwellers or the indifference of one of Hardy's gods. Small wonder, then, that at the very least Barthelme does, from time to time, actively recreate his sense of the ordinary or obliquely redefines his attitude toward it by setting off against them the dogmatisms that menace their integrity. But under the pressure of a more transitive irony, the ordinary may itself become the source not of resigned contemplation but of positive irritation, as it does to the letter writer of "The Sandman," who angrily asks his girl friend's psychiatrist: "What do you do with a patient who finds the world unsatisfactory?" and answers peremptorily: "The world *is* unsatisfactory; only a fool would deny it" (S, 93).

The answer is important, symptomatically, since any assertion of judgment necessarily threatens that resignation, which, rather than its emotional by-products, sadness or dailiness or the muted "lack of angst," determines Barthelme's strategy of acceptance. Furthermore, any deviation from acceptance opens the way still further to an irony mediated by the impulse to correct or improve or assert—or, alternately, to a desire to abandon irony completely. In either case, to a position which contravenes the neutrality of the suspensive. So, to take the extreme case, a handful of Barthelme's stories (they are, for the most part, early ones) suggest, in Tony Tanner's words, "the countering instinct to get away from matter altogether.[21] The Baudelairean longing expressed by the old woman in "Florence Green is 81" *"to go somewhere where everything is different"* elicits from the narrator the statement: "A simple, perfect idea. The old babe demands nothing less than total otherness" (CB, 15)—and from Tanner the comment that "although the idea is mocked, like every other idea offered as idea in Barthelme, this note of yearning for an unknown somewhere else sounds throughout his work" (p. 404). (Tanner is discussing only the first three books.) The same note sounds again, and again ambiguously, at the end of "A Shower of Gold," where the protagonist, Peterson, asserts against the wildy absurd situation in which he is involved (an antic, existentialist television program) his own identification with Perseus and Hamlet, that is, with classical and Renaissance traditions. He "went on and on," we're told, "and although he was, in a sense, lying, in a sense he was not" (CB, 183). It is even tempting to imagine that in the title of the volume from which these two stories come (*Come Back, Dr. Caligari*) there lurks, though with an altogether conscious perversity, a comically nostalgic longing for a lost order.

In any case, although one could point to other examples of this anironic yearning in Barthelme's fiction—in "The President," for example, or in the ambiguously utopian portrait of "Paraguay," or, perhaps, in the remarks on equanimity in *Snow White* (pp. 87–88)—the strain is not, after all, as dominant as Tanner suggests, and it is effectively mocked in "A City of Churches," where both the heroine of the story and the discontent of the town itself refuse the completeness of perfection. Barthelme, is, then, less seriously attracted by an escape into the realm of total otherness than by the temptation to find *within* the ordinary possibilities of a more dynamic response. The distinction is important. Modernist irony, seeking in its opposite (in the anironic) some release from its own vision of fragmentation, characteristically imagines, as I suggested earlier, an image of total order. Whether the image is frankly of another world (Yeat's Byzantium) or of some symbolically sufficient enclave in this one (Howards End; the greenwood to which Forster's lovers flee in *Maurice*) or even of an ideal still to be, or only temporarily realized (Lawrence's star-balance; Woolf's lighthouse; Forster's "Only connect . . ."), in all of these cases the emphasis falls on a unity in which all discontinuity is comprehended and dissolved. Postmodern ironists are less sanguine; and rightly so, for the anironic has come to suggest in recent times not resolution but annihilation. Through the looking-glass of contemporary chaos, one glimpses death or the death of consciousness— which may explain the concern with the apocalyptic in much recent fiction or with the self-abnegations of the minimalist and the aleatory in painting and music.

Still, if the present surrounds the ironist with a different and less hopeful context and offers him fewer possibilities of reconstruction or escape, his problems are, nevertheless, in some sense the same as his predecessors'. The change in irony over the past two hundred years from technique to vision, its development from the chief instrumentality of satire into an autonomous sensibility, has had as probably its most interesting result the transformation of distance (then and still one of the main aesthetic conditions for the successful functioning of irony) into a metaphor for a series of psychological and moral problems. Briefly, among the German Romantics, a source of freedom, mastery, and joy, distance gradually becomes the symbol of estrangement and alienation; and by the beginning of the twentieth century, it is the figure of the outsider, the uncommitted spectator, longing to overcome his self-consciousness and make contact with the world outside his limited and limiting ego, that dominates the literary landscape of writers such as Eliot, Joyce, and Forster, to mention only the most obvious. If Barthelme differs from these authors, it is not because he perceives the tension between distance and involvement any less intensely. Indeed, he is in many ways far more conscious of the nature and implications of his irony. His originality lies, rather, as we shall see, in his treatment of the problem and in his solution to it.

But first the problem itself, which undergoes its most extended and ingenious exploration in "Kierkegaard Unfair to Schlegel." Against the background of a dialogue about the ineffectiveness of his political activities, "A," the transparently authorial respondent, gradually begins a defense of his own irony in terms of the power and control it confers on him. The introduction of Kierkegaard's *The Concept of Irony,* however, with its familiar but brilliantly summarized arguments about the ironist's subjective freedom, his alienation of existence, and his infinite absolute negativity, leads finally to A's admission that "mostly I am trying to annihilate Kierkegaard in order to deal with his disapproval" (CL, 97). The ultimate failure to do so becomes apparent in a conversation toward the end of the story between A and his interlocutor, Q:

A: But I love my irony.

Q: Does it give you pleasure?

A: A poor . . . A rather unsatisfactory. . . .

Q: The unavoidable tendency of everything particular to emphasize its own particularity.

A: Yes.

        . . .

Q (ASIDE):   He has given away his gaiety, and now has nothing. (CL, 99)

But that is not quite all. If the story charts A's loss of his freedom and particularity, it confirms, in its construction (the abrupt and apparently illogical cuts from one section to another, the absurdist elements, the narrative and tonal shifts), the power that Barthelme as author and ironist retains. The fundamental tension of "Kierkegaard Unfair to Schlegel" inheres, then, not in A's unwilling fall from ironic grace but in the disparity between that internal drama and the authorial techniques used to articulate it. Of course, much modernist literature exhibits the same tension—but with an important difference. Whereas Forster's formalist aesthetic acts as a continuous counterforce to his assertions of spontaneity and freedom (except when he lapses into a desperate sentimentality), Barthelme's more open form allows with a greater frequency for the congruence of the aesthetic and the experiential. To a degree at least, structure becomes a window not a frame. I don't want to exaggerate this point: a good deal of modern literature, as Mark Schorer has taught us, uses technique as discovery; and there is no lack of artifice in the fictions of Barth or Coover or Gass, not to mention the *nouveau* and the *nouveau nouveau roman.* A number of Barthelme's pieces too verge on the precious and the contrived, but what one senses in the best of his work is an effort to use art to overcome art (as the moderns characteristically employ consciousness to move beyond consciousness)—or, better still, an attempt, parallel to that in "The Glass Mountain," to disenchant the aesthetic, to make of it something not less special but less extraordinary.

The desire to tame the extraordinary relates back, in turn, to the question of irony and distance. Unlike the classic modernists attempting to annex the world to the self or to lose the self in the world (compare the crazed cry of Flaubert's St. Antoine: "descendre jusqu'au fond de la matière,—être la matière!" or Lily Briscoe's craving in *To the Lighthouse* for "unity," "intimacy," some "device for becoming, like waters poured into one jar, inextricably the same, one with the object one adored"), Barthelme has more modest aims. If, indeed, he is, as ironist, already part of the world around him and not its distant observer, if that world is, furthermore, perceived not as object but as field, and if, finally, the phenomenal presents itself not as the veil of appearance but as multiform, irreducible reality, then the notion of involving himself with, or of encompassing, all of life is in any case an impossibility. But the suspensive no less than the equivocal involves its psychological and moral distances, and Barthelme seems of late less willing or able to abide them. Forced to deconstruct the monster he has built "to instruct [him] in complacency," the narrator of "Subpoena" ends his story on a note of mounting hysteria: "Without Charles, without his example, his exemplary quietude, I run the risk of acting, the risk of risk. I must participate, I must leave the house and walk about." The last sentence may well cut two ways, slicing away at the narrator's objectless compulsion to act as much as at his earlier complacency; and the lesson he learns in looking at Charles—"See, it is possible to live in the world and not change the world" (S, 114)—may be read different ways as well: as an attack on those who seek to impose their certainties or as the refutation of the value of passive acceptance. It seems best, in fact, to let the ambiguities of the story stand and to see in it Barthelme's attempt to narrow (in the words of a pompous character of an earlier tale) "the distance between the potential knowers holding a common-sense view of the world and what is to be known, which escapes them as they pursue their mundane existences" (CB, 119–20)—between, that is to say, activity and awareness: the mutually implying alternatives of all ironists of this century.

But how then, exactly, does Barthelme go about narrowing the gap? In two ways. First, by a further series of rejections, which come, interestingly, among his several portraits of the artist. Earlier examples of these, especially "The Dolt" and "See the Moon?" have been extensively mined by critics seeking statements of Barthelme's aesthetic (fragments, collage, the difficulties of writing, and so on), but more revealing for purposes of the present discussion are the group in *Sadness*. All four, in one form or another—and in a way typical of twentieth-century considerations of the artist—concern themselves with the problem of the extraordinary. "The Flight of Pigeons from the Palace," the simplest and most immediately amusing (it is one of the picture stories) is a parable of the artist in an age of the conspicuous consumption of schlock, in which "the public demands new wonders piled on new wonders." "Some of us," the narrator admits ruefully, suggesting all those essays on the obsolescence or death of fiction, "have even thought of folding the show—closing it down"; and in its last lines, the story both confirms and mocks the notion of ever new wonders, which, "when you become familiar with them, are not wonderful at all," as, on a low-keyed, naive note of hope resurgent, it introduces one last marvel: "The new volcano we have just placed under contract seems very promising . . ." (S, 137). The reader, observing it, violently smoking, in the illustration just below, is left to judge the likely efficacy of this and other wonders constructed or discovered for the salvation of art.

Coming at the problem of the remarkable from a different angle in "The Genius" (the protagonist is in fact a scientist, but the equation with the artist will hold, I think), Barthelme exposes his much admired, much honored figure as self-conscious, vain, insecure, and inauthentic. At issue in both these very unlike stories is what may be called a *critique de la vie extraordinaire,* which is carried further in the far more subtle "Daumier," a wild farrago of a fiction, whose point is that "the self cannot be escaped, but it can be, with ingenuity and hard work, distracted. There are always openings, if you can find them, there is always something to do" (S, 181). The distractions are, of course, from the quotidian; the openings, for the most part, the ingenious inventions of art. "Daumier" traces its artist-hero's attempt to escape "the original, authentic self, which is a dirty great villain" through "the construction of surrogates" (S, 161). The surrogates are the vehicles for the fictions within the fiction, which are in turn punctuated by the original Daumier's reflections on the lively-dismal life around him and on the psychology of self-salvation implicit in his artistic efforts. To complicate matters, the two surrogates illustrate, roughly (since even in the first "desire has been reduced . . . to a minimum" [S, 162], the conflict between the active and the contemplative: a reechoing of the problem of the story itself. Further, the *mise en abyme* of "Daumier" outdoes even Gide and Huxley, as Celeste, a figure from the first surrogate's adventures, enters into the artist's "real" life—where she is last seen domestically preparing him a *daube*. But if, in this movement from fiction to life (or rather, from the secondary to the primary level of the fiction within Barthelme's story of Daumier), there seems to have been an accommodation of the aesthetically dramatic and the psychologically distant to the ordinary, nonetheless it is the second surrogate who, literally, has the last, unsettling word, as Daumier repeats verbatim his less than sanguine comment on the availability of "openings." And it is, finally, the second surrogate, "the second-person Daumier" (S, 180) who, talking to himself about his inability to sustain any attachments, recognizes that he is "a tourist of the emotions" (S, 177), thereby acknowledging both the price one pays for trafficking with the extraordinary and, too, the inescapability of that "dirty great villain," the self. Ultimately, "Daumier" is a stand-off: not a solution to but a dramatization of the maze-like interrelationships and the even more profoundly immiscible qualities of art and life, the uncommon and the ordinary, the distant and the still unsatisfactory. Even if one over-looks Daumier's avowal that "there would be a time when I would not be happy and content," the assertion that he now is, "temporarily" (S, 180), remains both fantastic (to the degree that it depends upon the doubly fictive Celeste) and suspect. "Daumier," even as it playfully seeks to disenchant earlier images of the artist, in some sort reenforces them, becoming, as it were, Barthelme's most suspensively ironic tribute to the equivocal: a boister-ous assault on, but never quite a disruption of, modernist poise.

"The Temptation of St. Anthony," on the other hand, whatever its difficulties, does take a stand. The story seems at first sight a fairly straight-forward contrast between the saint, who represents, according to the narra-tor, "something pure and mystical, from the realm of the extraordinary, as it were," and the townspeople he lives among for a time, who, in their dislike of the ineffable, feel, with varying degrees of belligerency, that "the things of this earth are good enough for them" (S, 150). As one becomes more aware of the narrator, however, things seem less simple. Seeing himself as "sort of like a friend" (S, 151) to St. Anthony, he is a reasonably intelligent man (though no intellectual), tolerant, sympathetic, capable of appreciating, if not alto-gether of understanding, the phenomenon he finds himself faced with. In-deed, his openmindedness, his attempts, marked by endless qualifications, to be fair to all sides eventually irritate and force the reader to question, if not exactly to distrust, his view of things. There is no reason, for example, to doubt his opinion of the community, or his assertion, apropos of his friend, that "in the world of mundanity in which he found himself, he *shone*" (S, 157). But it is not at all clear that he recognizes the judgment the story passes on the saint, even though it derives directly from his own central perception: that "St. Anthony's major temptation, in terms of his living here, was perhaps this: ordinary life" (S, 152). In short, "The Temptation of St. Anthony," although it is by no means an encomium to conformity, asserts, in its sympathetically critical portrait, the need for the extraordinary to find its place admidst the quotidian. And the retreat back to the desert, marking a failure to do just that, indicates another stage in Barthelme's questioning of the distance, the suspensiveness that Anthony—parabolically the saint as artist or the artist as saint—represents.

But if escape is unacceptable and if acceptance, in the sense of Ramona's acquiescence, is not enough, what then? The fact is that increasingly in Barthelme's work, if not consistently, acceptance is modified by a more positive, more affirmative attitude of *assent*. Some clarifications are needed at this point. In the first place, the objects of Barthelme's or his characters' assent are remarkable not by virtue of being outside or substantially different from common life. It is not a question of discovering Bell's "ultimate reality" but of agreeing with Wilde that "the true mystery of the world is the visible, not the invisible." The extraordinary exists as part of the phenomenal world or it doesn't, effectively, exist at all. In the second place, even the use of the word "discovery," as if one were constantly scrutinizing sidewalks and gutters for lucky pennies, is misleading. What is at issue is not an essentialist but an existential quest: a subjective, though not for that reason a random or arbitrary, conferring of value, based on a continuing sense of the nature of *la vie quotidienne.* So the letter-writing lover of "The Sandman," after his outburst at his girl friend's normalizing psychiatrist, goes on: "What I am saying is that Susan is wonderful. *As is.* There are not so many things around to which that word can be accurately applied" (S, 93). Susan may stand as another of Barthelme's emblems, this time of all the good a flawed world has to offer— *as is,* depressions and *chasmus hystericus* included—to someone who approaches it not, like her psychiatrist, *ab extra,* as from some fixed and distant point in a conceptualized schema of classical perspective, but like her lover, whose approach is, by contrast, radically intentional and direct.

Assent, then, is dynamic, exploratory, on-going, experiential: the supervenient alternative Ramona was unable to imagine. In some sense, of course, Barthelme's fictions are themselves the best examples of his own particular form of assent—the prevalence of short stories itself, perhaps, the sign of a preference or an affinity for mixed and modest pleasures, as opposed to the larger and more final satisfactions sought by an earlier time. "How joyous," ends "Nothing: A Preliminary Account," the notion that, try as we may, we cannot do other than fail and fail absolutely [at the task of defining nothing] and that the task will remain always before us, like a meaning for our lives" (GP, 165). Less derivatively and archly and in a more up-beat way, Barthelme suggests the nature of assent in "Engineer-Private Paul Klee Misplaces an Aircraft between Milbertshofen and Cambrai, March 1916," one of the most amusing and successful of his works. The incident to which the title of the story refers is the pretext for a contrast between Klee, the artist or man naturally at home in the world, an instinctive inhabitant, unlike St. Anthony, of the *Lebenswelt,* and, on the other hand—or rather, at a considerable remove—the Secret Police, who watch him as he discovers the loss of his plane and then as he decides to "diddle the manifest" (S, 69) in order to cover the loss. The Police, melancholy and inept, hidden from the world it is their duty to observe but by which they "yearn to be known, acknowledged, admired even" (S, 66), are the very type of distance and disengagement: unhappy gods exiled from the fullness of the creation. "We are secret," they announce lugubriously, "we exist in the shadows, the pleasure of the comradely/brotherly embrace is one of the pleasures we are denied, in our dismal service" (S, 70). Klee, by contrast, is an adept at pleasure, modest pleasures. Moving, by order, through the absurdity of a world at war, he finds time for "bread and wurst and beer" (S, 65), for paintings and reading, and for meetings with his Lily. Having reached his destination, he says to himself: " I wait contentedly in the warm orderly room. The drawing I did of the collapsed canvas and ropes is really very good. I eat a piece of chocolate. I am sorry about the lost aircraft but not overmuch. The war is temporary. But drawings and chocolate go on forever" (S, 70). I don't want to burden so light and joyous a story with the ponderous vocabulary of existential analysis. Enough to note that if Klee is inexplicably thrown into an absurd world, he manages nonetheless to enjoy thoroughly the openness and fecundity he also finds (or creates) in it, agreeing apparently with Heidegger that "the ordinary is basically not ordinary; it is extra-ordinary." Neither a rebel nor an accomplice, he accepts what he must and assents to what he can: a totally ingratiating model of *Dasein,* the contingency of being-in-the-world.

As one of the most attractive and attractively rendered figures in the stories, Klee offers himself as an obvious antithesis to Barthelme's Kierkegaard, the two suggesting in some ways the oppositional archetypes of their author's fictional universe. Humanistic, tolerant, non-directive, Klee intimates the possibility of irony as a graceful, even integrative gesture toward the world. Kierkegaard, on the other hand, religious and prescriptive, presents irony, disapprovingly, as we've seen, as an infinite absolute negativity. However, as one traces Barthelme's movement (admittedly a serpentine and by no means consistent movement) from acceptance, through the rejection of dogmatisms and certainties, to assent, Kierkegaard gradually takes on a less monolithic typological significance. Leaving aside the religious question— and that is a large omission, of course—one can see that, in fact, Kierkegaard pronounces what Klee, less magisterially, to be sure, enacts: "What is wanted, Kierkegaard says, is not a victory over the world but a reconciliation with the world" (CL, 95–96). To put it another way, as the self-viewed antagonist of Barthelme's ironic distance, his defensiveness, his infinite absolute negativity, Kierkegaard (or, more accurately, I suppose, the tradition he in part initiates) supplies precisely that existential-phenomenological background out of which Barthelme operates, even as he, not infrequently, parodies it. "As to 'deeper cultural sources,' " Barthelme said in response to one of Jerome Klinkowitz's questions, "I have taken a certain degree of nourishment (or stolen a lot) from the phenomenologists: Sartre, Erwin Straus, etc." (TNF, 52).

My argument, then, is that the modification of Barthelme's suspensive irony is precipitated by exactly that current of thought which has supplied twentieth-century artists with their visions of dailiness, absurdity, and drift. And inevitably so. For the postmodern writer, at least for those who refuse the lure of a new, ultra-formalism, there is no consolation in the thought of other, more perfect worlds—those heterocosms that haunt the modernist imagination. There is only the open, temporal field of the phenomenal, with which, in Barthelme's case, "reconciliation" is achieved through the homeopathic agency of his critiques of *la vie quotidienne* and *la vie extraordinaire.* Not, it needs to be stressed again, that assent (still sporadic, in any case) *replaces* acceptance in Barthelme's more recent work. No; if Barthelme differs from not only Sukenick but from Ricardou, Sollers, and *Tel Quel* in his refusal of a purely aesthetic surface, he differs no less from the Forster of *The Life to Come* in denying that what Forster calls "the smaller pleasures of life" constitute the whole of it. For Barthelme, assent is added to without cancelling the more generalized attitude of acceptance, as stories like "The Sandman" and, of course, "Engineer-Private Paul Klee" make clear.

To speak once more in terms of irony: no doubt much of the explanation for Barthelme's characteristic suspensiveness is to be found in his response to the confusion and fragmentation of his world, but more striking, if more speculative, is his effort to resist the subject-object dichotomy we have learned to recognize, in man's metaphysical imperialism, as the baneful inheritance of Cartesian and Romantic dualism: an attempt, in other words, to remain open to the experience of (non-metaphysical) otherness. But if, to quote Pierre Thévenaz, one of the less well-known phenomenologists, "the world gives itself to consciousness," it is also the case that, Thévenaz continues, consciousness "confers on it its meaning"[22]—gives it, in a movement of reciprocity, its value. It is just possible that with figures such as Klee, Barthelme helps to define still another stage in the development of irony— one in which the gaps and discontinuities of twentieth-century literature, heretofore the mark of absence or negation, become instead the sign of a not yet constituted presence. Thus, no longer the familiar cause of horror or paralysis or suspensiveness, they are transformed rather (as they are already in Woolf's *Between the Acts*) into the source of a continuing activity predicated on the need to choose, to confer meaning: to add to the humility of acceptance (even, or especially, of those gaps in which future meaning lies latent) the irreducibly human function as assent.

Both modern and postmodern literature are less homogeneous than some critics like to imagine. Within the modern camp, even within the fortress of Bloomsbury, as many still see it, counterforces to the ruling orthodoxy are discernible, not least the phenomenological strain that overtakes Woolf's work after *The Waves*. And among postmodernists, it is equally clear that the ascendency of the subjective, the open, and the temporal is threatened by a contemporary and exotic version of a supposedly discredited aestheticism. Sharp distinctions, then, are difficult and suspect. What *has* changed, or become apparent, in the course of the century, from Gide to Cortázar, is our sense of the space in which art and literature operate, that is, more fundamentally, the nature of our perceptions; and the lesson—if one can use so old-fashioned a word—of Barthelme's work is that a writer can, rejecting illusionist and psychological depth in fiction, nonetheless avoid the all too frequent banality of flatness, not by reimposing a metaphysical perspective or a theologically schematic worldview but by recognizing in what ways the dynamics of surface (of moral as well as aesthetic surface) are determined by an acknowledgment of the "horizons of the flesh."[23] Surface, in other words, may generate a particular, complex dimensionality of its own— or a depth of a kind different from that of classical perspective. So, as Merleau-Ponty writes: "The perceived thing is not an ideal unity in the possession of the intellect, like a geometrical notion, for example; it is rather a totality open to a horizon of an indefinite number of perspectival views which blend with one another according to a given style, which defines the object in question," (PP, 16). In a novel like *A Passage to India,* it is precisely the geometrizing of the universe—or the inability any longer to retain a belief in the Newtonian cosmos—that leads to breakdown, to a corrosive view of infinity. But the horizon of the phenomenal world is not an objective thing or place "out there"; it is the subjective, but no less real, result of being in the world: the shifting boundary of *human* depth, the pledge of man's necessary interaction with a world of which he is not only part but partner.

Barthelme's assumption of that partnership is manifest precisely in the movement from the relative passivity of acquiescence to the activity of decision and judgment (however tentative or qualified), which is implied in the transvalued irony of his assent and which is nowhere better illustrated than in the recent, uncollected story, "Rebecca."[24] Burdened by her "ugly, reptilian, thoroughly unacceptable last name" (p. 44), Lizard, by a judge's rufusal to change it, by her equally unchangeable greenish complexion, and by a series of less dramatic frustrations, Rebecca precipitates a quarrel with her lover, Hilda, watches her world collapse around her, and sees it reconstitute itself, provisionally, imperfectly, but lovingly, with Hilda's invitation: "Come, viridian friend, come and sup with me" (p. 45). Funny and sad, the vignette is in itself testimony to the fragile, dubious strength of human relationships and to an acceptance of life altogether different from Ramona's. But the story, despite the apparent centrality of the two women, belongs, in fact, to the narrator, the intrusive, playful, partisan figure, whose comments manage to engage the reader's sympathy and whose digressions and reflections avert its spill over into the sentimental. It is the narrator, always letting the reader know that he is in charge of, indeed the creator of, his fiction, who reserves for himself the last, nicely balanced, astringent and affirmative remarks: "The story ends. It was written for several reasons. Nine of them are secrets. The tenth is that one should never cease considering human love. Which remains as grisly and golden as ever, no matter what is tattooed upon the warm tympanic page" (p. 45). The final sentence, with its reminder of the ambiguous relations, or disjunctions, between life and art, provides besides, in its image of mechanical process (the tympanic page) and its moderating suggestion of human response (the warm page), a comment on the complexity of surface: the warm tympanic page, which, whatever its "objecthood," is also the sign of a vital depth, or, better still, the horizon of Barthelme's assent.

Barthelme's tympanic page is about as different as one can imagine from Sukenick's ideal of opaque surface, and it may be that he is, bit by bit, writing himself out of membership in the bossanova club. Not that his work lends itself to a division into discrete, sequential stages. Ramona, Amanda, and Klee, though in different degrees at different times, all populate the Barthelmean landscape, suggesting the varied, overlapping impulses to accept, to reject, and to affirm. The ludic strain in his work persists, not as a denial of meaning, of referentiality, but as an assertion of the artist's privilege to create meaning. And so too does the suspensiveness, at least in the sense that his work refuses the epistemological quest for ultimates and absolutes. Barthelme remains part of the world he perceives, approaching it through a process of interrogation to which he opens himself as well. Furthermore, life, as he sees it, not only refuses to offer up assurances and answers; it continues to be in large part, for human beings trying to make their way through it, frustrating, disjointed, and drab. "Rebecca" acknowledges the smaller pleasures against the background of a life still *fort quotidienne*. But, with all of this said, it is no less true that there is, at the least, a change of emphasis in Barthelme's later work: a sense that, Ramona notwithstanding, an alternative does exist. In the final analysis, the alternative presents itself, however malapropos or offensive the word sounds to many today, as a humanism of sorts—less anthropocentric, less hopeful, to be sure, than that of the modernists; based instead, like Sartre's or Merleau-Ponty's, on an ethic of subjectivity and risk. Thus, if the necessary incompleteness of Barthelme's world is in one sense the definition of its persisting sadness, it is, in another, the source of its pleasures. Still, no doubt, as the title of his latest collection suggests, guilty pleasures—but the signs too of a normative presence forging, tentatively, a morality and an irony for postmodern (or, possibly, post-postmodern?) man.

Notes

1. The Ironic Harvest: *English Poetry in the Twentieth Century* (London: Edward Arnold, 1974), p. 36
2. On the question of irony as technique and as vision, see my book, *Christopher Isherwood* (New York: Twayne Publishers, 1971), pp. 18–19, and the discussions of what he calls "General Irony" in D.C. Muecke's two books, *The Compass of Irony* (London: Methuen & Co., 1969) and *Irony* (London: Methuen & Co., 1970). In the earlier of the books, Muecke writes that General Irony "emerges . . . from an awareness of life as being fundamentally and inescapably at odds with itself or with the world at large" (p. 123). Muecke's studies remain the best on the subject.
3. For a more detailed discussion of this point and for a more specific consideration of the transformations of irony in the twentieth century, see my essay "Depths and Surfaces: Dimensions of Forsteian Irony," *English Literature in Transition*, 16 (1973), 257–74. The concept of the "anironic," to which I allude several times in the pages that follow, is treated more explicitly in my essay "Desire and Consciousness: The 'Anironic' Forster," *Novel*, 9 (Winter 1976), 114–29.
4. "Art for Art's Sake," in *Two Cheers for Democracy* (New York: Harcourt, Brace and Co., 1951), p. 95. The collection of essays will be referred to hereafter as TC.

5. See *The Garden and the Map: Schizophrenia in Twentieth-Century Literature and Culture* (Urbana, Chicago, London: University of Illinois Press, 1973), especially Chapter 1.

6. Richard Gilman, in *The Confusion of Realms* (New York: Vintage Books, 1970), accurately describes the "new reality" he sees Barthelme articulating as characterized "by horizontal impulses rather than vertical ones" (p. 43).

7. *A Writer's Diary,* ed. Leonard Woolf (New York: Harcourt, Brace and Co., 1954), p. 27.

8. Robert Coover, *Pricksongs & Descants,* (New York, Toronto, London: New American Library, 1969), pp. 204, 202, 188.

9. References to Barthelme's works will be given in the text and are to the following editions (the abbreviations used are indicated): CB: *Come Back, Dr. Caligari* (Boston, Toronto: Little, Brown and Co., 1964); SW: *Snow White* (New York, Toronto, London: Bantam Books, 1971); UP: *Unspeakable Practices, Unnatural Acts* (New York, Toronto, London: Bantam Books, 1969); CL: *City Life* (New York, Toronto, London: Bantam Books, 1971); S: *Sadness* (New York, Toronto, London: Bantam Books, 1974); GP: *Guilty Pleasures* (New York: Farrar, Straus and Giroux, 1974). The original publication dates of the books are, respectively, 1964, 1967, 1968, 1970, 1972, 1974.

10. *Anti-Story: An Anthology of Experimental Fiction* (New York: The Free Press, 1971), p. xx.

11. "The New Tradition in Fiction," in *Surfiction: Fiction Now . . . and Tomorrow,* ed. Raymond Federman (Chicago: The Swallow Press, 1975), pp. 43–44.

12. The interview (with Jerome Klinkowitz) appears in *The New Fiction: Interviews with Innovative American Writers,* ed. Joe David Bellamy (Urbana; Chicago, London: University of Illinois Press, 1974), p. 52. The interview will be referred to hereafter as TNF.

13. On collage, see Richard Schickel, "Freaked Out on Barthelme," *The New York Times Magazine,* Aug. 16, 1970, 42, and Barthelme's remarks in his interview (TNF, 51–52). In the same interview (p. 53), Barthelme denies that the statement "Fragments are the only forms I trust" (UP, 164) is "a statement of [his] aesthetic." It is worth reading the fantastic "recantation" he then goes on to make.

14. Edmund Carpenter, *They Became What They Beheld* (New York: Ballantine Books, 1970), n. pag.

15. "Modernist Painting," in *The New Art: A Critical Anthology,* ed. Gregory Battcock, rev. ed. (New York: E. P. Dutton & Co., 1973), pp. 68–69.

16. "Mr. Bennett and Mrs. Brown," *Collected Essays,* I (New York: Harcourt, Brace & World, 1967), 327.

17. "Indirect Language and the Voices of Silence," in *Signs,* trans. Richard C. McCleary (Evanston: Northwestern University Press, 1964), 54. Further references to Merleau-Ponty will be given in the text and are to the following works (the abbreviations used are indicated): PhP: *Phenomenology of Perception,* trans. Colin Smith (London: Routledge & Kegan Paul, 1962): PP. *The Primacy of Perception,* ed. James M. Edie (Evanston: Northwestern University Press, 1971).

18. *American Pop Art* (New York: Collier Books, 1974), p. 7.

19. *Art* (New York: Capricorn Books, 1958), p. 54.

20. See my essay "Language and Surface: Isherwood and the Thirties," *Contemporary Literature,* 16 (Autumn 1975), 478–91.

21. *City of Words: American Fiction* 1950–70 (New York: Harper & Row, 1971), p. 402.

22. What is Phenomenology? and Other Essays, ed. James M. Edie (Chicago: Quadrangle Books, Inc., 1962), p. 50.

23. The phrase is the title of a collection of essays on the thought of Merleau-Ponty edited by Garth Gillan (Carbondale and Edwardsville: Southern Illinois University Press, 1973).

24. *The New Yorker,* Feb. 24, 1975, pp. 44–45.

Postmodern Realism: Discourse As Antihero in Donald Barthelme's "Brain Damage"

MARY ROBERTSON

Donald Barthelme has often been valued mainly as a fantasist, part of a generation of writers whose "pure writing" productions kept alive the imaginative powers against all odds in a thoroughly technocratic, literalist culture.[1] Such "fabulation" is normally placed at the farthest end of the spectrum from the classic realist depiction of society, since the former is autotelic and the latter instrumental and referential. Willingness to frame a reading of Barthelme as surreal fantasy has helped some readers to "just relax and enjoy" his wildly amusing creations because it liberates them from grappling with the otherwise difficult question of what his fictions say.

Yet the sense of society's importance to Barthelme's fiction is too overwhelming to ignore. Most critics do not deny that Barthelme seems to have "something to say" about our modern world. Usually they decide that he writes some version of the old, familiar theme that the modern world is absurd and the people in it anomic because of this absurdity. Larry McCaffrey is typical in saying, for example, that "Barthelme's metafictional concerns are intimately related to his other thematic interests: the difficulties of expressing a total vision of oneself in a fragmenting universe, the failure of most of our social and linguistic systems, the difficulties of making contact or sustaining relationships with others."[2] Lois Gordon, too, stresses the absurdity:

> Essentially both hollow and stuffed . . . modern man is the offspring of T. S. Eliot's hollow man and waste lander, buried under the very thing Eliot yearned for—tradition, systems of belief, meaning, and explanation. It is as if the ritual Eliot wished us to pursue had completely lost its substance and in our compulsive and habitual search for 'meaning,' we had gained the words and the process for search, but lost any significance that might have attached to either. We have lost our residual roots with humanity and instead become monsters of information, like computers. Such a portrait of modern life may indeed reflect a disjointed and fragmented contemporary condition—and perhaps this represents a new sort of mimesis. Though Barthelme never admits it directly, there is implied social criticism in all his work.[3]

This essay was written specifically for this volume and is published here for the first time by permission of the author.

The striking thing is the uneasiness with which most Barthelme criticism typically veers between emphasis on the autotelic "art object" and on the social meanings in the works, even within the same discussion when both dimensions are acknowledged. When technique and meaning are analyzed together, it is usually at such a general level that it does not help a reader very much to create a coherent reading according to a principle that works uniformly throughout a given story. For example, Gordon, whose analysis in some ways lays a pathway to the doorstep of this essay in its emphasis on the paralysis of contemporary people who are "stuffed with roles, words, and expertise,"[4] never finds the reading key to join up at the highest level her separate insights about Barthelme's alienated characters, dislocated form, and focus on language. Her discussion of technique, like that of many other Barthelme critics, consists of cataloguing different devices like making lists, interpolating unexpected words in a series, use of pop allusions and puns, and so on. Most discussions of the relation of technique and meaning in Barthelme tend to boil down to the proposition that dislocated form mimes a dislocated reality or that a metasticized parody exaggerates man's paralysis of meaning.[5]

There are two main problems with these approaches. First, the repetition of the theme of alienation through fragmentation of form, a staple of modernism, would hardly distinguish an innovative writer by the time of the 1960s. Second, everyone agrees that a focus on language is central in Barthelme in a way that was not the case even in modernist writing, but how a focus on language as dazzling technique and a focus on language as thematically important are related has not been clearly answered. If technique is the vehicle of the "new mimesis" of which Gordon speaks, how does that actually work in the stories? Many critics have pointed out *that* language is a focal subject in Barthelme, but none has identified *how* Barthelme's linguistic pyrotechnics link with his representational themes in the way this essay does.

The question of how Barthelme's mimesis works cannot be separated from a reader's quandary about deciding how to structure a reading out of this apparently free-form object. Several critics have commented on the deliberateness with which postmodern surrealistic writers like Barthelme challenge the reader to come up with his or her own reading method; however, result of such attempts has usually been very impressionistic and sporadic rather than rigorous efforts to follow even one story completely through to establish a convincing method for reading Barthelme.[6]

This essay proposes a method, inspired by structuralist and poststructuralist methods of reading symbolic objects,[7] that at once respects the postmodern bias against hegemonic systems in Barthelme and also reveals how his surrealist technique makes him one of the leading realists of our time. It will demonstrate very concretely how his "new mimesis" works. Rather than threatening one another, his surrealist inventive genius adapts realist traditions to our contemporary perspective on social phenomena.

To appreciate how this is so requires a switch in perception of the text's surface that is initially a little difficult but, once mastered, becomes easy to the point that we wonder why we did not see it all along. The first key to the perceptual switch is not to be fooled into grasping for possible symbolic meanings of the many incongruous images and surreal happenings in Barthelme's stories. We instinctively reach for symbolic interpretation, as with dreams or the film *Star Wars,* when we cannot construct a realist sequential narrative. "Brain Damage" consists of ten mininarratives, separated randomly by pictures and what I will call headlines (the large, bold print). Immediately the burden is on the reader to decide what, if any, relation exists among the narrative fragments themselves and among the fragments and the pictures and headlines. Intense scrutiny of the pictures and headlines reveals a few tenuous clues that might help us "shore these fragments" in the "spatial form" reading mode taught to us by modernism. A leitmotif of sexual fear connects the fear of the beckoning woman in the fourth narrative and the picture of the woman with masculine face and gigantic breasts. A Prufrockian tension between active fear and diffidence registers in the juxtaposed headlines of WRITHING, SEXUAL ACTIVITY, and YAWNING. The blue light and the blue flowers possibly signal a symbolic overcoding. But none of these patterns is sustained enough to build a reading of the whole story, as patterns are in *The Waste Land.* Barthelme breaks up symbolic patterns as much as he breaks up realistic syntax. Details seem gratuitously chosen so that even our best old methods produce little. If we naturalize that incoherence itself as the symbolic message, the story would only repeat the time-worn message of alienation or "absurdity."

Neither can we read Barthelme's work quite as we read the "magical realism" of a García Marquez. Barthelme's work does not depict paranormal phenomena as equally "real" as empirical phenomena. Barthelme's work may be joined at its philosophical roots with that of the magical realists in emphasizing the linguistically mediated nature of reality, but the interchangeability of history and myth might have an ontological status in the South Americans' work that is not even a concern of Barthelme's. Rather he prefers to make semiosis itself his object of scrutiny, leaving the more mystical possibilities to others.

The modernist message of cultural incoherence is perhaps the springboard that links Barthelme's postmodernism to modernism, but that generalization by itself does not convey the essence of his innovative realism. His prose anatomizes more concretely the *way* contemporary culture is mentally and spiritually incoherent. The second, more affirmative, key to reading Barthelme is to recognize that types of discourse are his true referents. Vestigial "characters" appear throughout, but the real "hero" of his fictions is language itself. One must learn to read past all of the amusing content of his stories just as a structural anthropologist reads past manifest cultural displays to discern the latent semiotic structure beneath them without transposing that structural enunciation into an alien *symbolic articulation*. If Barthelme's stories make us feel "lost in the funhouse," it is because he positions us in a defamiliarized way among the babel of modern and premodern discourses in which we think and speak and represent reality. That is realistic representation in a different mode. Realists have always attended to their characters' worldviews and fashioned language to convey them. But with Barthelme the relative salience of mind (worldview) and discourse (the expression of that worldview) is totally reversed. "Mind" is squeezed down to the merest relic—it is mere token stimulus to narrative propulsion—and discourse balloons up to fill the textual world-space. Barthelme's stories enact the proposition that language speaks us rather than the other way around.

The approach advocated here is not the same as the reductive proposition that Barthelme's stories are "writing about writing." The two approaches share the idea that writing can be about discourse, but to say that Barthelme is just self-reflexively preoccupied with the discourse of his own art severely understates the rich texture of his social awareness. He casts a wider net to catch the many specialized codes or discourse available to contemporary people and, in a tone constantly tinged with irony, to play them off against discourses no longer available to modern man. This focus on language as both symptom and source of mental, spiritual, and social incoherence links him to Hemingway, who, by Barthelme's own admission, had the strongest influence on him. People usually see the association only in their minimalism, but Hemingway's principle that "all our words from loose using have lost their edge" grows in Barthelme from Hemingway's indictment of certain notable spurious abstractions to fill the entire universe of possible discourses used by contemporary people. Hemingway still thought it was possible to locate a few words that were "real," and he used them magisterially. He still thought there was a language of nature that was authentic. In Barthelme that nature is nowhere to be found, and he shows that the very notion of "real" words is naive now, if it wasn't always so. Yet one never feels that he has just abandoned Hemingway's concern for authentic speech as certain other "fabulators" have—"authentic" meaning some necessary correlation between speech and fact. To demonstrate these propositions, a rather painstaking journey through "Brain Damage" as an exemplary story is necessary. The method here reveals the structural principles applicable to every Barthelme story, but this story is one of the purest examples of Barthelme's realistic concern with the problem of the panoply of contemporary discourses.

The ten narrative fragments of "Brain Damage" and the story's pictures and headlines are each like a bead on the string of a single structural enunciation that might be summarized like this: We think and speak now in a variety of discourses, but they all seem to be either too complacent in their narrow and reductive precision or too uneasy, inadequate, and decadent, yet still preserving some vestige of contact with the complexity of human affairs as they were once thought of. Of course, to put it thus is already to assume more than the story guarantees, since each unit just beckons to the reader to place it interpretively in relation to other units in the story and provides no assurance that a proposition exists at all. Yet in view of such strongly interrogative headlines as "In Whose Name?" and "What Recourse?" one also might suppose that the story asks if our only choice now is between these two main types of discourse. Each type is represented by a number of more particular discourses dramatizing themselves, so to speak, by means of the surrealistic dialogue and events depicted in the story.

The first narrative fragment, obviously alluding to the *Waste Land* tradition by beginning, "In the first garbage dump I found a book,"[8] dramatizes, in the movement from its first to its second sentence, the cardinal point of "Brain Damage," the colonization of personal voice by various discourses. The first instance is that same pervasive inane combination of mid-cult spiritualism and self-help that caused the *New York Times* to split its best-sellers' list into two and bookstores across the country to devote entire sections to its merchandising. The inaugural "I" is immediately swallowed up by this book's language of hype. Indeed, the "I" seems the merest conventional excuse to feature this discourse, which has attained so much power over speech and thought in contemporary life. Once noble abstractions like "achievement, prosperity and happiness" (p. 133) are, through the repetition, shown to be empty clichés used to trap the unwary. The book's promises reek of spurious concern for its hopeful reader. Quite soon the speaker is using written language to articulate what he wants to tell us: "An example" is written, not spoken speech. Nowhere does the voice of the "I" in this fragment demonstrate any skeptical distance from the book's rhetoric and logic. The narrator, already lost as a unique character from the story's opening, unquestionably assumes as convincing the book's phony ethical reasoning—the spirit teachers are useful because their "light" repulsed the thief. There is no transaction here between the speaker's mind and the book; the same discourse marks them as indistinguishable. The more the speaker adheres to the discourse of this book, the more he loses himself in any conceivable humanistic sense. Since such a discourse is ubiquitous now, it does not work merely to read this as a playful parody of genuine spirituality; Barthelme depicts here an object in the real world.

The second narrative fragment parodies in its overall movement the discourse of dialectic even as it dramatizes the workings of several other discourses: the empiricist, humanist, and aestheticist/liberal discourses. The action of plugging in the flowers makes no sense in the normal realistic frame for reading, but it makes sense as a sign of the kind of enunciation that empiricist discourse forms all the time in its effort to understand the world. Empiricism is a way of talking and thinking about the physical world. Its experimentalism is a speech act of sorts that articulates its questions just as Gregory does: "What kind of current is this . . ." (p. 134). The reasoning is that type of inference taught by empirical science: "That was what we all thought because most of the houses in this part of the country were built in compliance with building codes that required AC" (p. 134). The humanist discourse takes a different approach, talking about the world as a good in itself. The contemporary world vacillates in liberal ineffectuality between the two, just as the speaker does here. His "own" idea is clearly not unique; the contemporary masses are confused somewhere between empiricism's instrumental rationality and humanism's reverence. The lame compromise choice to speak and think about the world in debased aestheticist terms ("The blue of the flowers is extremely handsome against the gray of that area" [p. 134].) is linked up here with such liberal indecision and compromise. Liberal academic hesitancy is also bound up with this discourse; Barthelme catches its indecisive tone in the pacing, diction, and subject of the sentence, "Toynbee's notions of challenge and response are also, perhaps apposite" (p. 134). A reciprocal implosion of discourses into irrelevance, such as we find in the five hundred pages of *The Magic Mountain,* here takes one short page.

The grotesque mock-heroic obsequies of Guignol the waiter are used to project the discourse of "objective" reporting, pervasive in both journalism and behavioral studies. True, the surrealistic situation alone would parody our contemporary inability to render moving human experiences like death with appropriate dignity and individuality, but the passage emphasizes that this inability results from a loss of appropriate solemn language. The account of the funeral is sanitized of all personal feelings and limited to a tone and diction bent on just "reporting the facts." The use of the passive voice bleeds all agency out of the report. The ludicrous but dull epithet "great waiter" (p. 136) reports received opinion with no attempt at evaluation. The report concentrates on fidelity to the gastronomic code instead of a reflection on the waiter's former personal qualities. The traditional moment to remember something good about the deceased in a colorful anecdote is taken over by the language of a trite advertising slogan for dishsoap—"Cuts the grease" (p. 134). Barthelme's focus in this passage is not so much on pickling a waiter in aspic as on the discourse by which such solemn realities as death are trivialized in our contemporary culture.

The fourth fragment contains two significant deictics—"A dream" and "An experience"—that tell us we should examine the two parts in relation to each other. A debased version of the discourse of Freudian interpretation has metasticized in the last forty years, interpreting much that was explained otherwise before Freud. Many people would not know how to speak and think about reality without it. The point seems to be the parallelism between what happens symbolically in the dream and "really" in the experience. The rusty ship loaded with explosives is that cliché dreaded now by English teachers, a "phallic symbol," shown to be practically engulfed by the vaginal "cliffs [that] rush forward threateningly" (p. 137). The experience too finds the sexually disinterested narrator being threatened by an invitation from an "older woman" to "pick up a penny from the gutter." Surely Barthelme's main interest in not in reiterating Eliot's old message of sexual fear and true passion's enervation; rather he features one of the main languages that has, in spite of Freud's intentions, enabled a further alienation of the self from its own springs of passion. Freud knew that all such symbols must be interpreted in relation to an individual's own system of dreams, but the point in this narrative passage is the utterly hackneyed reduction of Freudian interpretation. It suggests that this is *the* discourse in which we are likely to try to understand our sexuality, and that we do it by having already been colonized in our thinking by the Freudian clichés.

These clichés insulate us from direct exploration of our terrors when we have them in dreams because we have a ready-made framework in which to place them. "Oh, yes, this dream means I am resistant to sexual involvement," we hear ourselves say. Furthermore, because the juxtaposition of the dream and experience is just that—a juxtaposition without further comment—the passage suggests even further that perhaps we are not even capable of *having* an experience with the opposite sex in certain situations without reacting to it as if it were a Freudian cliché. The stereotyped discourse, having been that in which we for so long processed sexual matters in our minds, influences the nature of the experiences we do have. For example, the speaker does not see an older woman and wonder what will come of that; he sees an "older woman" as cultural stereotype of distasteful sexual predation and the incest taboo.

The pervasiveness of Freudian clichés is confirmed by the fact that the reader can so easily decipher the symbolic material here. We might look down on the poor wretch who is trapped in that discourse until we realize that these clichés are the first thing to have come to our mind because they are now part of the intersubjective code governing such contexts in the contemporary world. Our limited freedom as readers to make something of this passage signifies our limited freedom as people living in a sexual world. One only has to say "A dream" or "older woman" and responses are automatic.

The litanic confession was once a viable specialized discourse in which people established a relation to their conscience and their god. The fifth narrative fragment parodies it by emphasizing how lack of a formal discursive framework can affect our ethical bearings. We can manage now only a disjointed listing of items when, for whatever reason, we are called upon to turn our attention to our sins. (The absurdity of some of the sins adds to this effect, of course.) What strikes us here is the mechanical quality of the confessional litany. Just as with Guignol the waiter, the flat language without judgment is misapplied to a potentially solemn situation. This confession, with its flat effect, reminds one more of the ominous cadences of the brainwashed political recantation where the prisoner says whatever he is told to say. But it lacks even that justification. It is really just a list that confuses the important with the trivial and is guided by no tradition that would help the speaker distinguish between the two. Several times the speaker uses the word "truth," but we see that it is just a word that means nothing to the speaker. Cut loose from its social moorings, it floats free. The litanic confession implied a coherent ethical code behind it; it was a ritualized form that worked because a system of shared beliefs backed it up. Because we no longer agree on what is sin, or even that the concept is appropriate, the discourse once used to express that agreement is a mere shell of itself. Yet the effect on the individual is just as devastating as when he uses a discourse that is active among us; we see that without such a social language, he will be unable to truly locate his conscience.

The sixth fragment obviously parodies the discourse of contemporary anthropology, particularly its resolute attempts to remain "value free" by restricting itself to minute observation without adding judgment. Part of the fun here is the irony that the disinterestedness is not maintained because the very categories of analysis are biases from the observers' culture (it reminds one of the Saul Steinberg New Yorker's map of the United States); the gesture of inquiring beyond one's own border is neutralized by the parochialism of comparing everything to "our" culture. Again, the flat, one-dimensional idiom is the thing to hear in the passage. It can be contrasted with, for example, a Victorian missionary's account of savages, or Herodotus on Egypt, Gibbon on Rome, or DeToqueville on America. (Semioticians would say that they are in the same paradigmatic series; therefore, they are the "absent brothers" of this passage.) All significant value judgment has been erased from this discourse. Indeed, the anthropologist's "value-free" description has become the prime model for much of twentieth century cultural discourse.

By this point in the story, we begin to see a pattern emerge that contrasts two kinds of discursive impotence: the first is a flat positivism that robs experience of all spiritual resonance; the second is slightly more complex and resonant, but usually incoherent because it operates without roots in the present culture. We also begin to see that structurally, this text concerns the problem of the bewildering variety of discourses available to us at the same time that so many rich discourses of the past have been reduced to a homogeneous positivism.

By reducing it to the absurd, the seventh fragment parodies the idiom of pure descriptive economics that has for the most part replaced a more capacious political economy in our culture. The framing signal is "Behavior of the waiters," another abstract nominal, like "A dream" or "An example," that makes it impossible to identify personal point of view upon the material. The surreal action clearly alludes to Sartre's observations on a waiter's inauthenticity (Barthelme studied existential philosophy) and jokingly remarks upon the pyramid of exploitation in capitalism, whose ultimate jewel is filthy lucre. The style, as usual, severely understates the drama and significance of what is happening. It might be contrasted with the analytic but committed and figural prose Marx used to diagnose capitalism. What is the probability of revolutionary energy being applied to economics when the discourse used to discuss economic phenomena is so unfervent and innocuous?

The eighth fragment highlights what has become of metaphorical capacities in our culture and links their decadence to the failure of the contemporary university to promote effective moral and humanistic discourse. The first three lines, "The cup fell from nerveless fingers . . . The China cup big as an AFB fell from tiny white nerveless fingers no bigger than hairs . . ." (p. 143) catachrestically demonstrate the failed attempt to articulate something poetically. We hear in these three lines the whole gradual fall of figural discourse into literalness, and we have another example of an incoherent, once powerful discourse that strains to be relevant to the modern world. We are confused about whether to read "nerveless" literally or metaphorically, just as "Brain Damage" can be read either way. Further on, a terribly bad pun, "Department of Romantic Poultry" maintains this confusion of levels even as it satirizes the cowardice of literati in the university. Timidity characterizes both the poetry and the university personnel here. The tenured faculty is portrayed as a cautious centipede hugging the "plane of the feasible" (p. 143); the humanists are like chickens that cannot escape being devoured by the octopi sciences. Neither the language of poetry here nor the university president can establish a footing; the concrete always dissolves into the vague. The discourse of the tea ceremony—really a whole social language when you think of it—is obsolete and has nothing to do with real life any longer. The "blush" that ends the fragment is the appropriate figure for such discourses that have deliquesced into abstraction. Both poetry and the university, which is supposed to be society's visionary institution, have lost the power to produce convincing discourses to guide the modern imagination.

The ninth fragment mainly enacts the discourse of television, while at the same time it presents several subcodes like advertising, the adventure show, and TV drama. The TV characteristically portrays everything at the same plane of importance without syntactic subordination, which accounts for the rapid jump in prose here from one episode to the other without explicable transitions. The narrator is channel-hopping and the shows are being interrupted by the ads. Finally, the narrator shuts off the TV and attempts to create his own fiction, failing, of course, while delivering his pathetic little minimalist defence of poetry—"Some people feel you should tell the truth, but those people are impious and wrong, and if you listen to what they say, you will be tragically unhappy all your life" (p. 145).

In this section Barthelme attends to the uniformity and pervasiveness of the discourse of advertising by showing that all the ads exhibit the same essential structure—a shapely girl in bodily interaction with a product—and reminding us that they are regularly interspersed among the shows' episodes. Thus the inferior fare offered in the TV shows is further debased by being spliced with inappropriate commercial speech that, presumably, some viewers fail to distinguish from the shows themselves.

The adventure show and the TV drama are themselves stereotypical. Their triteness motivates the speaker to go to the garage and attempt some of his own storytelling. Again, we find a gesture in "Brain Damage" that attempts to infuse formerly powerful discourses like fiction with some potency, only to see that they have become weakly uncertain of themselves to the point of near-extinction or self-parody. Barthelme intersperses the inanity of the TV and advertising discourse with words like "real," "melancholy," "agony," "impious," "wrong," and "tragically," all of which are relics from anachronistic discourses. He allows us here to feel the Saussurian insight that words only signify within a system; without being embedded in an entire cultural discourse that uses such terms meaningfully and to which everyone subscribes, these words are like dead lions in a chicken yard. In a relativistic culture, "real" cannot signify in a meaningful way as it did in ages where standards of "truth" were accepted. "Impious" belongs to an age when piety meant something. Without the whole sustaining belief of a religious culture that could treat decisions about vocations as objective, the mother superior's assurance that she believes the young nun's renunciation of the world to be "real" seems empty. Likewise, a diagnosis like "Nun's Melancholy" would have seemed appropriate in an age when "melancholy" was a current psychological term. After Freud, it seems quaint. "Tragically," used as part of the phrase "tragically unhappy" has that peculiar odor of spiritual superficiality that both causes and results from the overuse of the word by inane self-help authorities.

Thus, the whole ninth fragment shows the vague, unnamed dissatisfaction contemporary people feel with the discourses that dominate their world. The speaker here shows the barest urge to impose his own form on things through storytelling, but the culture does not support it and he himself is at a disadvantage because his language is either barren and unexpressive or dotted with outdated terms that have lost their context.

One might call the tenth fragment a pop jeremiad. As such it is another separable code in its own right as well as a résumé of all the discontents registered in the first nine fragments. It is a motley lingua franca composed of scraps of the same sort of discourses—Winston advertisements, literary and cinematic allusions detached from their contexts, disingenuous euphemis ("You know what" [p. 146]), scraps of jungles. Unlike in *The Waste Land,* there are no echoes of coherent past discourses that provide a perspective exit to another coherent linguistic world. The postmodern hero, fashioned as he is of the discourses that have colonized him, is always within the horizons of the problem: "I could describe it better if I weren't afflicted with it" (p. 146). No detached, aloof paring of fingernails here.

Even the jeremiad of alienation has now become a cliché, and the more the voice complains, the more we hear it as one of Bellow's "cheap stimulants of alienation." This fragment would have to be placed with the second and eighth fragments as one of the uncanny, uneasy discourses as opposed to the positivist discourses, because it aims higher than mere description. It too cannot establish its authority. The main phrase, "brain damage," hovers, like "nerveless fingers," uncertainly between the literal and metaphorical. Just as we expect the metaphorical crescendo after the first three and a half lines, the narrator refers to Apollinaire's bandage and the last four minutes of *Bonnie and Clyde*. Either way, the text reduces the speaker to the status of the village idiot who hears everything and understands nothing.

And yet . . . and yet . . . what could it mean to say "Skiing along on the soft surface of brain damage, never to sink, because we don't understand the danger—" (p. 146)? This is like the Cretan liar's paradox. Only one who understood the danger could say this. It is the only detail in the story that even potentially establishes a foothold outside of the linguistic chaos of which the story is made. Yet the meaning of the words denies the possibility of a perspective outside. This is the paradoxical situation of the contemporary voice—there is a vague memory and intuition of some other more coherent discourse system, but it is too far out of sight and experience to constitute anything more than a frisson of dissatisfaction.

A number of fragmentary motivic connections exist between the words in the headlines, the images in the visual part of "Brain Damage," and the narrative sections. For example, the "rhythmic handclapping" might be associated with the litanies of sins in ritualistic public confessions; the sexual innuendo of the dream fragment might connect with "sexual activity." The most important connection is between the series "To What End?/In Whose Name?/What Recourse?" and the general problem throughout the text that the multiplication of discourses has resulted in the loss of a secure, coherent, hegemonic discourse in which to perceive and talk about things.

The imagery in the pictures likewise alludes sometimes to narrative motifs. The sexual imagery of the cane laid before a monster woman's head, or over the casket, the Edenic imagery of apples and foliage receded to the barest vestige at the edge of the frame, the fuses about to go off, the gigantic threatening breasts below the ambiguously gendered creature in front of whom a nun holds an apotropaic umbrella—all these resonate with the sexual fear expressed in the "dream" fragment. The pastiche of the Hellenistic sculpture of Promethus with the eagle at his breast can be linked plausibly with the recital of transgressions in the fifth narrative, and the blinded girl to the skier's blindness to danger in the tenth fragment, and perhaps even marginally to Apollinaire's bandage.

Yet just as none of the surreal narrative adds up to much of a story, the tempting motivic connections in these headlines and pictures do not represent anything coherent at the level of symbolic interpretation. One needs to read their form semiotically. Passing over our awareness of the referential themes and images, we should look at the relations of parts for their resemblance to what we saw happening in the narratives. The same problem presents itself—discourses that used to be powerfully coherent but are now loosed from their moorings.

The large print would normally be read as a gloss of the narrative texts (though the fact that the narratives are printed in italics also creates the possibility that they are a gloss to the headlines and pictures—no hierarchy is assured). Newspaper headlines are a kind of gloss to news stories, and such large-print gloss would normally serve as an intensified explanation of the text it accompanies. But this gloss system promises more than it performs. It is subject to the same discursive incoherence we found in the text. This gloss reminds us of other gloss systems we have been exposed to, such as various glosses on the Bible, poems like, "The Rime of the Ancient Mariner," the Greek chorus, or the medieval manuscript gloss. The function of those glosses was to help the reader clarify meaning. Barthelme keeps this form, but empties it of its power to clarify.

Imagine if we opened our newspaper every day to find more than one large headline of the same type size. If headlines came in series of three, our normal waking muddle would be exacerbated and our view of world events would be subtly altered. The very purpose of a headline is to establish a hierarchy of significance, to define for us what is the biggest news of the day. The convention of the single headline helps us unconsciously over time to plot our sense of history. Barthelme's use of the series of mysteriously related headlines signifies the loss of any such stabilizing convention. No one perspective point is established. If anyone doubts the prescient realism of Barthelme's "surrealistic" technique, consider the current *USA Today* front page format which broke with traditional front page conventions. This popular newspaper's front page now reflects the fact that there are no shared substantive values that could establish hierarchy, only the formal stance of impartiality that links liberalism and positivism. The form chosen for the headline words in "Brain Damage," the nonfinite gerund, bolsters this effect of ungroundedness. It robs the verbs of any concrete time and place, usually used to "ground" headlines, and generalizes without any sense of particular agency. Double nouns like "crowd noises" do the same, as students of jargon have long known.

The percentage of truth in the cliché that one picture is worth a thousand words should be bolstered when the subjects are gaping mouths or a titanic struggle or enlarged breasts leaping off the page. Alas, the discourse on pictorial and plastic art in "Brain Damage" is also riddled with the problems of the discourses portrayed in the narratives. Pictures too are often a gloss system in a written text, but these fail to clarify anything and exhibit the same uncanniness that we found in the ambiguous headlines and narratives. For pictures, perspective is the spatial equivalent of verb tense in writing. It limits the infinite circularity of details, announces the point where the picture's own "proper" finite field begins. It is the grounding for interpretation of the picture. All of the visual components of "Brain Damage" deny us perspective by which to interpret them. In fact, they "read" like visual lists.

Lacking sufficient space to explore these visual elements of the text in great detail, I will select items exemplifying the principles at work in all of them. No perspective points unite the three figures in the first picture, nor the apple borders with the sphinx/stairs figure in the second. The field is limited only by the semantically arbitrary rectangular borders, which are associated with the discourse of the book rather than the discourse of the pictorial etching. The Promethean sculpture, the pictures of the woman weeping in the chair and the blindfolded girl, and the duet of nun and breast-woman all are torn from some unspecifiable discursive contexts and deposited gratuitously here on the pages of this "short story." Internally the composition of the Prometheus defies perspective too—is it with the eagle drama above, the inexplicably female pietà-like figure in the middle, or the bathetic foot inspection below? The pastiche makes no symbolic sense. Conventionally, the eye travels from lower left to the focal point in the upper right of a picture, but in the nun picture that visual rule is violated. The lower right breasts are most prominent, working against our intuitive way of reading the picture. Yet the umbrella in a more forward plane tops the breasts. The head and shoulders dominate the umbrella; however, by comparison to the breasts, they are too narrow to produce a satisfying aesthetic focus. These pictures all activate the visual impulse to synthesize a "spatial form" that will stay put, but they are really just visual lists, lacking a definitive perceptual, and thus conceptual, resting place. They "speak" incoherently as pictures just as the catachresis about the cup as big as an air force base did in the narrative fragment about the university.

The tonal techniques of the pictures likewise work against privileging perspective. The first picture is comprised almost entirely of stark horizontal lines that have no continuity with the three-dimensional figures set next to them. Compare, for example, a James Ensor or Edward Munch woodcut where the same gaping expressions are repeated in the lines of the background, thus unifying it with the foreground into a coherent, expressive whole. Or in contrast, compare a Dali background with no shadowings at all to reinforce the figures. Usually in surrealism we find a distortion or convolution that makes a point either by extreme overstatement or understatement; in "Brain Damage" we find neither. The binary opposition "understatement/ overstatement" is itself undone. There are shadings under the pedestals in the first two pictures and the last, but they are nondescriptive, mechanical, utterly conventionalized, flat, and simplistic. They suggest the beginning, or perhaps only the memory, of such a thing as imaginative shadowing, but they do not develop it into any particular expressivity. Their expressivity relative to the high art of etching is like corduroy's to fine tapestry.

Thus the form itself of these pictorial elements reveals the same abstracting impulse we found in the narratives and headlines. Rather than being fully what they are, say a news headline, or a page of sociology, or an eclectic etching, they are illustrations of or allusions to those things. The illustration is a form that must pretend to speak in an expressive voice, but whose voice is already colonized by some other unattributable, usually generalized voice. The forms here reveal the semiotic paradox of any well-done illustration—its choked-off expressivity, the fact that it manages to neutralize emotion or aesthetic response in the very act of expressing or alluding to even extreme gestures, emotions or actions. If we "read past" the ostensible surreal content, then, we can see that Barthelme is suggesting that all our visual discourses have become neutralized into the relatively abstracted status of unpassionate illustrations.

Of course, we cannot even be sure that the visuals should be read generically in the same discursive mode as pictures, since the outer boundaries of each of the visuals create an ambiguous relation between them and the discourse of the "book" in which they find themselves. Just as within each narrative or picture we find the different motifs put into circular play with each other, so in the three-cornered colloquy among narrative, headlines, and pictures that comprises this text, each representative form is "flattened" into a signifier for that cultural semiotic system and signifies in the syntagmatic arrangement of the story only vis-à-vis the other two such flattened signifiers. The structural principle of the text consists of habitually juxtaposing, in the syntagmatic dimension, two signifiers that are normally paradigmatically oppositional: nun/sex goddess; cane as potency/cane as infirmity; Greek column/industrial smokestack; horror/yawn; book/picture. On the widest level of narrative pattern, it is the string of normally competing discourses. The text joins them, not in the easy organic unity of a new metaphor or a seamless, expressive allusion to past discourses (as in Eliot's *The Waste Land*), but in an ungrounded freeplay among elements that make superficial gestures of being integral units (the "whole" statue, the "whole" headline series, the "personal" speaker)—elements the in fact reveal only their self-marginality and marginality to the text's other elements.

The above exposition demonstrates the way Barthelme's story is a paradigm of postmodern form in its freeplay of signifiers. But the important point is that this freeplay displays the realistic situation of contemporary men and women. In the mid-sixties, all of this might have seemed aimed at reinstating the fantastic, an attempt to restore enchantment to the world. Now, in the nineties, we can see that this enchanting storytelling was also an important strain of social realism. It represents what was already actually happening to culture and the world. The loss of hegemony of any and all discourses here is now fully observable in the new economic, political, and social map of the world that will be the reality of the nineties. So, undoubtedly, it is not *only* loss Barthelme gives us in "Brain Damage"; it is also preparation for a more realistic attitude toward the way things are and will be in the electronic global village. This is not to say, as Klinkowitz, Gordon, and others have, that the value of Barthelme's absurdity is to insert imaginative new variations into the incoherent babel (an attitude that still approaches the variety in that babel from a superior point of view), but rather that its value is in helping us self-consciously to experience and accept that babel as a reality of the postmodern historical period, as Ramona in "City Life" accepts her impregnation by the "mysterious muck" of the city when she says, "I accepted. What was the alternative?"

Notes

1. Critics of this orientation have read Barthelme primarily as part of a movement of contemporary writers offering their self-conscious artifice as an antidote to an exhausted tradition of realism. Behavioral descriptions of social phenomena in Barthelme's works are treated by these readers mostly as grist for an aesthetic mill of imaginative transformation. "Reality" is used for the sake of tales whose "absurdity" is the very confirmation of our imaginative powers. See, for example, Jerome Klinkowitz, *Literary Disruptions* (Urbana: University of Illinois Press, 1975), 80, and Robert Scholes, *Fabulation and Metafiction* (Urbana: University of Illinois Press, 1979), 115.

2. Larry McCaffery, *The Metafictional Muse* (Pittsburgh: University of Pittsburgh Press, 1982), 100.

3. Lois Gordon, *Donald Barthelme* (Boston: Twayne, 1981), 22–23.

4. Gordon, 22.

5. Subsequent to Alan Wilde's early distinction between the ludic and the representational aspects of Barthelme stories in "Barthelme Unfair to Kierkegaard: Some Thoughts on Modern and Postmodern Irony," *Boundary 2,* 5 (Fall 1976): 45–70, McCaffrey and Gordon, among others, assign social realism at least as high a place as creation *de novo* in Barthelme, but at moments they, too, each sound as if the autotelic nature of the stories is the main point. While some of Gordon's insights are very close to those of this essay, her inability to show concretely how the language games *are* a reflection of the (nonorderly) external world differentiates her reading of Barthelme from this one. The purpose of this essay is to undo the habitual opposition between the postmodern collage art-object and the "orderly reflection on an . . . external world" (Gordon, 28). The difference between this essay and those underlining Barthelme's parody is also worth pointing out. One way of putting the central idea of this essay is that Barthelme parodies certain types of language, or "discourses," because he takes their structure and fills it with trivial or surreal content. Charles Molesworth, too, in *Donald Barthelme's Fiction: The Ironist Saved From Drowning,* (Columbia: University of Missouri Press, 1982), emphasized Barthelme's parody. But, rather than treating this parody as an accurate representation of actual cultural discourses, as I do, Molesworth sees Barthelme's parody as a vehicle leading us into a wilderness of decentered meaning that tells us nothing.

6. Admonitions to the reader to take responsibility for cocreation are numerous in the criticism on postmodernism, but hardly ever does the critic go on to give a demonstration of a complete reading of a single story that would enlighten his reader as to just how one might go about making this meaning. See Klinkowitz, 62, and McCaffery, 119–20.

7. Barthelme's work has been called the "literature of surface," yet, amazingly, no one has recognized the inherent suitability for such a literature of methods of reading founded on the structuralist caveat that meaning is a matter of differences among surface signifiers more than of symbolic depths of correspondence. This essay's reading proceeds from the structuralist premise that one should eschew looking for signifier-signified correspondences—the typical way of reading mimetic realism—and concentrate instead on the play of differences of surface forms. The principle of the "circulation among signifiers" is a poststructuralist variation on that basic premise.

8. Donald Barthelme, *City Life,* (New York: Farrar, Straus and Giroux, 1970), 133; hereafter cited in the text.

A Highly Irregular Children's Story:
The Slightly Irregular Fire Engine

DAVID GATES

It's difficult, initially, to imagine Donald Barthelme as an author for children. True, his first novel was called *Snow White,* but his Snow White is to the Grimm-Disney heroine as Lolita is to Little Nell. Barthelme's *Snow White* is a fairy tale for overeducated adults. As in his shorter fictions, the apparent irrationality and disconnectedness of the "plot" and the strangely mixed diction hold up a broken mirror to a world in which (as a character in the early story "The Piano Player" says) "everything is in flitters." This is hardly a new perception:

> Things fall apart; the centre cannot hold;
> Mere anarchy is loosed upon the world. . . .

But Yeats's grave and resonant mode of expression is at odds with what he's saying; certainly it reflects his complacent certainty that it's all happened before and will all happen again. Barthelme, by contrast, has scavenged "flitters" from the rag-and-bone shop of the language, creating a dissonant tone that echoes the disconnectedness of which his characters complain.

Barthelme's writing is as much about writing itself as about its ostensible subject matter. But if, in his fictions, the writer is a magician conjuring up an alternate reality, he's a comically inept one: we're continually shown the wires that hold up the naked lady, and the rabbit drums in boredom on the false bottom of the hat. Among the other things Barthelme can't take quite seriously is the concept of the writer as omnipotent illusionist. The once-inhabitable world of conventional fiction, like his "Tolstoy Museum," is now a charmingly grotesque anachronism: a resort, but no longer a refuge. How does a literary subversive manage to mind his manners with young readers? Barthelme's answer: No need to. *The Slightly Irregular Fire Engine* is an appropriately gentle book, but Barthelme doesn't condescend to children by watering down the wit and irony; kids, in Barthelme's view, should

Reprinted from *Virginia Quarterly Review* 52, no. 1 (1976): 298–308. This essay has been substantially revised by the author for inclusion in this collection.

certainly be playful enough to enjoy a book in which narrative conventions aren't to be taken absolutely seriously.

The conventional children's book is Wordsworthian: the adults who write them are haunted by their knowledge that the child will not always *be* a child. Behind the Alice books, the Mary Poppins books, and *The Hobbit* is the author of the "Intimations" Ode lamenting the loss of the visionary gleam:

> "Listen, listen, the wind's talking," said John, tilting his head on one side. "Do you really mean we won't be able to hear that when we're older, Mary Poppins?"
>
> "You'll hear all right," said Mary Poppins, "but you won't understand."[1]

The typical children's-book plot is therefore a journey (to quote *The Hobbit's* subtitle) "there and back again." The hero visits Wonderland, the Lonely Mountain, or the Zoo at the full of the moon, and returns to the older sister on the bank, the Shire, or Number Seventeen Cherry-Tree Lane; the exotic world of vision and imagination dwindles into the everyday world of adulthood. Some slight token is usually brought back from the visionary world: Jane and Michael Banks, for example, are always able to find some irrefutable bit of evidence that what they saw was true. The intention is to integrate the visionary and the everyday. The effect is still disappointing, a Pyrrhic victory for maturity and rationality.

The Slightly Irregular Fire Engine trusts the reader, child or adult, to be familiar with the basic conventions of children's literature: it's a witty impersonation of a conventional children's book. Its main character is a young girl named Mathilda, whose Victorian costume and diction—as well as her appealing combination of pluck and politeness—remind us of Lewis Carroll's Alice. (The diction and deportment, though, keep slipping into 1970s American: Alice would never scratch herself or say "uh.") One morning in 1887, Mathilda wakes up to find "a mysterious Chinese house, only six feet high,"[2] in her back yard. Although what she had *really* wanted to find was a fire engine, she enters the house, which obligingly expands to accommodate her. (These shifts in relative size of heroine and surroundings also evoke the Alice books, though Barthelme doesn't use the machinery of cakes and mushrooms.) Guided by a djinn, she meets such denizens as a pair of Chinese guards, a rainmaker, a pirate, and a one-man band. After lunch—a ceremonial meal like the Mad Hatter's tea party is a usual feature of the conventional children's story—comes "Entertainment," in the form of "jugglers dancers and elegant fencers and every kind of flawless flourishy footlooseness." ("If there is anything better than lunch," says the djinn, "it is Entertainment.") Mathilda is offered various souvenirs to take away with her, but a fire engine is not among them. Eventually her nurse calls her home, and the following morning a bright green—not red—fire engine is standing where the Chinese house had been.

Mathilda's visit to the Chinese house purports to be an "escapade," which the djinn defines as "something you didn't expect . . . which surprises you, pleases you, and frightens you, all at once." But it's an escapade framed by the safe, mundane reality to which adults have become resigned. Despite its apparent delight in disorder, *The Slightly Irregular Fire Engine* is rigorously structured. The first and final pictures are of Mathilda's parents, "that gay and laughing couple" (in the pictures they are plainly not laughing), and beneath the final picture, in appropriately antiquated lettering, are words suggestive of accommodation to the workaday world:

CONTENTMENT
Industry and Frugality.

The legend (in similar lettering) which appears at the beginning of the texts suggests what's wrong with that workaday world:

SLENDER-WAISTEDNESS
Corseted Divinities with Waspish Affinities
Worrying, Flurrying.

Imagination is the conventional antidote to the constriction of our higher selves by the here-and-now, and the Chinese house, with its connotations of exoticism and gratuitous delight, appears to be its emblem. The first picture of the Chinese house is accompanied by the legend SUBURBAN DISTURBANCE: it's an intrusion into, and a potential escape from, the world that's too much with us.

But again and again, the Chinese house keeps reminding us of that world. The predictable "fabulous treasure," for example, is kept in "the Gray Room," so called, the djinn explains, "because it doesn't make up happy, particularly." The pirate—such a well-known figure of fantasy in children's literature that his first words to Mathilda are "No interviews!"—is a model of "Industry and Frugality" who literally tends to his knitting as he reminisces about his plunder and longs to get his cutlass back. The one-man band—Mathilda, quite accurately, notes that he "doesn't look too happy"—started out as a piccolo player, but is now encumbered (thanks, perhaps, to his industry and frugality) with an accordion and a full set of drums strapped to his back. Even the djinn himself, an archsymbol of the imagination's primacy over reality (our wish is his command), must bow to the world of industry and frugality: the elephant, he tells Mathilda, is "closed Mondays," and the escapades he's peddling "come in two styles—fancy and more fancy." Indeed, the expression "slightly irregular" in the book's title should be understood in its merchandising sense: because the fire engine is green rather than red, it's a less expensive keepsake for the djinn to give Mathilda.

Like the "sour and severe citizen" sitting on a barrel of pickles and the "statue of the Chief of Police, heroic style, solid marble" (the catalog-style description, of course, is the djinn's; he's describing a head of Zeus), most of Mathilda's new acquaintances are thinly disguised representatives of the adult world in which she must take her place. It's no surprise that one of the diversions offered her is the chance to be "a grown-up tennis-playing hat-wearing woman." And it's appropriate that she be rudely summoned from the Chinese house by her bawling nurse, who looks like Margaret Hamilton in *The Wizard of Oz* and whose profession reminds us of Blake's envious and malicious (but probably frugal and industrious) Nurse in *Songs of Experience,* who calls her young charges home by telling them that "your spring & your day are wasted in play."

The Chinese house's parodic resemblance to the gray world of adulthood is not the only indication that Mathilda's escapade is no escape. Not only does it fail to take us far away, it fails to take us there convincingly. Barthelme deliberately undercuts what little plausibility his narrative has by illustrating *The Slightly Irregular Fire Engine* with collages made up of nineteenth-century engravings. These pictures give the story an air of improvisation. They not only follow the text but often determine it: the plot, finally, comes to seem little more than a way of stringing together a random sequence of illustrations. Why does Mathilda decide, on the first page of the text, to go "hooping"? Because it seems to be "good hooping weather," she says. Because a hoop is a convenient image of the book's circular structure, a sufficiently sober-sided critic might say. But we suspect it's mostly because Barthelme found a picture somewhere of a little girl playing with a hoop.

And even if the reader could suspend disbelief, Mathilda herself cannot: she seems well aware that she's a character in a children's book. "I suppose I'd better go inside and see what strange things happen" she says dutifully when she discovers the Chinese house. As she acts out her role in what she knows is a conventional literary situation, her boredom is politely concealed but never dispelled. The entertainment she's offered is a higgledy-piggledy as the "show" in Barthelme's contemporaneous collage-story for adults, "The Flight of Pigeons from the Palace," whose narrator complains that "the public demands new wonders piled on new wonders. . . . Often we don't know where our next marvel is coming from. The supply of strange ideas is not endless."[3] Mathilda is a stand-in for the jaded reader, surfeited with wonders: the reader as consumer. The wonders in the Chinese house are mostly shop-worn: "We have Chinese acrobats. I think that the cat-seller will be around before lunch. We have an elephant that falls downhill, head over heels. That's rather interesting. We have some flying machines, although they're somewhat primitive. We have Chicken Chow Mein."

The Chinese acrobats come straight from the Ed Sullivan Show (the subject of a deadpan Barthelme piece reprinted in *Guilty Pleasures*). The Chicken Chow Mein is blatantly ersatz exotica and, considered in conjunction with the cat-seller who "will be around before lunch," somewhat suspect. And even if the flying machines weren't primitive, it's doubtful that they'd impress a child of the seventies who had seen a man walk on the moon. Mathilda and the reader both recognize that convention demands they be fascinated. They're not.

Of course, Barthelme's failure to fascinate is a calculated failure. His work calls into question the enterprise of creating more and more Tolstoy Museums of representational, inhabitable fiction. But if the pleasure of suspending disbelief in a fictional world can no longer be savored wholeheartedly, at least we still have the pleasure of the imaginative act itself, of ficiton as artful dodge. In Barthelme's fiction, as in twentieth-century painting, artifice has been purged of representation. Imagination, for Barthelme, isn't just a faculty that comes in handy when it's time to sit down and write. It's what the writing is about, because it's what makes us fully human. *The Slightly Irregular Fire Engine* appears to be a conventional Wordsworthian parable in which imagination withers in the process of growing up. But that convention is self-contradictory: the "Intimations" Ode and *Mary Poppins* are both products of the very imagination whose loss they lament. What's delightful about *The Slightly Irregular Fire Engine* isn't the obsolete pleasure of total immersion in illusion, but the pleasure of being in the company of an illusionist. True, his repertoire is a little dull, and he keeps reminding us that his tricks are just tricks. But he persists in believing that "if there is anything better than lunch, it is Entertainment."

Notes

1. P. L. Travers, *Mary Poppins* (New York: Harcourt, Brace and World), 142.
2. Donald Barthelme, *The Slightly Irregular Fire Engine; or, The Hithering Thithering Djinn* (New York: Farrar, Straus, and Giroux, 1971); not paginated.
3. Donald Barthelme, *Sadness* (New York: Farrar, Straus and Giroux, 1972), 137.

Irony and the
Totalitarian Consciousness
in Donald Barthelme's *Amateurs*

Wayne B. Stengel

At his best Donald Barthelme was a highly moral and political American short story writer. Moreover, for a decade or so—from the mid-sixties to the late seventies—in a plentiful, inventive stream of stories that often appeared first in the New Yorker, Barthelme challenged and enlarged the possibilities for short story form and short story expression. As the seventies proceeded, Barthelme's imaginative energies altered substantially. This phenomenon is apparent in *Amateurs,* Barthelme's fifth collection of short stories, published in 1976. There are four or five first-rate stories in this group of twenty-one, and yet even in the best of these Barthelme's vision seems tamed, controlled, even restrained by some of the very forces that his earlier writing so brilliantly destroyed or at least called into question. If the two most important vectors in Barthelme's short fiction are irony and human consciousness, as well as the relationship between the two, many of the stories in *Amateurs* impinge irony on their subject matter from so many perspectives as to be finally not so much deeply ironic, or even anironic, but merely controlled by Barthelme's willful subjugation to his own dazzling, dexterous use of a variety of ironic stances. Likewise, if Barthelme's stories prior to *Amateurs* consistently reject the tendency of human consciousness to force imaginative writing into conventional, preordained shapes and containers, some of the most effective tales in this collection are about the triumph of groupthink, the victory of a particular, collective attitude to reality that squelches the desires of individuality, language, and perverse lone resistance to its kind of conformist tyranny. Furthermore, there is far too little, and far too ambivalent, a sense of the irony of just these defeats within these stories. By analyzing three vivid, representative tales from *Amateurs,* "The School," "Some of Us Have Been Threatening Our Friend Colby," and "The New Member," I think it is possible to see a large and significant fault line between early and later Barthelme. In recognizing this graphic distinction,

This essay was written specifically for this volume and is published here for the first time by permission of the author.

critics might begin to assess the gains and losses in Barthelme's attitude toward his own ironic attempts to forge a reconciliation with the world and toward his vision of human consciousness as fostering a kind of intellectual totalitarianism among otherwise independent, free-spirited, and civilized men and women.

"The School" is one of Barthelme's most frequently anthologized works, appearing as a representative sample of Barthelme's art and as an exemplum of post-modernist short story practice in a wide variety of freshman composition texts and short story collections. Yet what is one of Barthelme's smoothest, glibest, and rhetorically most confident tales is a curiously self-defeated model as well. Told by a male grade school teacher, this tale recounts, in a kind of mellifluous, catalogued ironic lament, a series of deadly mishaps involving first plants and animals, then parents, and finally reaching their children, who are students in the narrator's elementary school class. As the mayhem and horror of these spiraling disasters mount, the teacher, with only occasional qualms or nervousness, proceeds with his lesson plans, insistent that these disruptions are inevitable in a modern education and, perhaps, are irrelevant to it. When his terrified students demand to know why the school has been besieged with these unremitting catastrophes, the narrator can offer them no satisfying explanation. Furthermore, they insist that he offer them proof of the power of regeneration, the force of life over death, by making love to their attractive teacher's aide before their innocent eyes. Horrified by their request and yet fearful of ignoring their anxiety, the narrator begins to embrace the student teacher as his students become excited. Suddenly, there is a knock at the door. The narrator opens it to find a new pet gerbil waiting to enter his classroom. Barthelme concludes his parable with the sample declarative: "The children cheered wildly."[1]

Doubtless the smug, mostly self-assured voice of the narrator is meant to represent those modern educational administrators who insist on procedure, order, and ritual under any circumstances, choosing to ignore the death, violence, and chaos of the society around them as they hurry through their daily drills, schedules, and standardized agendas. Where is the humanity and ultimate purpose in an education that so ignores the brutality of the world, Barthelme asks? Yet what finally fails this story is its lack of surface tension and its ironically smiling conclusions.

Anyone who teaches this story must ask who has placed this new gerbil outside this desperately smiling instructor's door so that he can begin yet another round of falsely confident, cajoling lessons in animal and human ecology—the glib, manipulative teacher, his fellow instructors and administrators, or worse yet, Barthelme, the looming authorial presence in the tale? What is wrong with both the consciousness and the irony in this work is that it becomes, at once, too little and much too much. Barthelme is at great pains to show that the sweetly domineering consciousness of this grade school teacher is not a monstrous force but an individual, with his own uncertainties and insecurities. Still, his victory achieved by someone placing before the students new life, and thus diverting them from their meaningful, hard-headed questions about life and death and human values, is a triumph for just the collectivist brain damage that so many of Barthelme's earlier tales have assailed. Moreover, in conclusion, the children cheer wildly at what? It is the simple arrival of a new living creature, the endless ability of their teacher to deceive them, the duplicity of their school in cheating them out of a meaningful education, or, in essence, the force of Barthelme's imagination in finishing his tale with such multiple, whimsically ironic endings that even his readers become a tool of his skillful rhetorical persuasion?

What is most wrong about his charming, acccomplished cautionary fable is not just its protagonist's easy acquiescence to the forces of control and submission—although earlier Barthelme stories like "City Life," "Paraguay," "The Explanation" and "Kierkegaard Unfair to Schlegel" refute just the totalitarianism to which this narrator succumbs—but the smoothness of its droning narrative listing of disaster, its almost musicialization of grief and disaster recorded as a harmonic Vonnegut-like "so it goes." In one of his finest stories, "Engineer Private Paul Klee Misplaces an Aircraft between Milbertshofen and Cambrai, March 1916," from *Sadness* (1972), Barthelme recreates abstract expressionist painter Klee's experience as a thoroughly reluctant inductee in World War I and sketches a great artist's ability to make the best of any nightmare through the sheer force of his imagination. On the other hand, "The School" displays the power of a teacher and a writer to hoodwink his pupils and audience through the power of his pet gerbil, his linguistic magic acts, parlor tricks done with mirrors, and self-reflexive language. In stories before *Amateurs,* Alan Wide recognizes a significant shift in the writer's attitude to his use of irony: "The fact is that increasingly in Barthelme's work, if not consistently, mere acceptance is modified by a more positive, more affirmative anironic attitude of assent . . . Klee intimates the possibility of irony (irony completed by the anironic ideal it implies) as a graceful, even integrative gesture toward the world."[2] Yet the voice of "The School" has no desire to integrate his view of education as rote procedure with the tragedies that beset his school. Rather, he wants to superimpose his rules and guidelines on his students as a means of ignoring and suppressing the painful incongruities of experience.

What's worse, this story has absolutely no rough surfaces. Barthelme's best tales have the jagged edges, the musical flat notes of jazz and collage, two of Barthelme's favorite art forms. Because of their raggedness and asymmetry, encountering such stories from any angle draws blood, invokes the shock of recognition that here is an artist deeply suspicious of the detritus of American pop culture and mass consumption, a writer who is forcing the short story into a symbolist, highly poeticized verbal and formal stylization to dramatize his anxieties about the vulgarity and emptiness of contemporary American experience. "Fragments are the only forms I trust,"[3] insists the narrator of "See The Moon," deeply aware of the moral responsibility of the legitimate craftsman to shape the fragmentation of his culture and experience into a sum that is more than the holes in its parts. "Strings of language extend in every direction to bind the world into a rushing, ribald whole,"[4] the narrator of "The Indian Uprising" contends as he watches the takeover of New York City and his own imagination by a savage, terrorist band of Comanche Indians expertly trained in guerrilla warfare and brutal counterinsurgency techniques. With this story Barthelme clearly recognizes that though language may be capable of destroying the meaning and value of experience, the moral and political demands of art dictate that the consummate writer retain his identity and purpose, whatever the forces of oppression or liberation, justice, or injustice a society creates or inherits.

Yet despite these fictive recognitions of the writer's moral and political responsibility, by the time of *Amateurs* in 1976, there seem to be unsettling confusions in Barthelme's style and subject matter. No critic has analyzed Barthelme's aesthetic late career quandary as forcefully as Jack Hicks in his study of contemporary American fiction, *In the Singer's Temple*.

> These twenty fictions [*Amateurs*] lack the structural and linguistic energy of Barthelme's most significant work. There is no experimentation with typography or engraving, nor is there widespread use of literary fragmentation or collage, as in "The Falling Dog" or "Departures." . . . Barthelme's fiction . . . is a precarious balancing between lyric poetry and narrative prose; it depends on the tension between the necessary baggage of character, plot line, sustained mood, traditional syntax, and consistence of verbal style and the correcting need to deny, modify, or escape from those holding cells. It thrives on the eternal dichotomy between fiction as artistic sublimation ruled by logic, order, and coherence, and verbal expression as the more unrestricted play of the mind, particularly in its preconscious and subconscious aspects, daubing as an idiot savant at the palette. However accessible and affirmative, . . . the stories [in *Amateurs*] often lack the richness of texture and narrative invention that characterized Barthelme's finest work.[5]

With equal acuity, Hicks summarizes the philosophical tensions implicit in *Amateurs* and all of Barthelme's fiction: "Barthelme regards literature as a single, hierarchical system within a vastly oppressive mega-hierarchy. The act of writing is a projection of human consciousness; what is needed is a form of literature that releases consciousness from the burden of the past and from its own self-destructive tendencies."[6]

Yet the legitimately menacing quality of "Some of Us Have Been Threatening Our Friend Colby," an occasionally anthologized story from *Amateurs* and arguably one of the cleverest and most ominously controlled stories Barthelme ever composed, depicts the desiccation of individual consciousness as a creatively gleeful act. In this tale a coterie of aesthetes gathers to discuss the fate of their friend Colby, who has obviously gone too far. Collectively, their totalitarian impulses dictate that Colby meet with death by hanging and the entire duration of the story, as narrated by one of their circle, consists of their discussion of the graceful, aesthetic forms, the polite, easeful considerations they can amend to their decision to destroy their friend's right to be. A variety of special arrangements are proposed as humane accoutrements to his beheading. One friend wonders what kind of classical music—exalted or severe—should accompany the event; another speculates how the invitation to the ceremony should be worded, while yet another ponders if wire or rope is the most painless method for Colby's demise. Not only does this story brilliantly demonstrate the total triumph of the artiful, artificial forms of modern life over any moral content, but the story demonstrates the unabashed victory of a horrific consensus consciousness that can easily obliterate meaning and purpose in a decadent, overcivilized society.

Yet the ultimate confusions of the tale lie in its contradictory, self-consuming senses of irony. Its smiling nihilism, this Kafka-without-claws quality, lies not exclusively in what Hicks perceives as the strength of its forces of logic, order, and coherence, personified by Colby's would-be friends, but also in Colby's enervated inabilities—and Barthelme's limited desire—to have Colby fight back, escape, or evade their grotesque but fine-tuned reasoning. Colby hardly constitutes the vital Barthelme ego, what Hicks calls an "idiot savant daubing at the pallet of his very unique consciousness." Thus the greatest terror of the story is that finally it is consumed by what Hicks recognizes as its own self-destructive tendencies. "Some of Us Have Been Threatening Our Friend Colby" is a masterful, hilarious, smooth-as-glass depiction of how gracious and urbane citizens perform complex, strategic, and heinous acts, losing their individual identities to the dominant consciousness of a death-obsessed, death-worshipping culture. Unfortunately, one can't help but feel that completely appreciating this story means losing some small portion of one's own consciousness and irony to enjoy Barthelme's linguistic destruction of Colby as much as the narrator and Colby's other friends relish tightening the rope around his neck.

If a denuded Kalfkaesque spirit hovers over this story, the full-fledged energy of Poe, Barthelme's other influential literary benefactor, gives real dimension, even poignance, to "The New Member," one of the most unappreciated stories in *Amateurs*. "The New Member" is never anthologized in short story collections, has been critically avoided by scholars, and is hardly deemed essential reading for anyone attempting to assess the Barthelme canon. Yet this tale, once again about horrifying committee decisions and the partial triumph of committee consciousness, has an exuberantly playful, highly unpredictable sensibility and a well-contained sense of irony. The story ultimately demonstrates that the forces of totalitarianism threatening to engulf modern life are susceptible, even vulnerable, to their own fears, tremors, and demons of control. In this tale, which is a deadpan spoof of those collective mental processes so conditioned by Roberts' Rules of Order that they are unable to think beyond it, either a committee of archangels, a gathering of exceedingly genteel mafioso bosses and matrons, or, most likely, a group of East Side Manhattan philanthropic benefactors, meet to decide the fate of their charges. These privileged executives and doyens are so consumed with ruling a motion proper or out of order, seconding or tabling it, that they have long forgotten that people's fates and lives hang in the balance. When a novice member of the committee looks apprehensively outside their meeting room to report a huge stranger lurking at the window, her fears gradually convince other committee members to invite the outsider into their enclave. By story's end, the tribunal offers this alien presence a seat on the committee so that one of the anonymous masses whose lives are so randomly disrupted by its causal pronouncements can at last take part in their decision-making process.

One of the wittily calculated concluding ironies of this tale is that the hulking stranger, now a part of one of his society's most important committees, its dominant thought processes, immediately emerges as an insufferable tyrant. Like many creatures who live for committee duties, he instantly becomes a whimsical autocrat given to absurd decrees and stringent regulations. The new member's saving grace is revealed in the last sentence of the story. Although he demands that all members wear gray overalls with gray T-shirts, that they say morning, evening, and lunchtime prayers and do calisthenics between 5 and 7 P.M., and despite his forbidding boutonnieres, nose rings, and gatherings of one or more persons, "on the question of bedtime, [he is] of two minds."[7]

Very few Barthelme stories achieve such a perfect balance of his concerns with human consciousness and irony with such grace and astringency. If the great danger for human consciousness in the modern world is society's terrifying drive to make all individuals think as one, how, Barthelme asks, does literature effectively dramatize that threat, and how can irony ridicule this compulsion without making the ironic impulse just another aspect of the collectivization of human thought? With this story, Barthelme makes his new member as guilty of the deadly pragmatism and fatalism as the narrow circle of lawmakers he enters, while giving this newest dictator some of his colleagues' trepidations and uncertainties. Barthelme ultimately declares here that the hope for all totalitarian systems, as the West has just recently seen with communism, is that, eventually, they may be "of two minds."

After an initial series of stories and short story collections that viewed experimentation, formal innovation, fragmentation, and collage as fundamental means for analyzing human perception, Barthelme's later writing enters the enemy camp. What is it like to be part of absurd mental constructs like educational administration, a deadly, claustrophobic clique of aspiring artists and aesthetes, or any committee that makes life and death judgments, Barthelme asks in "The School," "Some of Us Have Been Threatening Our Friend Colby," and "The New Member." The danger in these tales is that in visiting their tyrannical collective social consciousness, Barthelme fraternizes far too much with his antagonists' dilemmas. In revealing ironies within ironies inside their hierarchical systems, Barthelme can make totalitarianisms that wish to devour us seem all too humane, amusing, understandable, or aesthetically appealing. Ultimately one can ask, at least about "The School" and "Some of Us Have Been Threatening Our Friend Colby," where does Barthelme stand in relation to these stories? Isn't he too sympathetic with his instructor's evasion of responsibility to his students in "The School," and don't we, us the audience, as well as Barthelme, eventually enjoy threatening our friend Colby? In *Amateurs,* only in "The New Member" does Barthelme have the wit, moral vision, and controlled irony to explain the origins of his pet gerbil while vividly illustrating the dissension in the ranks that the sudden appearance of this beast on the threshold creates. In this ingenious fabliau, the figure hovering in the doorway is our own need to continue the lesson, to proceed with the story, to be ironically entertaining before our audience at all costs, even though we know we are as capable of manipulation, threat, and the desire to control others as individuals within the most insidious totalitarian environments. Our redeeming trait may be that, on some issues, we are of two minds.

In an otherwise felicitous essay honoring Donald Barthelme's career, John Barth in the September 19, 1989, *New York Times Book Review* called Barthelme the thinking man's minimalist.[8] For all of Barthelme's economy and miniaturization, he can never accurately be called a member of the minimalist school. Nor did he strive for limited effects in a limited short story form. Indeed, Barthelme was interested in evoking major aesthetic realignments, crucial shifts in our attention spans, and substantial inversions in our grasp of language and cognition. Recognizing that the human thought process in all its scope, grandeur, and wackiness is a huge and complex subject, Barthelme could be better termed the thinking man's essentialist. He is forever a writer who realizes the need for individuality, persistence, and the constant struggle of every unique human consciousness in asserting itself against many of the monolithic, pernicious, deadly "isms" of twentieth-century life.

Notes

1. Donald Barthelme, *Amateurs* (New York: Farrar, Straus and Giroux, 1976), 41.
2. Alan Wilde, *Horizons of Assent* (Baltimore: Johns Hopkins University Press, 1981), 183–84.
3. Donald Barthelme, *Unspeakable Practices, Unnatural Acts* (New York: Farrar, Straus and Giroux, 1968), 157.

4. Barthelme, *Unspeakable*, 11.

5. Jack Hicks, *In the Singer's Temple* (Chapel Hill: University of North Carolina Press, 1981), 35.

6. Hicks, 35.

7. Barthelme, *Amateurs*, 164.

8. [*Ed. note:* Barth's essay is reprinted at the head of this volume.]

Donald Barthelme:
The Aesthetics of Trash
(*Snow White*)

LARRY MCCAFFERY

What does a writer do when he thinks that language no longer communicates effectively, that words have lost their power to move or amuse us, that reality is no longer capable of sustaining mythic devices, that telling traditional stories of any kind is suspect? As though in answer to these questions, Barthelme presented us in 1967 with *Snow White,* an overtly metafictional work which seeks to exploit the decay of language and literature. Like the longer works of Coover and Gass, *Snow White's* principal subject matter is the relationship between man and his fictions. It is not the "real world" which it seeks to represent but the status of art in general and of literature in particular. Rooted deeply in a fundamental distrust of most of the conventional principles of fiction, the book also shows an understanding of Wittgenstein's famous distinction between what can be told and what can be shown. Not a description or theory of the conditions of language and literature, *Snow White* portrays these features in its metafictional fabric.

In an essay describing the views held by many contemporary "literary pessimists," George Steiner states:

> There is a widespread intimation, though as yet only vaguely defined, of a certain exhaustion of verbal resources in modern civilization, of a brutalization and devaluation of the word, in the mass cultures and mass politics of the age. . . . It is grounded in historical circumstance, in a late stage of linguistic and formal civilization in which the expressive achievements of the past seem to weigh exhaustively on the possibilities of the present, in which word and genre seem tarnished, flattened to the touch, like coin too long in circulation.[1]

Obviously, there are enormous problems for a writer who accepts the notion of the "brutalization and devaluation of the word." Essentially three courses are open to such a writer: he may, like Rimbaud, and, to an extent, like

Reprinted from *The Metaficitonal Muse: The Works of Robert Coover, Donald Barthelme, and William H. Gass,* by Larry McCaffery, by permission of the University of Pittsburgh Press. © 1982 by University of Pittsburgh Press. First published, in a slightly different form, in *Critique* 16 (April 1975): 19–32.

Beckett, choose what Steiner calls "the suicidal rhetoric of silence";[2] he may, like Gass, Coover, and Ishmael Reed, attempt to revitalize the word and call for strategies which can replenish the power and poetry of language—such pleas have been issued by a variety of writers in the last two centuries: by Wordsworth, by Whitman, by the French Symbolists, by the surrealists; and, finally, the writer may adopt the strategy of self-consciously incorporating the decayed, brutalized elements into his own particular idiom and make the new idiom part of his point. Such strategy is employed by Céline, by Burroughs, and as we have seen, by Barthelme.

Although 180 pages in length, *Snow White* is not so much a novel as a sustained collection of fragments, organized loosely around the Snow White fairy tale in what [has been] described as Barthelme's "collage" method. Barthelme's rendition of the myth is, of course, peculiarly modern. As Richard Gilman has said, "That tale is here refracted through the prism of a contemporary sensibility so that it emerges broken up into fragments, shards of its original identity, of its historical career in our consciousness . . . and of its recorded or potential uses for sociology and psychology."[3] Thus, as Coover does in nearly all his fiction and as Joyce does in *Ulysses,* Barthelme has turned to a familiar myth rather than to "reality" to provide a basic framework for his tale, although the "material" which he places into the framework is drawn from a wide range of literary and cultural sources.

Despite its mythic framework, *Snow White* is likely to leave an initial impression of shapelessness. As in *The Public Burning, Ulysses,* and works by other writers of encyclopedic tendencies—one thinks of Pynchon, Gaddis, McElroy, Nabokov—*Snow White* presents us with a profusion of bits and pieces drawn from books and other literary storehouses such as folktales, movies, newspapers, advertisements, and scholarly journals. Just as he does with his short fiction, Barthelme often incorporates into *Snow White* the sorts of events, names, fads, and other data which can be found in any daily newspaper. Even more often, however, these fragments are drawn from clichés of learning and literature. We find, for instance, parodies of specific literary styles and conventions, pseudo-learned digressions about history, sociology, and psychology, mock presentations of Freudian and existentialist patterns, and inane concrete poems. Barthelme's use of this heterogeneous mixture of learning and verbal trash does not contribute to any truly mimetic design but brilliantly recreates a sense of what it was like to be alive in America during the mid-1960s.

If we examine the structure of *Snow White* more closely, we find that like Coover, but unlike Joyce in *Ulysses,* Barthelme prevents his perspective from being seriously mythic to any extent. The big problem for Barthelme—as for any writer today who wishes to rely on myth in one way or another—is a self-consciousness about myth that has reached such paralyzing proportions that most myth is now employed only for comic purposes.[4] Like Coover, Barthelme obviously feels that previous mythic structures no longer can serve the writer as useful framing devices; instead the original mythic structures are mocked, parodied, and transformed (with the assistance of various elements accumulated from contemporary myths and clichés) so that in John Leland's words, "*Snow White* becomes a form of a form, absorbing the aspirations of the original structure yet surviving only as it endlessly repeats itself without resolution."[5] Indeed, in many respects *Snow White* seems to be deliberately mocking Joyce's painstaking efforts at creating mythic parallels, suggesting perhaps that the conditions of both language and reality make such devices unavailable to the modern writer.

With the example of *Ulysses* in mind, we can find parallels between the events and characters in *Snow White* and those of the established versions in Grimm's fairy tale and the Disney film. The action of the story often twists and halts unexpectedly, but eventually it fulfills the basic situation of the fairy tale. Snow White, now twenty-two years old and beautiful, has grown tired of the words she always hears and has rebelled by writing a dirty poem. She is currently living with seven men (the dwarf figures) who daily sally forth with "heigh-ho's" "to fill the vats and wash the buildings" of a Chinese food factory (SW, p. 8). Concerned about her promiscuity (she has sex with her roommates daily in the shower room), Snow White has rationalized that her men really only add up to two "real men"—hence their dwarfishness. Later on, the rest of the familiar cast is completed with the appearance of Jane, a young woman who is the witch figure, and Paul, the prince for whom Snow White is waiting. While Jane begins to spin her wicked web, Paul digs a bunker, sets up a dog-training program, and keeps watch over Snow White with a self-devised Distant Early Warning System—all designed to help him watch and eventually win her. Paul finally makes the fatal error of eating the "poisoned apple" himself (in this instance, the "apple" is presented in the form of a poisoned Vodka Gibson) which the evil Jane has intended for Snow White. As the story concludes, Snow White is left to cast flowers on Paul's grave and, "revirginized," she rises into the sky.

One should quickly note that any summary of this sort is extremely misleading, for Barthelme is much more intent on creating a collage effect than on permitting a story line to develop in any straightforward fashion. The progression of events in *Snow White* is, for example, continually interrupted by digressions, catalogs, lists, and seemingly gratuitous trivia. Each of the heterogeneous fragments is given its own individual section or "chapter" rarely more than a few pages long; several are only one or two lines. Transitions between the sections, sketchy at best, are often entirely lacking; to establish a time scheme, for example, is quite impossible. Relying mainly on juxtaposition rather than on the more usual novelistic principle of transition, Barthelme creates the verbal equivalent of a collage whose elements will, in the words of the narrator of "See the Moon," "merge, blur—cohere is the word, maybe—into something meaningful" (UP, p. 152).

Aiding this collage effect are alterations in typography between conventional type and large black upper-case letters—much like silent film titles. The titles seem to provide objective or authorial perspectives on the action— a technique used, for instance, by Dos Passos and more recently by Julio Cortazar in *Hopscotch*. This device, however, is also being used parodically, so that the authorial insights are themselves feeble imitations of the confident pronouncements of past authors. Thus the text is constantly interrupted by such banal and inconsequential asides as:

PAUL: A FRIEND OF THE FAMILY

(SW, p. 47)

PAUL HAS NEVER BEFORE REALLY SEEN SNOW WHITE AS A WOMAN

(SW, p. 150)

Likewise, the background sections typically turn out to be cliché, scholarly-sounding assessments of literature, history, or psychology—sometimes attributed to specific writers, but usually not:

THE SECOND GENERATION OF ENGLISH ROMANTICS INHERITED THE PROBLEMS OF THE FIRST, BUT COMPLICATED BY THE EVILS OF INDUSTRIALISM AND POLITICAL REPRESSION. ULTIMATELY THEY FOUND AN ANSWER NOT IN SOCIETY BUT IN VARIOUS FORMS OF INDEPENDENCE FROM SOCIETY: HEROISM ART SPIRITUAL TRANSCENDENCE

(SW, p. 24)

THE VALUE THE MIND SETS ON EROTIC NEEDS INSTANTLY SINKS AS SOON AS SATISFACTION BECOMES READILY AVAILABLE, SOME OBSTACLE IS NECESSARY TO SWELL THE TIDE OF THE LIBIDO TO ITS HEIGHT, AND TO ALL PERIODS OF HISTORY, WHENEVER NATURAL BARRIERS HAVE NOT SUFFICED, MEN HAVE ERECTED CONVENTIONAL ONES.

(SW, p. 76)

At other times, the passages seem to trail off into total incoherency, as when the following neatly centered list of words appears:

EBONY
EQUANIMITY
ASTONISHMENT
TRIUMPH
VAT
DAX
BLAGUE

(SW, p. 95)

Such digressions and irrelevancies, of course, considerably impede the narrative movement of the book and prevent Barthelme from relying on conventional novelistic devices of tension, development, and linear plot. Indeed, even the characters in *Snow White* openly conspire to refuse to cooperate with our expectations. Since for Barthelme the changes in modern society make the holding of any mythic center impossible, we find that the mythic parallels here follow the story only up to certain points and then find appropriate alterations. As a result, the characters openly defy the traditional roles established in the fairy tale and undercut nearly all of our expectations about them.

Like every other literary device in *Snow White,* the characters are clearly parodies of their archetypes. Because of their uniformly flat, almost comic-book nature, any sense of their actual "identities" is minimal and the whole realistic notion of developing a history for them is ignored. The book is almost devoid of the sort of details usually provided by novelists to help realize the action, such as the name of the city in which they live, physical descriptions of the characters or settings, or indications of a daily routine. Any background information that Barthelme chooses to provide is usually obscure and serves to mock and defeat our expectations. Of the dwarfs we know only that each was born in a different national forest. We are told: "Our father was a man about whom nothing was known. Nothing is known about him still. He gave us the recipes. He was not very interesting. A tree is more interesting. A suitcase is more interesting. A canned good is more interesting" (SW, pp. 18–19). Since we are given no physical descriptions, no backgrounds, and no idiosyncratic traits, we can "know" the characters only through the words they speak—and even here we can make only minimal distinctions. Indeed, at times even the dwarfs seem to have a difficult time identifying each other, as Kevin's remarks to Clem at one point indicate: " 'That's true, Roger,' Kevin said a hundred times. Then he was covered with embarrassment. 'No, I mean that's true, Clem. Excuse me. Roger is somebody else. You're not Roger. You're Clem. That's true, Clem' " (SW, p. 67). Thus the dwarfs' personalities are blurred and indistinct; they are characters made up entirely of society's stock provision of jealousies, cliché opinions, psychological afflictions, and linguistic oddities. On the other hand, they are obviously grotesquely unsuited for the unself-conscious, selfless roles that the original myth asks them to play.

Even more unsuited for his role than the dwarfs is Paul, whose princely mission is to rescue Snow White from her captivity with the dwarfs and save her from the murderous intentions of the witch-like Jane. But Paul is destined to be defeated in both his attempts, apparently doomed by the conditions of contemporary life that make it impossible for him to sustain the archetype which he should embody. The type of figure Paul should be, Barthelme suggests, has been driven underground—or into parody—by the neuroses and self-consciousness facing all modern men. Paul is perhaps the most notable of a long line of Barthelme characters who are doomed to personal and sexual frustration because of their own perverse hyper-awareness. From the beginning of *Snow White,* Paul is concerned about the implications of Snow White's appearance for his own life. He seems to sense immediately that involvement with her will impose on him obligations and responsibilities he is not certain he can fulfill successfully. Thus, after he has seen Snow White suggestively hanging her black hair out of her window, Paul remarks: "It has made me terribly nervous, that hair. It was beautiful, I admit it. . . . Yet it has made me terribly nervous. Why some innocent person might come along, and see it, and conceive it his duty to climb up, and discern the reason it is being hung out of that window. There is probably some girl attached to the top, and with her responsibilities of sorts" (SW, pp. 13–14).

Possibly because he is overly aware of the Rapunzel myth, Paul's response to these obligations is to flee, although he retains considerable awareness of the implications behind his actions. He realizes, for example, that conditions in today's society militate against true princeliness. In rationalizing his decision to hide in a monastery is western Nevada, Paul stops for a moment to consider the lack of opportunity for heroic action today: "If I had been born well prior to 1900, I could have ridden with Pershing against Pancho Villa. Alternatively, I could have ridden with Villa against the landowners and corrupt government officials of the time. In either case I could have had a horse. How little opportunity there is for young men to have personally owned horses in the bottom half of the 20th century! A wonder that we U.S. youth can still fork a saddle at all" (SW, p. 78).

After brief sojourns in France as a music instructor and in Rome as a member of the Italian post office, Paul decides to abandon his efforts to evade his duties as a prince. As with Bloomsbury and many of modern literature's comically conceived antiheroes, Paul is totally incapable of responding naturally to any situation because his decision-making capacity has been deadened by the sludge of literary and cultural conventions. Rather than meeting his challenges directly, Paul vacillates, mediates, and filters his responses. Comically, he digs a bunker outside Snow White's house and installs an observation system which includes mirrors and dogs attached to wires. When the moment of crisis arrives, bungling Paul drinks the poisoned Vodka Gibson intended for Snow White; muttering banalities to the very end—"This drink is vaguely exciting, like a film by Leopoldo Torre Nilsson" (SW, p. 174)—Paul dies "with green foam coming out of his face." So much for Prince Charming.

Snow White, meanwhile, has patiently been waiting for reluctant Paul to complete his duties. As she explains to one of her anxious wooers: "But this love must not be, because of your blood. . . . I must hold myself in reserve for a prince or a prince-figure, someone like Paul. I know that Paul has not looked terribly good up to now and in fact I despise him utterly. Yet he has the blood of kings and queens and cardinals in his veins" (SW, p. 170). As Paul soon demonstrates, Snow White is overestimating the ability of royal blood to produce a contemporary prince-figure. We may question whether such concepts as "royal blood," "princeliness," and "heroic action" were viable in any age, but literature—including history books—has conditioned us to think otherwise. We are led, like Snow White, to react to Paul through these filtered, largely literary stereotypes. As Snow White realizes, the fault may not lie so much in Paul as in our own expectations of him: "Paul is a frog. He is frog through and through. . . . So I am disappointed. Either I have overestimated Paul, or I have overestimated history" (SW, p. 169).

The obvious suggestion being made here is that reality can no longer sustain the values needed to create either a hero-figure or the proper ending to a fairy tale. Snow White seems to realize this when she decides to pull in her long black hair and sadly remarks: "No one has come to climb up. That says it all. This time is the wrong time for me. I am in the wrong time. There is something wrong with all those people standing there, gaping and gawking. And with all those who did not come and at least try to climb up. To fill the role. And with the very world itself, for not being able to supply a prince. For not being able to at least be civilized enough to supply the correct ending to the story" (SW, p. 132).

Snow White, then, is doomed to disappointment because heroes are now created *only* in books and movies—and even there they are found less and less because reality is losing its capacity to support fictions of this kind. Consequently, we have to content ourselves with media-produced substitutes. Speaking of the dwarfs, Snow White summarized this dreary prospect: "The seven of them only add up to the equivalent of about two real men, as we know them from the films and from our childhood, when there were giants on the earth. It is possible, or course, that there are no more real men here, on this ball of half-truths, the earth, that would be a disappointment. One would have to content oneself with the subtle falsity of color films of happy love affairs, made in France, with a Mozart score" (SW, pp. 41–42). In many respects, we are expected to share Snow White's realizations as we respond to Barthelme's book: our expectations, created by previous encounters with literature, are left unsatisfied. If we are, like Snow White, disappointed with this prospect, we have overestimated language (because it can no longer communicate effectively) and reality (because it no longer produces the kinds of heroes, logical progressions, and predictable feelings which are the stuff of traditional novel).

If we turn to the central question of the role of language in Barthelme's book, we find that, more than anything else, *Snow White* seems to be "about" the current condition of language and the possibilities which exist today for a writer for communicating something meaningful to his readers. Throughout the book a variety of very topical subjects are brought up: the Vietnam War, crowded street conditions, air pollution, political corruption. But as Gilman has observed, "The novel isn't about these things, not about their meaning or even their phenomenological appearance. It is about their status in the imagination."[6] Barthelme is, therefore, not so much interested in using such material for satiric analysis as he is in seeing how such things have affected the public consciousness, especially in how that consciousness is reflected in language. *Snow White,* then, metafictionally deals with the problems of its own composition, often analyzing itself as it moves forward—all the while mocking our interpretations and attempts at making "outer referents."

At times this anticipatory mocking has quite specific targets. As Barthelme is aware, our reaction to any work of fiction is influenced by a wide variety of literary and critical suppositions. Readers, no less than writers, have become so self-conscious about literary and critical conventions that writers have difficulty in creating anything which is not already a cliché. Having accepted this fact, Barthelme (and most of the other contemporary metafictionists) decides to have some fun with it by directly playing with these anticipations. The most obvious example is the questionnaire which Barthelme inserts in the middle of the novel. This questionnaire not only makes fun of the critical machinery we are probably using to "interpret" *Snow White* but also serves as a delightful parody of the language-form of a questionnaire itself. Like Nabokov, Barthelme also takes special delight in poking fun at Freudian psychology, as when he occasionally presents us with passages which are so teasingly Freudian that they slip over into parodic self-commentaries:

WHAT SNOW WHITE REMEMBERS:
THE HUNTSMAN
THE FOREST
THE STEAMING KNIFE

(SW, p. 39)

In other sections of the book the characters themselves either anticipate our interpretations of what is happening or create their own. One of the dwarfs, for instance, says of the women they watch while they are at work, "We are very much tempted to shoot our arrows into them, those targets. You know what that means" (SW, p. 8). And, of course, we do. Not surprisingly, Snow White is very much aware of the literary significance of letting down her hair from the window: "This motif, the long hair streaming from the high window, is a very ancient one I believe, found in many cultures, in various forms. Now I recapitulate it, for the astonishment of the vulgar and the refreshment of my venereal life" (SW, p. 80). Bill, the most self-conscious dwarf, is also the book's most expert symbol hunter and, at times, he even anticipates the probable sources which readers will rely on to give "meaning" to a scene. When Bill notices the long black hair hanging out of the apartment window, he asks himself whose hair it might be: "The distasteful answer is already known to me, as is the significance of the hair itself, on which Wurst has written. I don't mean that he has written *on* the hair, but rather about it" (SW, p. 92). This kind of arcane, scholarly knowledge proves to be quite useless for Bill, just as it is in assisting our own interpretations. In this instance, Bill's awareness of the variety of meanings he can attribute to Snow White's actions in no way helps him decide what to do about them, for, as he soon admits, "It is Snow White who has taken the step, the meaning of which is clear to all of us. . . . In the meantime, here is the hair, with its multiple meanings. What am I to do about it?" (SW, pp. 92–93).

In addition to mocking our interpretations, the novel contains various other self-referential qualities. The most important of these are the many digressions about language, including discussions of the language of *Snow White* itself. Like the fiction of Coover, Barth, Borges, and Gass, *Snow White* embodies in form as well as content the difficulties of writing in the modern age. One such "self-discussion" occurs when Dan presents a Borges-like (Klipschorn?) discussion about the nature of language:

> You know, Klipschorn was right I think when he spoke of the "blanketing" effect of ordinary language, referring, as I recall, to the part that sort of, you know, "fills in" between the other parts. That part, the "filling" you might say, of which the expression "you might say" is a good example, is to me the most interesting part, and of course it might also be called the "stuffing" I suppose, and there is probably also, in addition, some other word that would do as well, to describe it, or maybe a number of them. . . . The "endless" aspect of "stuffing" is that it goes on and on, and in fact, our exchanges are in large measure composed of it, in larger measure even, perhaps, than they are composed of that which is not "stuffing." (SW, p. 96)

Barthelme, of course, is a master of creating exactly the sort of "filling" and "stuffing" that Dan is talking about—as this very passage indicates. As we have seen from our earlier discussion, Barthelme resembles Pinter, Beckett, and Ionesco in his continual interest in the linguistic idiosyncracies and banalties which people use to express themselves—and which have made the creation of literature and even communication of any sort increasingly difficult. When, as Wittgenstein says, the "language machine" begins to "run idle," not only do people become increasingly isolated from each other but also writers find that they can take nothing for granted from their readers. Thus the narration of *Snow White* is frequently interrupted so that Barthelme can explain the specific meaning of words or phrases which might be confusing or misleading. When Barthelme describes Henry's process of examining his weaknesses as "weaknesses pinched out of the soul's ecstasy one by one" (SW, p. 29), he becomes worried about our possible objections to his metaphor and decides to explain himself. Here, as elsewhere when he speaks with his own voice, the tone has the flat, elevated ring of a scholarly essay which is exactly suited for the mock-serious treatment he is presenting: "Of course 'ecstasy' is being used here in a very special sense, as misery, something that would be in German one of three aspects of something called the *Lumpwelt* in some such sentences as 'The *Inmitten*-ness of the *Lumpwelt* is a turning toward misery.' So that what is meant here by ecstasy is something on the order of 'fit,' but a kind of slow one, perhaps a semi-arrested one that is divisible by three" (SW, p. 29).

Another indication that language is not functioning properly can be found in certain passages which lose direction and slide into pure irrelevancies. The digressive method used here is not the one found, say, in *Tristram Shandy*, for it is not based on an associational logic and does not lead anywhere. A certain passage will begin with fairly ordinary novelistic intentions such as providing clarification or additional description and then uncontrollably wander off into regions of "pure blague." The following discussion of Bill by his fellow dwarfs demonstrates this method quite well. After learning that Bill is absent "tending the vats," we have an apparent digression about his clothes turn into a random selection of verbal garbage:

> Bill's new brown monkscloth pajamas, made for him by Paul, should be here next month. The grade of pork ears we are using in the Baby Ding Sam Dew is not capable of meeting U. S. Government standards, or indeed, any standards. Our man in Hong Kong assures us, however, that the next shipment will be superior. Sales nationwide are brisk, brisk, brisk. The pound is weakening. The cow is calving. The cactus wants watering. The new building is a building with leases covering 45 percent of the rentable space already in hand. The weather tomorrow, fair and warmer. (SW, pp. 119–20)

Problems with language are even more apparent in certain sections (see, for example, pp. 31, 63, 164–65) in which broken and incomplete thoughts and sentences strain to become realized but manage to appear only in incomplete, syntactically fractured fragments. The method, which has some obvious affinities with Beckett's later writing and with Burroughs's "cut-up" technique, sometimes uses ellipses to separate widely different thoughts. Like the final "Etc." in "Views of My Father Weeping," these ellipses suggest that we should assume what is being left out is not worth being printed in its entirety.

Finally, the most pervasive way in which Barthelme demonstrates the bankruptcy of language and literary traditions is the more familiar approach of parodying well-known literary styles and methods. Like the "Oxen of the Sun" section of *Ulysses, Snow White* is created out of a wide variety of narrative styles traceable to specific literary sources; in addition, allusions to these works, some direct and others veiled, are sprinkled liberally throughout the book and serve to reinforce the self-referential nature of the work. Often the short sections are created from a hodgepodge of styles, modulating rapidly between specific literary parodies (of Stendhal, Rimbaud, Shakespeare, Loren Hart, Burroughs, Henry James), current slang, academic clichés, and advertising jargon. The style, whatever its source, is usually wholly inappropriate to the subject at hand, as with an elegant sermon being delivered against "buffalo music" or a learned commentary on "The Horsewife in Modern Society."

The reversals and inconguities in Barthelme's *Snow White* and in his short fiction as well should remind us of the difficulties involved when any contemporary writer attempts to build a work of art from the words at his disposal. Certainly it is significant that Snow White's first words are: "Oh I wish there were some words in the world that were not the words I always hear!" (SW, p. 6). As John Leland suggests, throughout the novel "it is as if Snow White wishes to escape from 'her' fiction—the words which speak her and which she must speak—to find an existence beyond the voices articulating her existence. Snow White, however, is unable to imagine anything better; she is locked within the texts she attempts to transcend."[7] Barthelme's novel, however, proves that although fiction may not be able to transcend the limits imposed by its trashy, too-familiar materials, it can accommodate itself to this condition by metafictionally incorporating this same debased condition into its very fabric.

Notes

1. George Steiner, "Silence and the Poet," in *Language and Silence* (New York: Atheneum, 1967), 46.

2. Steiner, 46.

3. Richard Gilman, "Donald Barthelme," in *The Confusion of Realms* (New York: Random House, 1969), 45.

4. Robert Scholes discusses this parodic use of myth by contemporary writers (especially with regard to Barth's *Giles Goat-Boy*) in *The Fabulators* (New York: Oxford University Press, 1967).

5. John Leland, "Remarks Re-marked: Barthelme, What Curios of Signs!" *Boundary 2* 5 (1977): 804.

6. Gilman, 50.

7. Leland, 801.

Donald Barthelme's *Snow White*:
The Novel, the Critics,
and the Culture

ROBERT A. MORACE

Delight in formal experimentation is one characteristic of much of our contemporary American fiction. Another, either explicit in the choice of subject matter or implicit in the narrative treatment, is the scornful criticism of the popular culture and its audience. While the former has received considerable attention from critics, the latter has more often been cited as a given than discussed in any detail. Perhaps the reason for this reticence lies not so much with the critics as with the writers themselves, who prefer to deride the popular culture rather than to analyze it or their basic assumptions about it. In the peremptory words of William Gass, "This muck cripples consciousness."[1] Gass, appropriately, is presently writing a novel he hopes will be so good no one will publish it. Other writers associated with the new fiction, such as Jerzy Kosinski, attack the mass culture reductively, while still others, Robert Coover and Ishmael Reed for example, resort to caricature (not without good reason). Kurt Vonnegut is both more sympathetic and, in his way, more analytic. But the most important exception to the general rule is, I believe, Donald Barthelme, especially in his curious little novel *Snow White*.

The very unconventionality of this oddly mimetic book has obscured for many readers the degree to which it serves as a remarkably detailed, and in some ways even melancholy, critique of the reductive linguistic democracy of the comtemporary American mass culture. To those already disposed towards innovative fiction, *Snow White*'s being "stylistically appropriate" and "a remarkably entertaining performance" are sufficient to ensure its worth.[2] To those who wonder where-have-all-the-Tolstoys-gone, *Snow White* is merely slick and self-indulgent. Neither view does justice to the complexity, as distinct from the technical proficiency, of Barthelme's writing, which at least to some readers is very clearly the work of a "conventional moralist."[3] More to the point, when Tony Tanner compared Barthelme's fiction to the Watts

Reprinted from *Critique: Studies in Contemporary Fiction* 26, no. 1 (Fall 1984): 1–10. Reprinted with permission of the Helen Dwight Reid Educational Foundation. Published by Heldref Publications, 4000 Albemarle St., N.W., Washington, D.C. 20016. Copyright © 1984.

Towers in Los Angeles,[4] he in effect set the stage for what has emerged as the single most important question for readers of *Snow White*: to what extent is the novel a surrender to the contemporary culture or a criticism of it? For the more tradition-minded reader, the answer is simple. According to John Gardner, Barthelme "reflects his doubting and anxious age because he is, himself, an extreme example of it," one whose only advice is "better to be disillusioned than deluded."[5] Gerald Graff goes a step further. Although in his ambivalent and even contradictory remarks on the novel, Graff does admit that Barthelme's style parodies empty language—language as gesture rather than language as communication—and acknowledges that *Snow White* is "finally a form of cultural statement," he criticizes what he considers the author's "irreverent stance toward his work" and "the novel's inability to transcend the solipsism of subjectivity and language. . . ." In sum, the novel does not entirely succeed in playing the "adversary role" prescribed by Graff because Barthelme "lacks a sufficient sense of objective reality" and therefore does not fully resolve what Graff identifies as "the writer's problem": "to find a standpoint from which to represent the diffuse, intransigent material of contemporary experience without surrendering critical perspective to it."[6]

The tendency to read *Snow White* as a sign of an ethically bankrupt age rather than as a critique of it culminates in Christopher Lasch's controversial study, *The Culture of Narcissism*. Those characteristics Lasch associates with pathological narcissism—"dependence on the vicarious warmth provided by others combined with a fear of dependence, a sense of inner emptiness, boundless repressed rage, and unsatisfied oral cravings . . . pseudo self-insight, calculating seductiveness, nervous self-deprecatory humor . . . intense fear of old age and death, altered sense of time, fascination with celebrity, fear of competition, decline of the play spirit, deteriorating relations between men and women"—these are the same characteristics noticeable throughout *Snow White,* as Lasch himself acknowledges. In what ways then has Barthelme failed? In Lasch's view, Barthelme's perfunctory ironic humor and refusal to present himself as an authority evidence the fact that he "waives the right to be taken seriously." Moreover, Lasch charges, in their fiction Barthelme, Vonnegut, and other innovative contemporary writers have abdicated their responsibility to provide psychologically and socially useful fantasies for their readers, readers who then turn to the escapist fantasies of the popular culture, which, Lasch says, are not only not psychologically useful but also socially dangerous in that they tend to increase the individual's dissatisfaction without suggesting to him viable ways to improve his condition.[7]

In order to understand just how mistaken is the view held by Gardner, Graff, and Lasch, it is necessary to examine the specific ways in which Barthelme analyzes in his novel the language used in today's society. For the most part, however, Barthelme's supporters have been as quick as Gardner or Lasch to deny the presence of *any* content, ethical or otherwise, in Barthelme's work.

Ronald Sukenick, for example, views Barthelme as the exemplar of the non-representational, improvisational, opaque "Bossa Nova" fiction that, according to Sukenick, began sweeping the country in the late 1960s. By opacity, Sukenick means that the fiction and the experience of reading the fiction exist solely "in and for" themselves; moreover, "opacity implies that we should direct our attention to the surface of the work, and such techniques as graphics and typographical variation, in calling the reader's attention to the technological reality of the book, are useful in keeping his mind on that surface instead of undermining it with profundities." Although Barthelme does draw the reader's attention to the surface of *Snow White,* he does so chiefly in order to show the ways in which language and explanations mediate between self and experience and to make clear that the result of this mediation, in the contemporary culture at least, is the cheapening or perversion of words, experiences, values, and people. Unlike his surface-loving characters, Barthelme penetrates his novel's various surfaces—of character, of clichéd language, of printed page—in order to expose the melancholy absence of any deeper, humanizing meaning (the very "profundities" Sukenick wishes to exclude). It is the dwarfs, not their author, who love books that require them to do nothing more than read, or experience, the words printed on a page, the way a jaded traveler reads the print on a timetable. Barthelme dives beneath these surfaces—not so deeply as Melville perhaps, or at least not in the same ways—in order to expose the plastic (no longer pasteboard) mask of dwarf language and culture. Thus, to call Barthelme a "very bossanova writer," as Sukenick does, or an "action writer" whose aim, according to Jerome Klinkowitz, is "to create a *new* work, which exists as an object in space, not in discursive commentary on the linear elements that form it," only serves to emphasize the significant formal innovativeness of the fiction at the expense of what Gardner would term its "moral" content.[8] More importantly, Sukenick's formulation invites and indeed almost makes plausible the misguided criticism of Graff and Lasch, who argue for a literature in which the author presents this "moral" content to the reader directly, perhaps (considering Graff's praise of *Mr. Sammler's Planet*) even didactically.

A few reviewers and critics have managed to avoid this either/or approach to Barthelme's disconcerting little novel and have made at least passing mention of his critique of the language of the contemporary culture, but only one, William Stott, has attempted to define its specific nature.[9] Stott persuasively argues that Barthelme's "stories are about what happens to fiction in a non-fiction world [a world in which "the facts of life" are supplied primarily by non-fiction], or—to put it another way—what happens to private values when all facts are treated as public." What happens is that private values can no longer be maintained because they have been supplemented by "non-fiction's public definitions." One effect of this cultural change is the perversion of private expression, and another is the devaluation of significant historical acts.

The method of radical devaluation noted by Stott is at the heart of Barthelme's critique of American mass culture in *Snow White*. The method is decidedly not "genially democratic," as one sympathetic critic has claimed.[10] Rather, it is precisely the reverse of what Pearl Bell finds so abhorrent in his fiction. Bell flatly asserts that Barthelme's stories do

> not pretend to any ideas, comic or otherwise, about the "trash phenomenon"— the steadily mounting detritus of words and things that forms Barthelme's image of American life—but are composed of the trash itself. . . . What could be more perfectly expressive of contempt for the ordering intellect, for the authority of culture, for any discriminatory distinctions between the multitudinous and the valuable—if all men are equal, all things are also equal—than a writer whose works consist almost entirely, or so he likes to claim, of the raw sewage of spontaneous expression.[11]

To a degree it is true that "Barthelme operates by a law of equivalence according to which nothing is intrinsically more interesting than anything else," as Gerald Graff has claimed, but this method is a criticism of, not, as Graff and Lasch have charged, a surrender to, the contemporary culture.[12] What we find in *Snow White* is, in fact, Barthelme's tracing of that leveling tendency which Tocqueville recognized as a danger inherent in a democracy. The purposely anonymous society sketched in the novel (one can hardly say "depicted") is characterized not merely by a reductive political equality but more importantly by a radical and insidious democratization of language—a linguistic democracy in which any word can be substituted for any other word, in which all utterances are equally empty gestures produced as if just so many plastic buffalo humps, and in which the hollowness of the mass culture is reflected in the hollowness of the characters' language and in the general "failure of the imagination" of a culture given entirely over to the mindless consumption of ideas as well as goods.[13] Such a world Donald Barthelme neither surrenders to nor endorses.

Snow White is, among other things, a one hundred-and-eighty-page verbal vaudeville show (itself a kind of theatrical collage) in which the form of the jokes often constitutes the author's critique of dwarf culture. In all speech, says Dan, one of Snow White's seven dwarf lovers, there is always "some other word that would do as well, . . . or maybe a number of them" (96). Promiscuous as the novel's characters may be, it is their linguistic promiscuity which titillates the reader. Incongruities abound, obscure and archaic words appear as often as contemporary slang, and literally anything can be obscene: consider Snow White's sexually loaded plea for "more perturbation!" and the "pornographic pastry" which, alas, is not "poignant" (34–35). And, of course, just the reverse can happen: a "cathouse" mentioned several times turns out to be a house for cats. Similarly, anything can be a dead metaphor. Characters are frequently "left sucking the mop" (7) or finding "the red meat on the rug" (10). One character becomes "a sack of timidities" (146); others worship "the almighty penny" (102). Filled with a dread induced in part by introductory courses in philosophy and psychology, they have no difficulty coming up with such existential aphorisms as "the *Inmetten*-ness of the *Lumpwelt* is a turning toward misery" (29).

"Give me the odd linguistic trip, stutter and fall, and I will be content," says dwarf Bill (139); and early in the story Snow White laments, "Oh I wish there were some words in the world that were not the words I always hear" (6). Both complaints are, in one sense at least, foolish, as Barthelme's fantastically inventive word-play makes clear. Whether such crippled imaginations as theirs can successfully struggle against the usurping, homogenizing culture which dwarfs them and make the Barthelmean leap of language is, however, more than just a little suspect. The Snow White who, apparently not having taken a course in modern poetry at Beaver College, has never before heard the expression "murder and create" (6) is nonetheless writing "a dirty great poem" about "loss" (10, 59). Given the would-be poet's lack of both a tradition and an individual talent, the reader may find "the President's war on poetry" a rather gratuitous undertaking. The dwarfs have certainly already surrendered, as the mixing of metaphors in the following passage attests: "Of course we had hoped that he [Paul] would take up his sword as part of the President's war on poetry. The time is ripe for that. The root causes of poetry have been studied and studied. And now that we know that pockets of poetry still exist in our great country, especially in the large urban centers, we ought to be able to wash it out totally in one generation, if we put our backs into it" (55). In addition to the swords, wars, ripenings, roots, pockets, and washings, the speaker's moribund recitation of political jargon and his unknowing allusions evidence Barthelme's critical stance towards the culture's junk-heap approach to language and history, the debased contemporary version of Ruskin's storehouse.

Freed at last and entirely from that retrospection flailed by Emerson in *Nature,* the trash civilization in *Snow White* is marked not by the Emersonian injunction "Build therefore your own world" but instead by the inability to discriminate as to either words or values. The dwarfs ponder the *bon mots* of Apollinaire and LaGuardia with equal deliberation, and Snow White lavishes equal attention on the cleaning of the books, oven, and piano (in that order) and includes in her catch-all list of princes the historical Pericles, the contemporary Charlie, the literary Hal, the comic-strip Valiant, and the Madison Avenue Matchabelli. The omnivorous dwarfs read novels aloud and in their entirety, even the "outer part where the author is praised and the price quoted" (105–6), while the prince-figure Paul is torn between acting heroically and eating a "duck-with-blue-cheese sandwich" (28). Worse yet is the narrator's unconscious and incongruous juxtaposition of the emotional and the anatomical in this passage: "At the horror show Hubert put his hand in Snow White's lap. A shy and tentative gesture. She let it lay there. It was warm there; that is where the vulva is" (41). Such are the fruits of what Barthelme's narrator calls "the democratization of education" (128) and Christopher Lasch terms "the mindless eclecticism" of today's brand of higher education. This radical and entirely reductive equality is applied not merely to words, including names, but to people as well who, as a result, are often confused with and reduced to the level of objects, future trash, as in the novel's opening sentence, which begins, "She is a tall dark beauty containing a great many beauty spots . . ." (3). Even when, on rare occasions, Snow White becomes uncomfortable with this kind of language, she is only able to substitute one form of it for another. Looking at herself in a mirror, she decides to "take stock. These breasts, my own, still stand delicately away from the trunk, as they are supposed to do. And the trunk itself is not unappealing. In fact *trunk* is a rather mean word for the main part of this assemblage of felicities. The cream-of-wheat belly! The stunning arse, in the rococo mirror! And then the especially good legs, including the important knees. I have nothing but praise for this delicious assortment" (144). Unwilling to be a cadaverous "trunk," Snow White prefers to think of herself, unwittingly of course, as a hot breakfast cereal and a Whitman's sampler.

Another way in which language is used by these unreflective consumers is as a means of deflecting from problems at hand. Just as most of the characters turn to drinking at one point or another, all of them turn to language as a means of escape. Troubled by their deteriorating relationship with Snow White, the dwarfs busy themselves with a description of a room's interior decor; Edward transforms their problem into a sermon on the "horsewife" (99), and Dan decides it is not really Snow White that troubles them but the red towel she wears. The best and funniest example of deflection is the dwarfs' "situation report":

"She still sits there in the window, dangling down her long black hair black as ebony. The crowds have thinned somewhat. Our letters have been returned unopened. The shower curtain initiative has not produced notable results. She is, I would say, aware of it, but has not reacted either positively or negatively. We have asked an expert in to assess it as to timbre, pitch, mood and key. He should be here tomorrow. To make sure we have the *right sort* of shower curtain. We have returned the red towels to Bloomingdale's." At this point everybody looked at Dan, who vomited. "Bill's yellow crêpe-paper pajamas have been taken away from him and burned. He ruined that night for all of us, you know that." At this point everybody looked at Bill who was absent. He was tending the vats. "Bill's new brown monkscloth pajamas, made for him by Paul, should be here next month. The grade of pork ears we are using in the Baby Ding Sam Dew is not capable of meeting U. S. Govt. standards, or indeed, any standards. Our man in Hong Kong assures us however that the next shipment will be superior. Sales nationwide are brisk, brisk, brisk. Texas Instruments is down four points. Control data is up four points. The pound is weakening. The cow is calving. The cactus wants watering. The new building is abuilding with leases covering 45 percent of the rentable space already in hand. The weather tomorrow, fair and warmer." (119–20)

The comic deflection evident in this passage serves a serious purpose. Like the questionnaire Barthelme inserts into his novel, the purpose of which is not, as Christopher Lasch believes, "to demolish the reader's confidence in the author," the situation report suggests the extent to which the Age of Journalism that Kierkegaard predicted a century and a half ago has come to pass: the age of quick information (not wisdom) and skimmed surfaces. Small wonder that the dwarfs find in digression so effective a means of evading the problem Snow White poses and of achieving the promise of better days to come. Barthelme's reader is delighted, but at the same time dismayed and provoked, by the ludicrous literal-mindedness of the characters in the situation report and, for example, the "interrupted screw" and "bat theory of child-raising" passages (29, 16). This same journalistic literal-mindedness leads to the explanatory overkill evident on virtually every page of the novel, including the first. There the reader is told not only of Snow White's "many beauty spots" but also, in the driest, most mechanically repetitive language possible, *where* these beauty spots appear, and just in case the reader still has not gotten the picture, the narrator appends that picture, a diagram showing the position, "more or less," of each of the spots (3). Such explanations are similar to the reading preferences of the dwarfs, who like

> books that have a lot of *dreck* in them, matter which presents itself as not wholly relevant (or indeed, at all relevant) but which, carefully attended to, can supply a kind of "sense" of what is going on. This "sense" is not to be obtained by reading between the lines (for there is nothing there, in those white spaces) but by reading the lines themselves—looking at them and so arriving at a feeling not of satisfaction exactly, that is too much to expect, but of having read them, of having "completed" them. (106)

Both the reading and the explanations take time, fill up time, thus creating the illusion of completeness and understanding.[14] And too they resemble those empty, usually verbal gestures sprinkled throughout the story: seasoning for Barthelme's readers but more of the word-bog for his dwarfish characters who are at once the victims and the perpetrators of such linguistic absurdities as Jane's signing her threatening letter to Mr. Quistgaard "*Yours faithfully*" or a conversation in which "somebody had said something we hadn't heard. . . . Then Bill said something. . . . Other people said other things. . . . But Bill had something else to say" (35). With conversations such as these can Vonnegut's verbal shrug, "so it goes," be far away?

"I just don't like your world," says Snow White at one point, "a world in which such things can happen" (68). Just what these "things" may be Snow White never makes clear, or perhaps never can make clear, given that increase in the "blanketing effect of ordinary language" which parallels an increase in the "trash phenomenon" in Snow White's world (96–97). The triumph of this "blanketing effect" will restore the dwarfs to their longed-for state of "equanamity for all" (87) and will put an end to Snow White's complaint. "Oh why does fate give us alternatives to annoy and frustrate ourselves with?" (157). But it will do so only at a price: the loss of their linguistic and (thinking of Orwell's equation) political freedom, including the freedom to choose the *extra*ordinary possibilities of language rather than accept the blanketed language of dwarf culture. The triumph of the blanketing effect will result in a society even more tasteless and unprincely than the one found in the novel where it is believed that "It must be all right if it is ordinary" (174), a society already deafened by amplified but meaningless sounds and inundated by trash, a society of over-heating "electric wastebaskets" (129) and "the democratization of education" (128), a society where the individual (or what remains of the individual) is subjected to public scrutiny, where "vatricide" is the "crime of crimes" (164) and blanketing the song of songs, and where there is heard the novels' melancholy refrain, "the problem remained."

"Language," George Steiner has noted, "is the main instrument of man's refusal to accept the world as it is."[15] The ultimate linguistic democracy of *Snow White,* however, is characterized not by any such active refusal but instead by passive acceptance, indiscriminate consumption, and echolalia ("I have not been able to imagine anything better," says Snow White; *"I have not been able to imagine anything better"* reads the next sentence," 59). The result is indeed a "failure of the imagination" (59) or, more specifically, a sadly reductive democracy in which all words, things, people, emotions, and values are finally equal—that is to say, equally worthless, equally insignificant and interchangeable, equally dehumanized and dehumanizing. Such "muck" does indeed cripple consciousness. Much to his credit, Donald Barthelme does not turn away from the contemporary mass culture, nor does he scornfully and condescendingly belittle it. As one aphoristic chapter near the very end of the novel warns, "ANATHEMIZATION OF THE WORLD IS NOT AN ADEQUATE RESPONSE TO THE WORLD" (178). For the characters in the novel, this means the uncritical acceptance ("Heigh Ho") of their situation. For Barthelme it means something quite different. *Snow White* is not a book "crippled by the absence of a subject," as Morris Dickstein has said,[16] but instead a fiction that is very much about a crippled culture, a book that uses parody and various innovative techniques to analyze the texture of contemporary life. The character who admits, "But to say what I have said, gentlemen, is to say nothing at all" (99), speaks for himself and his dwarfish kind but not at all for his author, whose purpose is to clarify the relationship between the state of the society and the state of its language. clearly and inventively, Donald Barthelme's novel suggests that in a dwarf culture of plastic buffalo humps, religious sciences, hair initiatives, unemployed princes, "hurlments," attractively packaged jars of Chinese baby food, *dreck* and *blague,* one well-aimned joke is worth considerably more than a thousand words from the collective mouth of Bill, Dan, Kevin, Edward, Hubert, Henry, and Clem.

Notes

1. William H. Gass, *Fiction & the Figures of Life* (Boston: Nonpareil Books, 1978), p. 275.

2. Jack Shadoian, "Notes on Donald Barthelme's *Snow White*," *Western Humanities Review,* 24 (Winter 1970), 74; Albert J. Guerard, "Notes on the rhetoric of anti-realistic fiction," *TriQuarterly,* 30 (Spring 1974), 27–31.

3. William Peden, *The American Short Story* (Boston: Houghton Mifflin, 1975), p. 179.

4. Tony Tanner, *City of Words: American Fiction,* 1950–1970 (New York: Harper & Row, 1971), p. 400.

5. John Gardner, *On Moral Fiction* (New York: Basic Books, 1978), p. 81.

6. Gerald Graff, *Literature Against Itself: Literary Ideas in Modern Society* (Chicago: Univ. of Chicago Press, 1979), pp. 226, 227, 53, 238.

7. Christopher Lasch, *The Culture of Narcissism: American Life in an Age of Diminishing Expectations,* (New York: Warner Books, 1979), pp. 74–75, 50–54, 173–74.

8. Ronald Sukenick, "The New Tradition," *Partisan Review,* 39 (Fall 1972), 580–88; Jerome Klinkowitz, *The Practice of Fiction in America: Writers from Hawthorne to the Present* (Ames: Univ. of Iowa Press, 1980), pp. 106–13. More recently, both critics have begun to sound a less polemical (and less contentious) note. In a review of Gerald Graff's *Literature Against Itself* in *American Book Review,* 3 (March–April 1981), 5, Sukenick refers to Barthelme as "the social critic he so often is." Klinkowitz, in his *The Self-Apparent Word: Fiction as Language/Language as Fiction* (Carbondale: Southern Illinois Univ. Press, 1984), p. 76, acknowledges much the same point: "Barthelme had wanted his fiction to be an object, an 'itself' to be encountered in the world, to be 'bumped into'; but in producing such fiction, he has often written social satire of such linguistic conditions already existing in contemporary American customs." And finally, in their introduction to *Anything Can Happen: Interviews with Contemporary American Novelists* (Urbana: Univ. of Illinois Press, 1983), p. 21, editors Larry McCaffery and Tom LeClair are surprised to learn that Barthelme now claims a social relevance for what before had seemed clever little word objects.

9. William Stott, "Donald Barthelme and the Death of Fiction," *Prospects: An Annual of American Cultural Studies,* ed. Jack Salzman, vol. I (New York: Burt Franklin, 1975), 369–88.

10. Neil Schmitz, "Donald Barthelme and the Emergence of Modern Satire," *Minnesota Review,* 1, iv (1972), 114.

11. Pearl K. Bell, "American Fiction: Forgetting the Ordinary Truths," *Dissent* (Winter 1973), pp. 27–28.

12. Graff, p. 53.

13. Donald Barthelme, *Snow White* (1967; rpt. New York: Atheneum, 1978), p. 59. Subsequent page references are to this edition.

14. Concerning Barthelme's use of verbal and social "arrangements which 'fill up' without fulfilling," see John Leland, "Remarks Re-marked: Barthelme, What Curios of Signs," *Boundary 2* 5 (Spring 1977), 796.

15. George Steiner, *After Babel* (New York: Oxford Univ. Press, 1975).

16. Morris Dickstein, *Gates of Eden: American Culture in the Sixties* (New York: Basic Books, 1977), p. 221.

The Dead Father:
Innovative Forms, Eternal Themes

RICHARD WALSH

The Dead Father, Barthelme's second novel, provokes extreme responses. Its reception by the literary establishment was more than usually mixed— polarized, in fact, between cold dismissal and often immoderate acclaim. Both of these positions seem to stem from largely *a priori* literary sympathies and in consequence their arguments seldom engage the text itself in an insightful way, but they do indicate something of the literary issues at stake. The negative responses are all to some degree determined by a perceived failure of Barthelme's novel to fulfill certain basic expectations, expectations that are most clearly apparent in the opinion of Maureen Howard in the *Yale Review:* "This cold short narrative is written at an extreme distance from life, out of literary models and the author's idea of a defunct avant-garde."[1] The objection is that the novel lacks engagement with reality, or "life," a loaded word that denies any distinction between being about "life" in terms of its argument or the issues it addresses, which *The Dead Father* is, and being about "life" in terms of narrative subject matter—that is, in some sense realist—which it clearly is not. Why the latter should be exclusively valued as a mode of engagement with reality is not clear, but the comment of another reviewer suggests a simple nostalgia for linguistic innocence: *"The Dead Father* presents itself on a larger scale, really as cryptic allegory. But it lacks any sense of jeopardy and urgency. We learn very early that it is all cardboard."[2] This appears to be a complaint that the novel fails to engage the reader because it does not create a narrative world and characters who matter in their own right; but the expectation of such a vicarious and illusory mode of engagement can hardly be a convincing literary criterion. If we are told it is all cardboard (which is not quite true), for this to come as a surprise or a disappointment suggests a credulous habit of reading that is rather more escapist (and so presumably farther from life, if we are to take the word seriously) than the alternative offered in *The Dead Father.*

Michael Mason in the *Times Literary Supplement* pursues further the literary heritage of the novel, arguing that "To set [*Molloy*] beside *The Dead*

This essay was written specifically for this volume and is published here for the first time by permission of the author.

Father is to see that Barthelme is not advancing experimental fiction one jot."[3] The question is one of literary evolution, not literary merit, and without confusing the two or invoking a model of innovation as simple linear progress, it is clear Barthelme is doing much more than repeating Beckett's achievement. The debt to Beckett is obvious and acknowledged, but their concerns and methods are widely divergent, Beckett gnawing obsessively at essentially metaphysical problems, Barthelme exploring the intricacies of experienced relationships (familial, political, sociological, psychological). Barthelme's novel is both more at home with its self-consciousness and, in answer to Maureen Howard's comment, closer to life.

The enthusiastic reviews compete in allegorical interpretation of the Dead Father, producing long lists of tentative solutions to the allegory, with the apparent hope that, if none of them seems adequate alone, a sufficiently extensive set may capture the novel's meaning. Some critics, uncomfortable with the text's inconsistency in invoking such a multiplicity of allegorical signification, seek to order them hierarchically beneath a single master interpretation. Richard Todd offers a representative list, then moves to a higher level of abstraction: "He is God first of all. . . . After that he's what you will: The novel, Western Culture, Truth, Duty, Honor, Country. He is the order that we seek, and the control we seek to escape."[4] This is nice in that it epigrammatizes the ambivalence with which the Dead Father is viewed, but it is also a long way removed from the page-by-page text of the novel. It is not that such an allegorical meaning is invalid, but that having been chosen, it imposes a logic upon the text that distorts or neglects its literal development. In other words, while it is clear that the literal sense is not of great consequence on its own (just as the vehicle of a metaphor is inconsequential aside from its metaphoric function), this literal narrative rather than its "translation" must remain the center of attention if the exploratory process it facilitates is not to be subverted by a prejudicial allegorical framework. The idea of fatherhood is a more fundamental unifying principle in *The Dead Father* than any abstract allegorical formulation.

There are some gestures in this direction among the reviewers: Neil Schmitz in *Partisan Review,* for example, suggests that "the Dead Father is finally everyone's father, the great mutilated self-important, self-indulgent Super-ego whom we pull along behind us."[5] The psychoanalytical slant is slightly limiting but does foreground Barthelme's examination of our mental experience of fathers, his "theme-and-variations approach to what fathers mean to us."[6] Support for such an interpretative emphasis is also available in Barthelme's own comments on the novel. Asked to explain the germinating idea for *The Dead Father,* he replied simply, "A matter of having a father and being a father."[7] This remark must be taken as rather disingenuous and insufficient grounds on its own for inferring authorial intention, but he is a little more expansive in another interview: "*The Dead Father* suggests that the process of becoming has bound up in it the experience of many other consciousnesses, the most important of which are in a law-giving relation to the self. The characters complain about this in what I hope is an interesting fashion."[8] The emphasis here remains upon essentially filial subjectivity, without excluding the (social, theological, political) analogues upon which the scenario impinges. It is clear, though, that these latter are derivative from the literal sense of paternity in the novel, not hidden codes that provide its driving force. The singular parallelism of simple allegory is inadequate to *The Dead Father* because no single interpretation satisfies; nor does it evoke any set of allegorical meanings with sufficient consistency to justify reading it as a multiple allegory. As with Kafka, whose paternity is apparent at more than one point in Barthelme's novel, the blunt dualism of allegory ultimately fails to account for the degree to which the literal sense generates the narrative. It is not allegorical parallelism that should be the center of critical attention, then, but the thematic framework the novel itself employs, the question of fatherhood. In it Barthelme has found his unifying master-theme, one which can be used not as an abstract thesis but as an open metaphor: a metaphor whose tenor is unspecified and unfixed while its vehicle is developed on its own terms, to its own ends, becoming in the process not just the vehicle of a trope but a vehicle of discovery.

The opening tableau of *The Dead Father,* in which his huge body is described lying prostrate across the city, is formally separate from the narrative that follows; it lacks a chapter number and is printed in italic type. It stands in relation to the rest of the text as the condition upon which its action is predicated, a sort of protasis, the Dead Father's enormous impassive presence in the city reminiscent of the situation in Barthelme's earlier story, "The Balloon."[9] Unlike the balloon, the Dead Father has not appeared one night, but preexists the earliest memories of the citizens; he is a constant, coloring the whole of their experience. The essential fact here is the overbearing timelessness of his presence, which is also expressed in the static structure of the piece, a formal description of the Dead Father (head, body, left leg, right leg) in which the effect upon the lives of the citizens appears only parenthetically. The description is matter-of-fact in tone while repeatedly nodding in the direction of the epic narrative the Dead Father himself would demand, admitting in this ironic stance a double-edged mythic dimension to the Dead Father: myth as both past and powerfully present, awesome yet ludicrously anachronistic. So, the Dead Father is granted the heroic attributes he is due, but they are presented less as archetypes than as clichés: "The brow is noble, good Christ, what else? Broad and noble. And serene, of course, he's dead, what else if not serene?" and "Jawline compares favorably to a rock formation. Imposing, rugged, all that."[10] The essential statement of the condition upon which the novel is built is isolated in a single line paragraph: "Dead, but still with us, still with us, but dead" (p. 3). That this is an unsatisfactory state of affairs, but also that nothing is being done about it, is the essential precondition to the expedition that follows. In their impotence, the citizens remain children. The problem for Thomas, in undertaking to dispose of the Dead Father, is that he must to some extent become him.

In the first chapter this process is already under way, with Thomas at the head of the expedition that will drag the Dead Father to his grave. What is at stake in the confrontation between these two is illustrated by their contrasting ideas of authority. In the case of the Dead Father, this is manifest in his long-standing imposition upon his sons of a humiliating uniform of cap-and-bells, "for the good of all," according to the paternalistic refrain that echoes from the protasis onward. Juxtaposed with this is an example of Thomas's leadership, his recruitment to the expedition of the drunk, Edmund, against his better judgment: "It would be the making of him, he said. Our march. I did not agree. But it is hard to deny someone the thing he thinks will be the making of him. I signed him up" (p. 7). In an absurd way Edmund's belief proves correct: the Dead Father unpredictably makes him his heir. But this outcome is not necessary to the contrast between the Dead Father's and Thomas's ideas of benevolent authority, the one abstract and formal, "A matter of Organization" (p. 7), and the other intimately informed by the consciousness of its subject.

Thomas's attempt to establish a new mode of authority exists in continual tension with the allure of the old order, however, and this ambivalence extends beyond the abstract question of forms of authority to the relationship that operates across the generation gap between Thomas and Julie and the Dead Father himself. Julie's whimsical narrative of the initiation of the relationship of fatherhood is a quasipsychoanalytical explanation of this ambivalence: "The fucked mother conceives, Julie said. The whelpling is, after agonies I shall not describe, whelped. Then the dialogue begins. The father speaks to it. The 'it' in a paroxysm of not understanding. The 'it' whirling as in a centrifuge. Looking for something to tie to. Like a boat in a storm. What is there? The father" (p. 77). The father is both the threatening other who generates difference (by speaking to the child) and the only possible means by which this experience can be assimilated. This primal scene has a fundamental relation to the problem of language: the father, in the very act of attempting to communicate, initiates the disjunction between self and other which makes it necessary and impossible. The gap is generated by the language that seeks to close it. The child is therefore confronted with the choice between language, which forever guarantees that gap in the impassable barrier between signifier and signified, or acceptance of the father as origin, the authority in which signifier and signified are unifed and by that tautology, the theological "I AM," the arbiter of truth. The child choses the latter. The father, then, offers both hostility and security, the impossibility and condition of meaning. Of course, to put it in this way is simply to juggle the buzzwords of Lacanian psychoanalysis, risking a substitution of jargon for values, which is avoided by Barthelme. It is a tendency he satirized in "A

Shower of Gold,"[11] where the subject was existentialism, or rather its popular degradation; but as he explains in an interview, "You could do the same story today and substitute the current vocabulary and very little of the structure of the story would have to be changed. Call it 'The Lacanthrope.' "[12] Barthelme's allusions to Lacan are too light and fanciful to risk any leaden incantation of his themes, or any uncritical acceptance of his narrative's validity. Julie speaks in the context of a parlor game of intellectual disputation—"Fatherhood as a substructure of the war of all against all, said Thomas, we could discuss that" (p. 76)—and it is the idiosyncracy of her own conceptual language that dominates. Bound up with the rejection of the old structure is the grounds for Oedipal or generational rebellion, the problem of the evaluative criteria for the new. Julie, like Snow White in Barthelme's first novel, is driven by ennui to a desire for the new as such, a value in itself. An undiscriminating appetite for the new is a contemporary malaise that has preoccupied Barthelme elsewhere, in "The Flight of the Pigeons from the Palace,"[13] for example, where its consequences in art are explored. The fact that Barthelme's own innovative fictions cater to this desire indicates his considerable sympathy, but he is also conscious of the need to espouse a value beyond mere newness. In the *Paris Review* interview he explains the inadequacy of the criterion of newness with reference to a story in *Great Days*: "Reynolds Price in the *Times* said of my story 'The New Music' that it was about as new as the toothache. He apparently didn't get the joke, which is that there is always a new music—the new music shows up about every ten minutes. Not like the toothache. More like hiccups." But he also offers an interpretation of its underlying motivation: "It equates with being able to feel something rather than with novelty per se, it's a kind of shorthand for discovery."[14]

While the Dead Father stands above all for the permanence of his power, then, he is confronted with the antithetical view that, insisting upon change as a value, negates him utterly. Against his own concept of his seniority as authority, Julie explains his demise in terms of the youthful view of age as obsolescence: "It is because you are an old fart, Julie explained" (p. 10). This triggers a reflex response that the same phrase, antithesis of paternal authority, will produce twice more in the novel: the Dead Father storms off, and is discovered "slaying" in a grove of musicians. An extravagant list of the slain is given, the linguistic foregrounding of which prepares for the textual trump by which Julie shrivels his achievement: "Impressive, said Julie, had they not been pure cardboard" (p. 12). By breaking the language contract guaranteeing the father's authority, the primacy of language is here exploited to counter the very physical but contingent power wielded by the Dead Father. The change of label for the Dead Father's victims from "musicians" to "artists" in this passage suggests a confrontation between art and authority (music is Barthelme's favoured representative art form, as in "The

New Music"[15]); but the victory is not so unequivocal, and language not so uncompromised. When the theme of art arises again, this time in terms of the visual arts, the Dead Father's control is absolute:

> Tell me, said Julie, did you ever want to paint or draw or etch? Yourself?
> It was not necessary, said the Dead Father, because I am the Father. All lines my lines. All figure and all ground mine, out of my head. All colors mine. You take my meaning.
> We had no choice, said Julie. (p. 19)

As Julie's response makes clear, the implication is that language remains an inheritance contaminated by its past. It is no more possible to disown completely the meaning endowed on it by the father than it is to disown the structure of fatherhood itself. This problematic tension is incorporated into the form of the novel in the continuous conflict it enacts between the need to describe in the interests of the narrative, and its resistance to a conventional realization of the object of description: "They packed up. Thomas gave the signal. The cable jerked. The sun still. Trees. Vegetation. Wild gooseberries. Weather" (p. 9). Such gestural travesties of an attempt to render indicate a significant dissent from the normal novelistic focus of interest. The burden of significance in the novel is carried almost entirely in dialogue and mono-logue; in language attributable to or indicative of a particular subjectivity. The narrative world is a shadow cast by language, ontologically posterior rather than prior to it, and while it is coherently articulated (it is a narrative) it implies no coherence in those of its aspects that are not specified in language. The Dead Father is explicitly 3,200 cubits long, but his behavior and treatment in the narrative would often require the inference (if it were to be made) that he is human in scale. The inference is not to be made, because this contradiction is simply an implicit by-product of language that addresses other issues.

There are several points in the novel where a requirement for contextual detail is met by an absurd and bizarre list. These resist the purposive assumptions by which we normally read literature, for they perform the general task of aiding verisimilitude only in their form, denying it in their content. Yet they are not pointed enough for parody, nor do they offer themselves for any other signifying purpose. On such criteria these lists must be judged arbitrary, in the perjorative sense of lacking intentional motivation. But since the narrative of the novel accepts in its form the necessity of some degree of rendition, without however committing itself to realism, the detail by which this rendition is achieved is, except in its functional aspect, inevitably arbitrary. If the detail is arbitrary, it should be strikingly arbitrary; this is the function of ornament, or play, in the narrative—the functional motivation for a textual maneuver being general, and not setting down limitations of content as in realistic narrative, the specific is an open field in which the liberated imagination can dance, affirming itself in excess of the bounds of the necessary. This is not the same as saying it is flatly unmotivated.

Barthelme uses language, then, as a means of outgrowing the structure to which it remains subordinated, as an instance of the ambivalent relationship of the novel's argument: the structural imperative of rendition is adhered to but its tendency toward realism is subverted in the particularity of the language used, just as Thomas accepts the structure of paternity but works within it to minimize its authoritarianism.

The boldest extension of language beyond the function of meaning in the novel is the series of almost abstract dialogues between Julie and Emma, which stretches language to its breaking point. In their refusal of the dictates of meaning, the dialogues offer, as a narrative mode, an alternative to the Dead Father as origin of meaning. As such they stand in parallel with the other models of fatherlessness that are offered in the course of the expedition, all of which prove inadequate. The first of these is provided by two children, both aged ten, in love. Their attitude toward the Dead Father shows a naive-utopian freedom from the thrall of his authority, but it is an inadequate model because it is utterly private, unable to survive exposure to society at large: "We are going to live together all our lives and love each other all our lives until we die. We know it. But don't tell anyone because we'll be beaten, if the knowledge becomes general" (p. 14). The Wends, through whose country the party passes, are another model of society free from the thrall of paternity: "We Wends are the fathers of ourselves . . . that which all men have wished to be, from the very beginning, we are" (p. 73). But this too is utopian, and unavailable to Thomas: "The mechanics of the thing elude me, said Thomas" (p. 73). In a book that centers obsessively on the male lineage of fathers and sons, patriarchy and paternity, particular significance hangs upon the fact that the set-piece dialogues occur exclusively between the novel's two female protagonists. They constitute another model of father-lessness, of nonpatriarchal society: an anarchist-feminist enclave within the narrative of the expedition, in which Emma functions as a foil to Julie, who is established throughout the book as the antithesis of the Dead Father and the principal advocate of the chaos of fatherlessness that Thomas must balance against the Dead Father's authority.

Introduced as "conversation," the dialogues are verbal collages in which neither speaker is bound by the context of the previous locution. The speeches are not attributed, and confusion about who is speaking is propagated as the dialogues progress by the shift of motifs from one to the other. There is, at least in the first dialogue, a basic thread of contextual sense: Julie is hostile to Emma and seeking to get rid of her; Emma is curious, especially about Thomas, and intent upon staying. But they are dominated by the effects of repetition and juxtaposition of a repertoire of refrains, some of which have an apparent relevance to the dialogues themselves—"Hoping this will reach you at a favorable moment" (pp. 23, 24, 86, 155); or to the narrative context—"I can make it hot for you" (pp. 24, 25, 26, 61, 150); but often they suggest no relevance whatever—"Thought I heard a dog barking" (pp. 25, 26, 26, 62, 86, 148). Such an emphasis involves a treatment of language that tends to disregard its referential function. Barthelme does not consider himself to be working in this way, but does acknowledge its attraction: "There's an urge toward abstraction that's very seductive . . . the sort of thing you find in Gertrude Stein and hardly anywhere else."[16] In fact the movement toward treating language as abstract, far from obscuring its referentiality, serves only to highlight it; in these dialogues successive locutions introduce new deictic implications so diverse, and in such rapid succession, that the effect is not an appreciation of language as music but an exasperated reaching after meaning. Although recognizable aesthetic criteria are at work in the incantatory repetitions and thematic recurrence to certain lexical fields, they do not usurp the sense of intent inherent in the referentiality of language. As a refusal of coherence rather than an alternative to it, the dialogues fail to establish an independent value structure and remain subordinate to the intentionality they defy.

The dialogues get progressively longer through the book, achieving their effects on an increasingly large scale against the background of better-defined reader expectation. The process of reading them is one of constantly delayed resolution, more and more material being held in suspension against the possibility of retrospective coherence. Ultimately these dislocations of meaning introduce into the interpretative act an irreducible element of play, the pursuit of meaning liberated from expectations of resolution. The reader is beckoned along semantic trails that do not end or meet (though they may cross), but are simply abandoned in the proliferation of alternatives. What is denied is the end-directed, the definitive and the singular in meaning, in favor of the exploratory, speculative and polysemic. With the usurpation of structure by play, however, the imperative to order, which remains of importance to Thomas, is completely abandoned.

As such, these dialogues stand in clear contrast to the monolithic epic narrative with which the Dead Father makes his claim to authority. Related as he is being dragged along, the Dead Father's narrative is a parody of several heroic conventions—catalogs of gifts and offspring, cunning disguises, descent into the underworld, intrepid escapes—and its message is singular and direct: that its protagonist (the Dead Father) is the hero. A comparable tautology is his pyrotechnic speech to the men, where in reply to Emma's inquiry as to its meaning, the Dead Father says "it meant I made a speech" (p. 51).

The narrative offered by Thomas in response to the Dead Father's does not repeat the narrator-as-hero model, but rather presents him as a Kafkaesque victim: it is a narrative of the psychology of sons, ending in confrontation with the phallic Great Father Serpent. To the riddle this monster poses, "What do you really feel?" Thomas gives the correct reply, which he has read, not felt—"like murderinging"—and is surprised at how well this articulates his suppressed Oedipal desires. He is left "with murderinging in mind—the dream of a stutterer" (p. 46). The Dead Father, recognizing the pertinence of the tale to himself, is disconcerted, and seeks to undermine the authority of the narrative. Thomas's reply changes the rules on which the objection is based, in the process shifting the burden of authority onto reader interpretation, a trap into which the Dead Father unhesitatingly falls:

> That is a tall tale, said the Dead Father. I don't believe it ever happened.
> No tale ever happened in the way we tell it, said Thomas, but the moral is always correct.
> What is the moral?
> Murderinging, Thomas said.
> Murderinging is not correct, said the Dead Father. The sacred and noble Father should not be murdereded. Never. Absolutely not.
> I mentioned no names, said Thomas. (p. 46)

The Dead Father has been flustered into acknowledging the particular significance of the moral to himself, and the breakthrough is followed by the first of a series of symbolic transfers of power that occur at key stages through the novel: silver buckle, sword, passport, keys.

The shape of the novel is determined by Thomas's efforts to complete the transfer of power without in the process becoming the image of the Dead Father, the crucial issue being whether it is possible to usurp the Dead Father's position without also taking on his monolithic perspective. The balance is very fine between transformation and repetition in Thomas's appropriation to himself of the role of father; he is seduced by some of its rewards, notably the pleasure of control, into a dangerous proximity with the position represented by the Dead Father. The significant difference, however, is that when confronted Thomas does not attempt a mystification of the role of fatherhood but frankly confesses its attractions, while the Dead Father's preferred policy is an obfuscation of the nature of power relations. Part of Thomas's approach to the problem of authority is this process of "full disclosure" (p. 66), a laying bare of the motives and grounds that form a self-conscious attempt to retain around the process the qualifying frame of its contingency and answerability. So Thomas counters the Dead Father's assertion of his larger perspective by claiming a greater understanding of the limits of perspective, limits that the Dead Father would rather not acknowledge:

> My criticism was that you never understood the larger picture, said the Dead Father. Young men never understand the larger picture.
> I don't suggest I understand it now. I do understand the frame. The limits.
> Of course the frame is easier to understand.

> Older people tend to overlook the frame, even when they are looking right at it, said Thomas. They don't like to think about it. (p. 32)

The Dead Father's reluctance to acknowledge the frame is his reluctance to acknowledge his own death, his attempt to impose upon the structure he dominates a timeless rigidity. On the other hand, Thomas's emphasis on the frame receives some modification at the hands of Julie. When she proclaims their unity, Thomas angers her by insisting upon seeing this in the context of mutability: his emphasis on the temporal frame here leads to a devaluation of the present, an abdication from involvement. Julie affects a reconciliation in sex, but exacts a succinct and didactic revenge which reasserts the primacy of the present.

Thomas demonstrates that he has assimilated Julie's teachings when he is called upon to allay the doubts of the men—"*are we doing the right thing?*" (p. 92)—about the expedition. He relates an anecdote in which Haydn refuses Martin Luther's telephone request that he "do a piece for *us*" (p. 93), to which Edmund reasonably objects "You have got the centuries all wrong and the telephone should not be in there and anyway I do not get the point" (p. 93). Thomas's answer is inviting as a central statement of the context in which moral engagement is placed in the novel, and in Barthelme's work as a whole. There is no abdication of responsibility here, but rather a heightening of it through an unswerving consciousness of the uncertain context in which it must operate: "You see! Thomas exclaimed. *There it is!* Things are not simple. Error is always possible, even with the best intentions in the world. People make mistakes. Things are not done right. Right things are not done. There are cases which are not clear. You must be able to tolerate the anxiety. To do otherwise is to jump ship, ethics-wise" (p. 93). This is Thomas's awareness of the frame integrated into a commitment to action, rather than as a pretext for passivity.

The question of the structure in which action is to be located is addressed by the "Manual for Sons," which brings the novel's argument to its crisis. The manual deals with the father-son relationship in diverse aspects, offering advice that assumes the normal power structure of that relationship in a tone (that of a manual for parents) which inverts it. Some of the sections, such as "Dandling" and "Sexual organs" appear to address themselves to fathers rather than sons, both of these offering advice on the niceties of a father's sexuality in relation to his children, daughters in particular. This anticipates the manual's conclusions on the transfer of paternal power, the central issue of Thomas's situation. The problem is not one of killing the father—"time will slay him, that is a virtual certainty" (p. 145)—but of liberation from his influence. Death is never the end of the father's authority: "Fatherless now, you must deal with the memory of a father. Often that memory is more potent than the living presence of a father, is an inner voice commanding, haranguing, yes-ing and no-ing . . . At what point do you become yourself? Never, wholly, you are always partly him. That privileged position in your inner ear is his last 'perk' and no father has ever passed it by" (p. 144).

The manual's conclusion then is that the inherited role of fatherhood is realistically not to be abandoned but rather ameliorated: "Your true task, as a son, is to reproduce every one of the enormities touched upon in this manual, but in attenuated form. You must become your father, but a paler, weaker version of him. The enormities go with the job, but close study will allow you to perform the job less well than it has previously been done, thus moving toward a golden age of decency, quiet and calmed fevers" (p. 145). The manual's program of reform is moderate rather than radical, not through choice but because it accepts the taint of inherited structure (psychological, conceptual, social, economic, political, aesthetic) as a necessary condition of subsequent action. The reception of the book by Julie and Thomas provides a measure of their respective positions on the question of fatherhood. They are unable to decide whether the book is too harsh or not harsh enough, an indeterminacy for which Thomas provides a rationalization deeply unsatisfactory to Julie:

> It would depend on the experience of the individual making the judgment, as to whether it was judged to be too harsh or judged to be not harsh enough.
> I hate relativists, she said, and threw the book into the fire. (p. 146)

That Julie's anger is directed at the book rather than at Thomas indicates a parallelism between the problem of its evaluation and the problem it addresses. Julie is caught between her desire for an absolute solution and her inability to provide one (the felt oppression of fatherhood and the anarchy of fatherlessness), while Thomas's pragmatic relativism aligns him with the manual's conclusions.

The success of the novel depends upon more than the resolution of its argument, however, and the question remains as to how much the reader is compelled by all this. Certainly little is offered in terms of involvement with the characters—in fact, this is actively discouraged. Barthelme has himself identified as one of the weaknesses of his writing that he does not offer enough emotion, his tendency to short-circuit it with humor. Given the character-antipathetic narrative style he favors, this is a necessary sacrifice rather than a failure. And the novel *does* appeal to the emotions in other ways. The novel's ending is moving without falling back on techniques that induce sympathy with the characters, who even by that stage have a functional rather than an individual status—the Dead Father in particular, though his demise is the center of reader involvement. The final chapter brings him to his grave, a great hole in the ground, and to a reluctant acceptance of his fate. The narrative maintains a tone of quiet pathos: "The Dead Father looked again at the hole. Oh, he said, I see" (p. 174). He climbs into the hole, his dignity greatest at his end. This is no gleeful conquest for Thomas, who as the standard-bearer of a new and finally ascendant order nonetheless mingles admiration with his rejection of the old:

> I'm in it now, said the Dead Father, resonantly.
> What a voice, said Julie, I wonder how he does it.
> She knelt and clasped a hand.
> Intolerable, Thomas said. Grand. I wonder how he does it.
> I'm in the hole now, said the Dead Father.
> Julie holding a hand.
> One moment more! said the Dead Father.
> Bulldozers. (pp. 176–7)

Notes

1. Maureen Howard, "Recent Novels: A Backward Glance," *Yale Review* 65 (1976): 408.

2. Roger Shattuck, *"The Dead Father,"* New York Times Book Review, 9 November 1975, 50.

3. Michael Mason, "Paternity Pursuit," *Times Literary Supplement*, 17 June 1977, 721.

4. Richard Todd, "Daddy, You're Perfectly Swell!" *Atlantic* 236 (December 1975), 112.

5. Neil Schmitz, "Barthelme's Life with Father," *Partisan Review* 46 (1979): 306.

6. Peter S. Prescott, "Pater Noster," *Newsweek,* 3 November 1975, 59.

7. Larry McCaffery, "An Interview with Donald Barthelme," in Tom LeClair and Larry McCaffery, *Anything Can Happen: Interview with Contemporary American Novelists* (Urbana: University of Illinois Press, 1983), 41.

8. J. D. O'Hara, "Donald Barthelme: The Art of Fiction LXVI," *Paris Review* 80 (1981): 199.

9. Donald Barthelme, *Unspeakable Practices, Unnatural Acts* (New York: Farrar, Straus and Giroux, 1968); reprinted in *Sixty Stories* (New York: E. P. Dutton, 1982), 53–8.

10. Donald Barthelme, *The Dead Father* (London: Routledge and Kegan Paul, 1977), 3–4; hereafter cited in the text.

11. Donald Barthelme, *Come Back, Dr. Caligari* (Boston: Little, Brown, 1964), 171–83.

12. O'Hara, "Donald Barthelme: The Art of Fiction LXVI," 207–8.

13. Donald Barthelme, *Sadness* (New York: Farrar, Straus and Giroux, 1971); reprinted in *Forty Stories* (London: Secker and Warburg, 1988), 130–40.

14. O'Hara, "Donald Barthelme: The Art of Fiction LXVI," 190, 189.

15. Donald Barthelme, *Great Days* (London: Routledge and Kegan Paul, 1979), 21–38.

16. O'Hara, "Donald Barthelme: The Art of Fiction LXVI," 197.

Post-Modern Paternity:
Donald Barthelme's *The Dead Father*

ROBERT CON DAVIS

Among late twentieth-century American novels, the one that most seriously attempts to define the father in recent, or post-modern, fiction, and possibly the most important "father" novel since *Ulysses* and *Absalom, Absalom!,* is Donald Barthelme's *The Dead Father* (1975). This complex and brilliant work accomplishes nothing less than a major redefinition of what the father in fiction is, and it does this as it forces novelistic attention to range back, over the structure of the father in English fiction. Difficult to approach—as are many other post-modern novels—Barthelme's novel forces one to rediscover how to read a novel, as the first lines, presenting a view of paternity that verges on patent absurdity, show this novel's resistance to any simple interpretation: "The Dead Father's head. The main thing is, his eyes are open. Staring up into the sky. The eyes a two-valued blue, the blues of the Gitanes cigarette pack. The head never moves. Decades of staring. The brow is noble, good Christ, what else: Broad and noble. And serene, of course, he's dead, what else if not serene. . . . He is not perfect, thank God for that. . . . No one can remember when he was not here in our city positioned like a sleeper in troubled sleep."[1]

Barthelme's portrait of the fictional father, for all of its detail, presents a cryptic caricature that teeters between profundity and nonsense. If one moves in for a close-up of the head, a shift that breaks up its continuous lines, then, as the noble brow and blue eyes dissolve, a rogues' gallery of many fathers takes shape in place of the single face. At the right end of this gallery stand Squire Allworthy, John Jarndyce, Edward Overton, and others who are stern but ultimately benevolent toward their children. To the extreme right of Jarndyce and the gallery's other saintly figures emanates the paternal white light that John Bunyan's Christian found in the Celestial City. At the gallery's left end stand Mr. Murdstone, Mr. M'Choakumchild, Sir Austen Feverel, Huck Finn's Pap, and Thomas Sutpen, and, to the extreme left of these child haters, a grim reaper (like Wash Jones or Percy Grimm) who, as the polar opposite of the celestial light, mindlessly sweeps a scythe through young limbs. But, with a shift back, this close-up of the rogues' gallery's many fathers dissolves and, once again, from a distance appears the single, sphinxlike head. Like a blank-eyed Greek statue who gazes at the world and flinches at nothing, his head turns toward an ultimate and elusive point that only he sees. How he can be dead, though "only in a sense" (14), suggests portentously a grasp of the paternal tradition in Anglo-American fiction.

A fiction that taps this tradition by daring to seize the father as a whole stands in peril of some presumption, as does the attempt to understand that fiction. Such a fiction, flirting with the absurd, invests everything in an attempt to leap out of and then to turn to embrace its tradition, in this case the paternal tradition and that of the novel itself. If the fiction cannot make the leap, then, like Herman Melville's *The Confidence-Man,* it breaks into pieces. From the perspective of a purely thematic criticism, it can be shown that the rogues' gallery figures exist separately and without meaningful relationship in a tradition: literary symbol and structure simply do not exist. But against such fragmentation and reduction literature brings symbols into existence by taking enormous chances with our understanding of tradition that become authentic fiction when they succeed.

The Dead Father begins in a description of the father's great body half-buried in the middle of a French city. Sitting motionless, "staring up into the sky," he appears to be dead, but the narrator cautions that he is not, not entirely. The details of his features soon make it apparent that his different parts are emblems of paternity and that this character is to be taken as a complex symbol. His noble brow stands for mental power and concentration. His rugged jawline indicates formidable will and endurance. His blue eyes and gray hair show his attractive and even dashing appearance. His "full red lips [are] drawn back in a slight rictus . . . disclosing a bit of mackerel salad lodged between two of the stained four," as absurd evidence of great appetite and desire. Although held in place by chains, like Prometheus, the figure in this audacious attempt to capture a literary symbol is easily recognizable as a father: authority, aloofness, great appetite—it is all here in a sketch. This being so, and granting what seems like true veneration in this description, it must be wondered why the narrator is quick to add that the father, though admirable, "is not perfect, thank God for that." In fact, he adds, "we want the Dead Father to be dead." And further, in a strident tone, "we sit with tears in our eyes wanting the Dead Father to be dead—meanwhile doing amazing things with our hands" (2–5). That the father is dead and that his children should want his death are facts, in Barthelme's words, "End-shrouded in endigmas" (172).

The fact to be dealt with here, as in much other post-modern fiction, is that literary paternity is not linked inextricably with "fathers" as figures in stories. Even though the relationship of children, mothers, and fathers at the thematic level of narrative constitutes the family material from which fictions are made, at the structural level of the text the meaning of that relationship takes shape as a "symbolic father," ultimately a function in narrative structure. This function floats freely, to a considerable extent, without mooring in images of the father, either social or personal, because it is a structural aspect of narrative: it prohibits mere repetition and mere sequentiality, lapses into narcissism, in effect forbidding an untold story, either in the form of silence or in the mechanical repetition that imitates silence. Specifically, it is the essential "no" expresssed as a dilemma (a riddle to be solved, a family member to be found, an injustice to be surmounted, etc.) that, as Vladimir Propp notes, comes at the beginning of every narrative to generate its structure. The problem of Barthelme's post-modern fiction is this: how does a novel, part of an English tradition of fiction (*Robinson Crusoe, The Ordeal of Richard Feverel,* etc.) that explicitly articulates the function of paternity both thematically and structurally, exist within its tradition without being overcome by it?

For, although in one way free of the tyranny of father figures, the post-modern novel still must deal with the residue of father images, mostly social and economic in origin, that belong to the English tradition of realistic fiction; indelibly inscribed in that tradition is the portrait of a mature gentleman in a suit with vest, with graying hair and glasses and perhaps a watch chain slung across his middle. He is Squire Allworthy, Sir Austen Feverel, Edward Overton, or Jason Lycurgus Compson, III—a composite of the rogues' gallery figures. His exclusive power to signify the paternal metaphor has been rescinded since James Joyce's *Ulysses,* but he and his special privilege are still there as a living memory in the English literary tradition. No longer recognizing that privilege, the post-modern novel, nonetheless, must continue to deal with it, since how it deals with tradition gives post-modern fiction its identity.

The Dead Father, for example, manifests wholly traditional structures. Primarily, there is the quest: the Dead Father seeks renewal in a search for the Golden Fleece, and on this journey he performs heroic deeds in combat and tells of past conquests in love. The fact of this mythic journey alone links Barthelme's novel to *Robinson Crusoe, Huckleberry Finn, Moby Dick, Ulysses,* and many others. Also in line with quest conventions, as the journey's end nears a female (her name is "Mother") is liberated, her entrance into the action obviously connected with the consummation of the journey. Further, the Dead Father has a helper on the quest in his son, who enlists nineteen men to tow his father toward his goal. Additionally, the son recounts undertaking an initiation directly connected with his ability to aid his father and to be on the quest. Along with the quest, there is the highly traditional novelistic device of the book-within-a-book. The novel's "A Manual for Sons" gives practical guidance, in the manner of a field manual, for identifying and dealing with what it calls the important nineteen of the twenty-two possible kinds of fathers. Both of these conventional literary devices, the quest and the book-within-a-book, create a picture, and an accurate one, of a novel solidly ensconced in the English tradition.

On closer examination, however, these aspects of the novel reveal profound irony in its traditionalism. First, although the novel contains a quest, it is one that casts suspicion on the status of its quester: he is at times comatose and at other times frenetic. To begin with, the Dead Father is being towed by nineteen men who pull a cable attached by a titanium band to his waist. Still, he does perform heroic deeds: when he is not being pulled along, the Dead Father goes "slaying" through the countryside with an enormous sword, slicing up exotic animals and men. After leveling one grove of musicians, the destroyer stands pleased with himself:

The Dead Father resting with his two hands on the hilt of his sword, which was planted in the red and steaming earth.

My anger, he said proudly.

Then the Dead Father sheathing his sword pulled from his trousers his ancient prick and pissed upon the dead artists, severally and together, to the best of his ability—four minutes, or one pint. (12)

He would like to go out of control in the use of his "ancient prick," but he can find no women to participate, and he is restrained constantly in his sexual advances by Thomas, son and helper. When the Dead Father misbehaves, sexually or otherwise, Thomas raps his father squarely on the forehead in a rebuke to his authority and to the seriousness of the journey. Thus, the "aid" Thomas gives him is double-edged, as Thomas compels his father to remain, in effect, a prisoner on the quest. In doing so, Thomas is "killing me" (158), as the Dead Father complains. "Not we," Thomas answers. "Processes are killing you, not we. Inexorable processes" (158).

In the second major irony of the novel, Mother's appearance at the end reflects a pattern of feminine experience that does not belong in the traditional masculine cast of the quest. Mother, in fact, travels with the Dead Father's retinue, not as a participant, but as "a horseman on the hill" (32) following and observing its progress from a distance. When she does join the group, she does so to make a grocery list for ther children. The Dead Father states, rather pointedly, as the mysterious figure on a horse rides away: "I don't remember her very well . . . what was her name?" (170).

And not only is Mother foreign to him; his daughters Julie and Emma he sees only as possibilities for sexual conquest and is virtually unable to communicate with them. Were the Dead Father to attempt to talk to them, he would find that they, while speaking English, have a language of their own. Instead of the Germanic assertion-question-response pattern of English conversation, Julie and Emma speak a language of free association mixed with guardedly private connotations—a language of the oppressed. In the first such conversation, Julie addresses Emma:

Whose little girl are you?
I get by, I get by.
Time to go.
Hoping this will reach you at a favorable moment.
Bad things can happen to people.
Is that a threat?
Dragged him all this distance without any rootytoottoot.
Is that a threat?
Take it any way you like it.(23)

The large margin of indirection in their talk, like Mother's erratic participation in the Dead Father's journey, veers away perversely from the predictable path of formal discourse. As if not dependent on the stringencies of verbal exchange, they communicate through what is unstated but recognized as mutual experience. They do reach a destination in their conversation, but the route they take cannot be known in advance. In sum, their oblique communication and Mother's roundabout way of traveling suggest an a-linear model of behavior foreign to the rational economies associated with paternal authority.

In a third major irony of the novel, Thomas' status on the quest as helper and apparent heir to the Dead Father's pre-eminence is shown to be suspect. For example, in response to the Dead Father's command, "explain yourself. It is always interesting to hear someone explaining himself" (56), Thomas responds with a stutter, "I was bbbbbbborn twice-twenty-less one years ago in a great city" (57). Finally, after a period of poaching from government fish hatcheries and spending several years in a monastery, Thomas began reading philosophy, only to discover "that I had no talent for philosophy" (58). Two salient aspects of Thomas's explanation of himself are that he has so little success in his endeavors, and that he can sustain himself with very limited successes. Thomas implies that his strength is to be found in his failures, as the first requirement of one who would become the father is that he is willing to undergo preparation, that is, to be a son, who by definition is in a passive or subservient position.

The hidden strength in Thomas' passivity is revealed in the initiation story he tells the Dead Father. He relates that he was kidnaped and tortured by a group of men who claimed simply that he "was wrong and had always been wrong and would always be wrong" (40) and that he would be held until he "accommodated" (41). After some time Thomas was brought to see the Great Father Serpent, who "would if I answered the riddle correctly grant me a boon . . . [but] I would never answer the riddle correctly so my hopes they said, should not be got up" (43). Standing before Thomas, the "serpent of huge bigness which held in its mouth a sheet of tin on which something was written" continually calls out "for the foreskins of the uninitiated" (44). As the Great Father Serpent makes preparation for riddling, Thomas slips beneath the tin sheet and finds the answer to the riddle that was "the most arcane item in the arcana," according to the serpent. Then, the riddling begins: *"What do you really feel?"* asks the serpent. Having seen the correct answer, Thomas responds immediately, with a stutter, "Like murderinging." Shocked by receiving the right answer, the serpent has no choice but to award Thomas the ability "to carry out this foulness," but rushes to caution that "having the power [to murder] is often enough. You don't have to actually do it." Thomas, too, is stunned, for even though he steals the riddle's answer, he is struck by what *murderinging* calls up in himself: "what I was wondering and marveling at was the closeness with which what I had answered accorded with my feelings, my lost feelings that I had never found before." Underneath the facade of an obedient son, Thomas finds that he is a murderer. Then, having submitted to the Great Father Serpent's riddling, the transformed Thomas is set free by the kidnappers to be, as he says, "abroad in the city with murderinging in mind—the dream of a stutterer" (46).

In the initiation rite, an exercise in creative passivity, Thomas taps the "lost feelings that I had never found before" and acknowledges guilt for a primal crime that he has no distinct memory of committing. Yet the admission of a murderous desire makes it unnecessary for him to murder: by accepting guilt for a crime that has already taken place, Thomas need not perform the act he has acknowledged responsibility for. In effect, because Thomas identifies the source of his aggressivity, he need not play out aggression by killing fathers. This admission, and the ability to accept guilt and limitation that it implies, place him in line for the Dead Father's authority.

The psychology of his initiation is enlarged upon in "A Manual for Sons"—a document that mysteriously falls into Thomas' hands. Here the initiate's confrontation with paternal opposition is described in psychological terms: "They [fathers] block your path. They cannot be climbed over, neither can they be slithered past. They are the 'past,' and very likely the slither, if the slither is thought of as that accommodating maneuver you make to escape notice, or get by unscathed. If you attempt to go around one, you will find that another (winking at the first) has mysteriously appeared athwart the trail. Or maybe it is the same one, moving with the speed of paternity" (129). Whether a single entity or a multiple projection, the father is a principle of opposition. He is always the past, as finding is necessarily an experience of refinding, just as Thomas "refinds" the desire for murder in his confrontation with the Great Father Serpent. The meaning of the father-as-obstacle is elaborated by Julie when she explains, in a crucial passage, that after "the fucked mother conceives" and "the whelpling . . . [is] whelped . . . then the dialogue begins. The father speaks to it. . . . The 'it' whirling as in a centrifuge. Looking for something to tie to. Like a boat in a storm. What is there? The father . . . the postlike quality of the father" (77). According to the metapsychology of Julie and "A Manual for Sons," the father's dual function is to be the one who intrudes in the child's free state and also to be the primary object in relation to which the child is established in the world. That is, as the child's first intruder who blocks continuance in the "storm," the father presents a solution to a dilemma he himself creates for the child.

This metapsychological account of the rise of mind can be organized as follows: (1) the first catastrophic encounter with the father-as-object is a confusing centrifugal experience both of being spoken to and of speaking, since in the first state there is no separation between agent and receiver of an action; (2) a horizon of object relations comes up at the moment when the child finds the father as a primary object in the world and in so doing separates him- or herself from that world; (3) then, a mooring in the father-as-object lays a basis for a relationship with that world, which in turn is the matrix for all that is humanly intelligible. This world, as Julie suggests, establishes itself on the ruins of the pre-world where the father first intrudes, and her calling the father the post that orients the "it" that becomes human is a recognition of the father as a primary principle of function in mind's structure.

This recognition of the paternal function takes shape as the awareness of a dead father, as Thomas's discovery of an archaic (and latent) desire to murder a father suggests. Likewise, "A Manual for Sons" recounts the origin of the father's power in an initial patricide, after which "you must deal with the memory of a father. Often that memory is more potent than the living presence of a father, is an inner voice commanding, haranguing, yesing and noing—a binary code, yes no yes no yes no yes no, governing your every, your slightest movement, mental or physical. At what point do you become yourself? Never, wholly, you are always partly him" (144). This is, in fact, Freud's dead father, a representation of the process of internalizing symbolic authority as conscience. As Jacques Lacan puts it, "the symbolic Father is, in so far as he signifies" the law of this process, "the dead Father."[2] The passage shows that Thomas's memory of his fantasized desire for murder is the archaic expression for the father as the source of opposition, the principle of the "binary code." And the manual clearly describes a theory of mind consonant with Julie's. From this point of view, the Dead Father's old prerogatives—to love all women, to go slaying, to have his own way—are vestiges of an imaginary show of power that has less import as he gets closer to the end of the quest, his symbolic function then appearing as the true legacy to the mental life of his children.

Thus, the several traditional elements of *The Dead Father*, while anchoring the novel in the English tradition of fiction, have an underside of meaning that subverts the significance they would have in realistic fiction. First, the quest is undertaken by one whose power to act is not commensurate with the romantic (in Northrop Frye's terminology) nature of the quest, since the Dead Father must be towed along. Second, the stature of a father figure is drastically diminished by Thomas's seizure and destruction of his prerogatives. Third, women, usually goals to be accomplished and treasures to be discovered on the quest, are found here in a sphere, outside of the paternal domain, that the Dead Father has no access to. Fourth, Thomas' initiation experience reveals a great antipathy toward the father, one that leads him to imprison the Dead Father on an ambiguous journey. Last, "A Manual for Sons" tells plainly what the rest of the novel suggests all along: the father's authority is not a social force—expressed by privileged males who perform particular acts in the world—but a function within the structure of the mind that can be depicted only symbolically. The primary "endigma," then, that this novel points to, is the meaning of the Dead Father—a figure the novel presents simultaneously as a character in a fiction and as a symbolic function.

Another look at the figure of the Dead Father is in order. He is like a god who has been brought down from a great height for ritual dismemberment on earth. In his lowly state, he is being towed, cable to waist, by nineteen men to a trench where he will be buried by waiting bulldozers. Still, he has "authority," as Julie says, "fragile, yet present. He is like a bubble you do not want to burst" (67). At the same time, she states bluntly, "The father is a motherfucker" (76). The divided response of his children reflects, in a general way, the creative and destructive aspects of the Dead Father's nature. For the first part, when he copulates he is a tremendous engine of culture. With his fertile "ancient prick" he creates objects in the world, various things like the poker chip, the punching bag, both light and heavy, the midget Bible, the slot-machine chip, the Saving & Loan Association, "Six and three quarters per cent compounded momentarily . . . I guarantee it," and people, "some thousands of children of the ordinary sort" (pp. 36–38). In his destructive phase, he turns around to plow under his creations with the same glee he took in making them. This rapaciousness, represented by his "ancient prick" and swinging sword, knows no restraint, only its own desire and expression. For instance, after he has given a speech of ponderous gobbledygook to the retinue pulling him and is asked what the speech meant, he answers, "Thank you . . . it meant I made a speech" (51). He believes that all utterance expresses himself. He says: "All lines [are] my lines. All figure and all ground mine, out of my head. All colors mine" (19). His is a primary encounter with the world by which he knows no bounds and strikes nothing to check his progress. Or, rather, he finds a way of discounting obstacles so that he appears to remain unencumbered. "Having it both ways," he says truthfully, "is a thing I like" (15).

This comic characterization is a rough but accurate representation of the paternal function, a self-contained opposition contingent on nothing outside of itself. Still, as one who swaggeringly copulates and slays, a variation of the composite authoritarian figure with glasses and suit and vest, he is only one image of opposition, one not precisely equivalent to the symbolic father. Suggesting more of the symbolic function (in a theory of mind) described by

Julie and "A Manual for Sons" is the operation that goes on in the Dead
Father's left leg. Inside it is a mechanism that works "ceaselessly night and
day through all the hours for the good of all." The leg contains "small booths
with sliding doors" in which people confess their sin and guilt. "The confessions are taped, scrambled, recomposed, dramatized, and then appear in the
city's theaters, a new feature-length film every Friday. One can recognize
moments of one's own, sometimes" (4). Thus, into the left leg's process of
transformation goes the raw material of guilt and pain, and out of it come the
articulations of being human and the connections with a deeper self, the
products of culture. To be sure, the Dead Father as a character is a megaloma-
niacal, narcissistic sacker of reality, that is, a hard-edged caricature of the
father, but his children need what he makes possible—culture.

It is curious that the paternal symbolic function is lodged casually in the
Dead Father's left leg; but then he only took on this function, as he explains
to his son, because "mechanical experience was a part of experience there was
room for, in my vastness. I wanted to know what machines know." And what
do they know? "Machines are sober, uncomplaining, endlessly efficient, and
work ceaselessly through all the hours for the good of all" (13). The Dead
Father manifests the symbolic process—the metapsychology Julie describes,
the creation of conscience "A Manual for Sons" explains, and the cultural
production derived from guilt, "a new feature-length film every Friday"—in
the innocuous left leg, a member of his body not connected with his particular swaggering personality (the leg, in fact, is detachable!). This tenuous link
emphasizes that the symbolic process, though based on paternal opposition,
is not synonymous with this image of the father, this paternal image being an
imperfect indicator of that process.

It is essential to the concept of the symbolic father that any one image
fall short of encompassing the symbol; in fact, an image of the father must
fail so that the place it leaves empty can indicate the symbolic function and
not the particularity of the agent of that function.[3] The Dead Father, for
instance, is classified by his children as "an old fart" (10), one whose time has
passed and who, therefore, is no longer needed: to ease him out, Thomas
systematically denies him privileges and, at last, any participation with his
children. The Dead Father even comes to view himself as inadequate, reflecting in a Molly-Bloom-like interior monologue on what he as a father did not
know: "There were things I never knew[:] . . . what made the leaves fi-
brillate on the trees . . . what made the heart stop and how unicorns got
trapped in tapestries. . . . But AndI dealt out 1,856,700 slaps with the open
hand and 22,009,800 boxes on the ear." In short, he was busy dominating
others and "never figured out figured out wot sort of animal AndI was.
Endshrouded in endigmas. Never knew wot's wot" (p. 172). At the end of
the quest, as the Dead Father is bulldozed into the trench, the symbolic
authority of his left leg is taken up, internalized, by his children; he dies, in
effect, so that his function can be reborn in those who have relations with

him. The narrator's relief that the Dead Father "is not perfect, thank God for that" alludes to the ncessity of paternal failure—death or absence—so that the symbol may be signified—somewhat as the death of an ancestor makes a totem possible. "We *want* the Dead Father to be dead," the narrator proclaims, so that the *father* may belong to his children.

This novel's manner of signifying the father structurally belongs to tradition: like the fathers in *Robinson Crusoe, Tom Jones,* and *Huckleberry Finn* the father must be lost so that, in his absence, his function can be known. From the structural point of view, in fact, it is father absence, not presence, that signifies the father: the father is lost so that his meaning can be found symbolically. At the same time, the manner in which the father is presented here is not a mere repetition. Barthelme draws his paternal material from the rogues' gallery of traditional images, compresses it into a single image of the father, then allows that image to fall like a straw man, leaving the locus of the father in its place. In this way, Barthelme's novel uses the material of the realistic novel to advance beyond the realistic novel and is at once thoroughly traditional and post-modern. Not truly satiric or parodic, possibilities that would orient *The Dead Father* toward a merely traditional depiction of the father, this fiction employs irony to undermine its own materials in order to signify the father anew.

So, simultaneously a representation of the rogues' gallery of fathers (the whole of the paternal tradition) and a denial of paternity, the Dead Father's character comprises a fiction at a high level of abstraction. A fiction dealing in these cerebral strokes—the whole of the paternal tradition in fiction is evoked and then desiccated—verges on defining itself more as criticism than as fiction. For one thing, to posit fiction at this level of abstraction is to gamble reader engagement on very thin odds: character, plot, theme, setting, and symbolism—all are tossed into a sea of abstraction that only specialized knowledge (a critical awareness) of the English tradition and its underlying structures can navigate. The danger of avant-garde fiction has been voiced before, about *Ulysses* and *Finnegans Wake,* about Faulkner's novels, and about many others; with Joyce and Faulkner, readers have come into being because their novels needed reading—they were too important to be left unread. The special boldness (and danger) of Barthelme's fiction is that it flirts with surface nonsense, as does much fiction by William Gass, Thomas Pynchon, John Barth, Hunter Thompson, and Tom Robbins. This flirtation creates the appearance of peripatetic elements (the name "Oedipa Maas" in *The Crying of Lot 49* is a good example) that are methodically drained of their significance, so that the father—as a principle of order—is continually promised, but his articulation is deferred, sometimes indefinitely. This narrative technique, an apparent abnegation of the father, can be deciphered as fictional sense only at another level very far removed from the play of images and from what is commonly known as texture—elements that traditionally convey the pleasure of the text for readers.

Of course, in the structural consideration of a text, the novel that can be comprehended never lacks an indication of the father. "Every narrative," as Roland Barthes says, "is a staging of the (absent, hidden, or hypostatized) father,"[4] and the loss of that staging "would deprive literature of many of its pleasures."[5] And it must be admitted that one alternative to the father in fiction could be to abandon pleasure and to strive for a blissful state of unintelligible rapture, a lyric gesture. It is here, then, between two fictional possibilities that Barthelme's novel is to be understood. On one side of it is what Barthes calls "pleasure"—*jouir,* the state of recognition and comprehension—and on the other is what he calls "bliss—*jouissance,* the ecstasy of being transported. Within these coordinates, nearly abjuring comprehension, *The Dead Father* hurtles toward blissful transport.

In this search for bliss, *The Dead Father* wagers the ancient bet that the father may be seized in his totality, directly: it tries to grasp his essential shape—in effect, to break through his pasteboard mask. This ambitious striving, a strike against tradition, necessarily requires a sacrifice of pleasure, one that Barthelme boldly makes. That the bet is lost and the father not seized are foregone conclusions; that loss is as much a part of the ritual of fiction-making as is the need to take such risks. Paradoxically, it is in that necessary "failure" at the level of narrative structure, wherein the father is not seized in his totality, that the novel signifies most directly the paternal symbol it cannot possess.

Notes

1. *The Dead Father* (New York: Farrar, Straus, and Giroux, 1975), pp. 3–4. Further page references to this novel will appear in the text.
2. Jacques Lacan, *Écrits: A Selection,* trans. Alan Sheridan (New York: W. W. Norton, 1977), p. 199.
3. Jacques Lacan describes this situation theoretically when he says, "the failure of the signifier in the Other, as locus of the signifier, is the significance of the Other as locus of the law." *Écrits,* p. 221.
4. Roland Barthes, *The Pleasure of the Text,* trans. Richard Miller (New York: Hill and Wang, 1975), p. 10.
5. Barthes, *The Pleasure of the Text,* p. 47.

Metamorphosis and Possession:
An Investigation into
the Interchapters of
Overnight to Many Distant Cities

MICHAEL TRUSSLER

Ernest Hemingway once described the structure of *In Our Time,* with its vignettes interspersed between the stories, as being similar to the effect of observing a coastline from a ship. A vignette, he suggested, offers a view of the "whole," as might be seen from a distance with the naked eye, and the story was an elaboration of detail that could be compared to viewing the same coastline with a pair of binoculars.[1] What is helpful to the reader about Hemingway's analogy is that it allows for the orchestration of various motifs and voices that occur throughout *In Our Time* by suggesting a consistent dualism: there is a coast; there is an observer. Barthelme, in *Overnight to Many Distant Cities,* parodies the textual architecture of *In Our Time* through the use of italicized interchapters, but in a way that exceeds the perimeters of the earlier text: Hemingway's vignettes, although composed of disparate voices, retain the shared reference of the difficulty of achieving *communitas* in a violent world and are subsumed by a final, possibly central voice; the interchapters of *Overnight to Many Distant Cities* barely possess a common syntax. Utilizing pastiche, they move from resonances of Milton to a reenactment of contemporary performance art, witnessed by Benvenuto Cellini, as might be photographed by Joel-Peter Witkin. The movement between coastline and observer, accentuating the vagaries of perception (helpful to an interpretation of Hemingway by providing a locus), shifts and blurs with Barthelme; instead of providing unity, the interchapters function tangentially.

Barthelme's ludic parody tempts the reader to locate, despite an uncertain cartography, the perimeters of his text by tracing its many origins and in so doing, to create a cohesive method of reading. This temptation is augmented by the repetition of various motifs, verbal and imagistic, that seem to streamline the text, but Barthelme's juxtaposition and resituating of the past result in an elasticity that defies narrative coherence. The text does

This essay was written specifically for this volume and is published here for the first time by permission of the author.

create an idiom suggesting the persistence of memory, but it is an idiom that places Nietzsche beside Beckett beside Cinderella, the hopes of modernist architecture next to the metamorphoses of the ancient Welsh poet Taliesin. Taking a suggestion from the title of the collection, this is a journey occurring overnight to many places, perhaps simultaneously, which suggests the significance of dreams and the internal lexicon belonging to them. There is the invitation to read *Overnight to Many Distant Cities* through, for instance, Hemingway's text, but doing so in a strict fashion would perhaps do little else than remind the reader of Hemingway's reliance on *The Waste Land*. This does not mean that *In Our Time* is intertextually absent, but through the elasticity of Barthelme's text, evocative of the collage technique he has used previously, the identity of the past is altered by being presented in a state of flux. Instead of an observer viewing a coastline, boundaries and perspective have been jettisoned, and the reader must hover over uncertainty.

Overnight to Many Distant Cities then, is a text that particularly denies possession by the reader. A stable identification of the perimeters of either a word or a motif is precluded, owing to a complex metamorphosis that affects the various components of the text. Recognition of the shape possessed by details in the text must be provisional since the shape is temporary; that which appears to "represent" a certain signification in one portion of the text becomes fundamentally altered in another. It is largely through the interchapters that this metamorphosis is most apparent.

I

It is axiomatic that in order to read one must recognize, in general terms, the code initially offered by a text. It is the subsequent transition, the reader's attempt to circumscribe the dimensions of the code of a particular text through a perception of context, that is Barthelme's gambit. Barthelme does not as much attack this attempt as he takes advantage of it. The reader is given, as Charles Molesworth describes, a narrative that incorporates a readily identifiable mode of discourse, only to discover that: "instead of a recognizable narrative logic, we get a series of gaps and discontinuities, which are felt as such because there is almost a sense of continuity in the description."[2] I would argue that part of the shape of Barthelme's discourse is dependent upon the oscillation between surprise and frustration in the attempt to determine, through an ever-expanding denial of the reader's ability to do so successfully, the meaning of context. One of the means that Barthelme uses to exploit this process would seem to be the creation of interchapters, since this technique creates the suggestion of a taxonomy; separating different forms of narrative invites the possibility that there are levels of narrative that may be seen against each other, thus delineating a shape to determine context. Upon investigation, however, it becomes evident that the interchapters themselves contain a proliferation of various modes of discourse, "a series of gaps and discontinuities" that dismantle the construction of a continuous "recognizable" narrative.

Overnight to Many Distant Cities begins with a voice recalling an event that precedes the narrative—"[t]hey called for more structure, then"[3]—immediately placing the reader's ability "to identify the deictic co-ordinates"[4] of the narrative in jeopardy. An anonymous "they" have somehow, in a distant time, influenced the shape of the narrative. The scope of the word "structure" is unknown; it may refer to the construction of presumably metaphoric cities; it may also indicate self-reflexivity but in an ironic manner, since a call for more structure "then" does not mean that it is necessarily being practised now.

The recounting of previous exploits, "Babel, Chandigarh, Brasilia, Taliesin," is perhaps the point where context is most radically redefined.[5] As a list in a series, there is the suggestion of commonality, but if this is so, the series follows an internal logic that defies external signification. Chandigarh, one of Corbusier's "radiant cities," meets, easily enough perhaps, Brasília, an example of twentieth-century urban planning, but the identity of Brasília is possibly unstable since there is a reference, in "The Sea of Hesitation," to an "architectural anomaly," a building constructed in the shape of a triangle. Since Costa's Brasília is designed also in the shape of an equilateral triangle, the reference to Chandigarh is different, since it is not an adumbration of something else in the text. Babel exacerbates the dilemma of interpretation, not only owing to the incipient suggestions of an atavistic plurality of discourses and subsequent commentaries—to name one, Barthelme's emphasis of the building materials coming from the "back sheds" recalls Kafka's parable of Babel, "The City Coat of Arms," where the emphasis is upon not the tower itself, but the construction of the city surrounding the edifice, which calls into question "what Babel is Barthelme referring to?"—but further, Barthelme's linking, through the series, of Babel with Taliesin perplexes the meaning of the spatial. On one level the word "Taliesin" refers to Frank Lloyd Wright's series of houses, but through Wright's admiration of Richard Hovey's masque based on the Welsh poet, which influenced his choice of names for the organicist architectural experiment, the word "Taliesin" in Barthelme's text takes on literary as well as architectural overtones. What does it mean for a group of architects to build, alongside Brasília, the name of an ancient Welsh poet, who, like Homer, perhaps did not exist but who is granted mythological authority over a group of poems? As a parody of the arcana involved in reading a modernist text, this is a critique by an author who knows that his work will be anatomized: "The forest will soon exist on some maps, tribute to the quickness of the world's cartographers" (p. 164); but it also suggests metamorphosis and the pleasure of creation, something not far from the voice of the first interchapter. Taliesin's birth was complex. Beginning as a blue salmon, moving to a dog, a stag, a piece of dirt picked up by a chicken, diamonding down eventually to a drill in a smithy, he finally achieved human incarnation, a process possible only through narration.[6] Babel, Chandigarh, Brasília, and Taliesin are, then, the accomplishments of an architect who labors to construct "invisible cities," cities which are the result of narrative.

The reader is confronted with the possibility that the interchapter is composed of a plurality of codes, although the sentences have the appearance of running together continuously. There is the suggestion of a symbolic use of language, the eight-mile run suggesting infinity, and the paradigmatic in a Joycean sense ("clad in red Lego, at the point where the new river will be activated"), offering Logos and riverrun past Eve and Adam's. Some of the sentences are proleptic, the areas of the city that "had been designed to rot" prefigure Alexandra, the "designer of artificial ruins." The phrase, "the pens containing the fawns" possesses overtones of metafictional discourse through the pun on the word "pens." Such a fracturing of levels of discourse, under the appearance of continuity, places the reader in a position of suspension: meaning is not as much deferred as it is scattered.

The layout of the city under construction, seen from a great height, suggesting the photogramic studies in perspective done by L. Moholy-Nagy in the twenties, demonstrates "the shape of the word FASTIGIUM," which is not the name of the city but a word from the interchapter and drags it through a dictionary, one discovers that it has architectural (fastigium being a gable or a summit) and historical (the word Babylon meaning the "gate of the gods") dimensions, as well as literary complications (fastigium meaning "the highlight of a story"). The idea of the city as a word that may be read, reminiscent of Campanella's *City of the Sun,* which demarcates a Utopian city that is to be understood as a book, involves lexicological pursuits that, threatening to turn the city into an iconic sign, collapse the act of reading into absurdity. Barthelme ironically entices the reader into performing an etymological excavation of the meaning of his text perhaps to suggest not the futility of doing so, but the enigmatic dilemma involved in reading contextually a piece of writing that eventually defies signification, for the word "FASTIGIUM" may have as its genesis only the elegance of its script; as a parody of the concrete poem, it may exist as an object that is "defamiliarized," resting on a landscape of words.

The first interchapter densely creates, not a cipher with which to read the developing collection, although I believe that metamorphosis plays a dominant role in *Overnight to Many Distant Cities,* but a ubiquitous confrontation of often contradictory codes that, when recognized, call into question the mechanics available for reading. The final words of the text, "[t]omorrow, fair and warmer, warmer and fair, most fair . . ." borrowed from the "situation report" in *Snow White,*[7] are a meteorological drawl that transforms "they called for more structure," through the colloquial use of "they called for" (suggesting the weatherman) into a playful forecast that delineates, among other things, the manner in which language overpowers the strictures of narrative. The attempt to determine context in this particular piece of writing entails breaking down the sentences, because of the fragmenting effects of excessive signification, into separate units, whether phrases or words. The effect of this is that the individual sentences are structured in such a way that they function as a collage more than as a means of conveying a continuous narrative. One way to describe this is to posit the existence of "gaps and discontinuities" within the narrative; another approach is to consider the sentences in the first interchapter to be surrealist constructions that are an imbrication of incongruous, although collaborating, juxtapositions.

II

In the first part of this essay I explored some of the complexities and ambiguities of context. This entailed, necessarily, stepping outside the "frame" of the interchapter in an attempt to demarcate not so much the limitations of the text but the many directions that it points toward. To expand a text in this manner is also to narrow the range of its narrative(s). A text does take place in language and history, but an overreliance on external signification when reading may mitigate recognition of narrative's provisional power to absorb meaning and signification. In other words, although a text may be splintered by either "difference" or an author's decision to present fragmentary discourse, narrative may also subsume meaning, not as an artifact nor as a repository, but as the means by which meaning/unmeaning is articulated.

Consider briefly the interchapter titled "Willie & Wade" (pp. 77–78). In this interchapter, which verges on being a parable, a fan imaginatively addresses a pair of mutually interchangeable recording stars, who are granted the ability to empathize with any given scenario. Not only does this dynamic duo have the ability to say "I know" to an expanse that encapsulates all human experience, but they also maintain the secret individuality of the fan involved. Willie & Wade are ordinary guys who are also—by extension—the ultimate audience; they understand the unique standpoint of the narrator and privilege him/her with their understanding to such an extent that the narrator could easily change places with them. There is, naturally, no need to actually do this, because Willie & Wade already understand this identification, thereby avoiding some economic unpleasantness. As social commentary, the interchapter "Well we all had our Willie & Wade records . . ." displays unequivocally the power of Nietzsche's "ascetic priest" in contemporary terms, making one wish that Alexis de Tocqueville could have witnessed the pivotal role that the entertainment industry plays in American culture; however, I would like to treat this interchapter as a springborad to discuss the enfolding aspects of narrative demonstrated in other portions of the text. Just as Willie & Wade can encapsulate reality for the believer, blurring the subjective and the objective, narrative may fold within its interstices both the razor-blading of discontinuous discourse and the panoply of containment.

In the interchapter "I put a name in an envelope . . ." (pp. 37–38), Prospero would seem to merge with Jacques Derrida. A mysteriously unnamed "name" is placed within an envelope and then, through an ever-expanding Russian-doll style of metamorphosis, finally usurps narratorial power by walking away "most confidently." It would appear that through this interchapter Barthelme balances metafictional artiflce against the loss of narratorial control: "it fell out of the history of art into a wastebasket, a thing I could not have predicted." The difficulty of extratextual signification is suggested by the envelope being sent to Fichtelgebirge, a mountain range in West Germany whose principal city is Bayreuth, linking it perhaps to Nietzsche and Wagner, but the emphasis in the interchapter is on a paradox: narrative may carry the "name" but not reveal it. The narrator's attempt to encase the name, to clothe it with discourse, is futile; like a dangerous acid that burns through all containers, the meaning of the name evades revelation. Proteus, in Barthelme, could not be forced to show his genuine form. The "aporia" that the name "represents" is situated somewhere in the narrative through a difficult dialectic: narrative as an empty mirror, a laughing staircase, a pair of invisible eyes, may elide meaning but it also absorbs it since the absence of meaning is dependent upon narrative to give it formlessness. Narrative may well be a mirage instead of a window, but the narrator is a voice and a structure that situate a place where questions of ontology have more relevance than questions of truth. My earlier suggestion that Barthelme's prose is saturated with a degree and variety of signification that destroy concatenation needs the corresponding idea that an interchapter may also possess an internal dimension of signification partially suspended from external reference. Different from the nondiscursive "strength of stones,"[8] narrative is a construct that temporarily creates its own order, an order that does not convey meaning as much as shape a place that takes part in language but is also removed from it. The name that cannot be read (or designated a place) engenders, in this interchapter, a narrative, which in turn seems to repudiate its origin. The futile attempt to place the name becomes a crystalline movement, suggesting Protean metamorphosis, that burrows through various levels of signification, then leaps finally to swallow itself by shifting into "the new blue suit" and walking away. This is not to say that narrative is sacrosanct, as are Willie & Wade, in that it is a magical mechanism that possesses the capability to say anything, however whimsical, but that Barthelme's narrative moves in two directions: it is an affirmation that undermines and negates itself. The three kings may be placed within a blue suit as monarchs, as face cards, or as words changing into other words; each transition is a metamorphosis, a light suggestion that narrative may be a statement and a question simultaneously.

III

In a text that refers to structure as frequently as this one does, there is always the possibility that an attempt to determine a specific structure may very well be a literary cul-de-sac. The temptation to regard *Overnight to Many Distant Cities* as different from Barthelme's previous collections of short stories is strong, since it possesses an overt structure with literary antecedents. It is helpful to recall, regarding this text concerned with the building of cities, that part of the ethos of modernist architecture, the urge to civilize people, is obliquely criticized in "The Sea of Hesitation": "I began to wonder if behavior *should be* changed" (p. 96). In *Paradise,* Simon refers to the "messianic-maniacal idea that architecture will make people better" and goes on to argue that contemporary architecture, rather than being "soulless," resembles a "circus."[9] It is helpful perhaps to link the structure of *Overnight to Many Distant Cities* to the manner in which postmodernist architectural theorists regard the past. Linda Hutcheon cites Robert Stern in *A Theory of Parody:* "Our attitude toward form, which is based in a love for history and an awareness of it, does not imply accurate reproduction. It is eclectic and is used as a technique of collage and juxtaposition, to give new meaning to known forms and thereby goes off in new directions. Our faith is in the power of memory (history). . . ."[10] I do not wish to identify Barthelme's text too closely with architectural theories; reproducing an architectural motif is considerably different from doing the same in literary terms and in some ways is much less complex owing to the difference in media. Words possess different perplexities than brick, concrete, and glass. However, Stern's discussion of eclecticism is valuable in that it suggests the way that *In Our Time* and other modernist words may have a ghostly presence in Barthelme's text: they are not "accurately reproduced" but are interwoven in such a way that they alter signification as much as they are changed, compounding the problem of making connections in the fluidity of a postmodernist text.

A dilemma facing the reader of *Overnight to Many Distant Cities* is that Barthelme's text teems with allusions, making it "a virtual anthology without a binding,"[11] but, through the modification of juxtaposition, the components of the anthology are themselves transformed. For example, in the story "The Mothball Fleet," the Admiral-waiter tells the narrator that he has "heard the singing of the wounded and witnessed the burial of the dead" (p. 130). T. S. Eliot is often not far from Barthelme's stories, either in *Overnight to Many Distant Cities* or elsewhere, and the Admiral's words would seem to be a juxtaposition of "Prufrock" and *The Waste Land.* (In effect, one could argue that Barthelme is parodying Eliot's technique of juxtaposition by neatly setting Prufrock against *The Waste Land.*) However, an allusion to Eliot in a story that involves the silent theft of a stockpiled armada (perhaps the story is a conceit that plays with Eliot's opinions regarding literary theft) seems to identify one of the intriguing aspects of the technique of juxtaposition: the "original" text is modified as much as it modifies. In other words, the presence of Prufrock and *The Waste Land* in the story invites an interpretation that incorporates these allusions, but this process of interpretation is frustrated since the matrix of the story alters the identity of the lines from Eliot. The juxtapositioning of Eliot and a waiter with "mustard on his coat" provides for humor, but it also suggests that the significance of Eliot's poetry has been irrevocably altered. Stern's remarking that collage gives a "new meaning" to the past is perhaps not explicit enough; postmodernistic collage, by resituating the past, fundamentally transforms it. The components of a collage are in a state of flux.

Further, the complexity involved in determining the significance of specific images or references in the text is compounded when one tries to isolate them. The story "Visitors" mentions "a fellow with oddly-cut hair the color of marigolds and a roll of roofing felt over his shoulder" (p. 16), which would appear to be a detail that the reader can identify as "realistic." To interpret this golden-haired workman as someone that Bishop could conceivably notice while "walking down West Broadway on a Saturday afternoon" is problematic when one considers that the previous interchapter is spoken through the voice of a worker who is involved with some rather complex architectural projects. Having a workman from the first interchapter wandering through another portion of the text would suggest that the text is an ongoing work-in-progress. Reminiscent of Macintosh in *Ulysses,* insofar as the man with the roofing felt demonstrates overt authorial control, perhaps this man's presence offers the suggestion that the borders of the interchapters and stories are a membrane through which different parts of the text may pass freely. To insist that there is a definite relationship between the interchapter and the short story would be unsound; nevertheless, a connection does appear to exist. The dilemma that faces the reader is that the status of any given portion of the text is always uncertain. Potentially each detail of the text may be affected by an image or a phrase that occurs elsewhere, making the act of reading a provisional process.

As with the package containing the name that falls out of a vault in a history of art into a wastebasket, something that the narrator could not have predicted, various motifs rove through the text. For instance, Bishop's daughter, "at vivid moments" in a horror movie, jumps "against him, pressing her breasts into his back" (p. 14); this mirrors the "bogle" Hannahbella sleeping with the Bottom-like Duncan: "move a bit so that your back fits better with my front" (p. 156). Streamlining, or "staining" (*Snow White*) a text with recurrent images, phrases, and such is not of course something that Barthelme has invented. It is perhaps a parody of the conventions of realism or a parody of Hemingway's technique of utilizing the leitmotif, but in a writer as self-conscious as Barthelme, such devices also raise questions regarding the status of discourse and the nature of structure. The use of parody in *Overnight to Many Distant Cities,* directed externally or bent inward toward the text itself, may not be making a facsimile as much as it is creating a kind of synthesis where the identity of the original begins to fade. The presence of either component wavers, and this undermines the structure of the text since little may be clearly extricated.

In a text such as Barthelme's *Overnight to Many Distant Cities,* structure may perhaps not be a grid that the reader, after recognizing a rudimentary, skeletal framework within the body of the text, provisionally superimposes upon the text. Patterns do exist, but I think that they exist to accentuate the problems of formulating structure when the bricks, glass, and cement of a literary narrative are words. The difficulty of reading words is adroitly depicted in *Paradise:* " 'The dust in your poems,' Simon asks, 'is it always the same dust? Does it always mean the same thing? Or does it mean one thing in one poem and another thing in another poem?' . . . 'My dust,' she says, 'my excellent dust. You're a layman, Simon, shut up about my dust' " (p. 157).

Simon's curiosity regarding the role that an arrangement of words plays in affecting the signification of a single word, possibly colored by his background as an architect, is an extension of the difficulties of formalism: "a word incorporated into verse is, as it were, wrenched from ordinary speech, [and] surrounded with a new aura of meaning. . . ."[12] The relationship between literary discourse and "ordinary speech" possibly deserves to be discussed eleswhere, but Exjenbaum's description of "a new aura of meaning" is relevant, through extrapolation, to a text that utilizes the technique of juxtaposition.

Overnight to Many Distant Cities frequently stretches the boundaries surrounding the signification of words. For instance, the relatively mundane but symbolically heavy word *blue* is able to uphold the suit that walks away as well as being a possibility for painting the trucks that may or may not exist in the story "Wrack." Is this creating "a new aura of meaning" for the word *blue* or is it dismantling what the word signifies? What is the relationship between the use of words by a character such as Bishop, who, as a "realistic" construction of words, seems to possess the ability to place his own particular stamp on words (the "Art History lecture"), and the disembodied voices in "Wrack" who speak often through association only, rather than from a position of control? For instance, they seem to care for a moment about Boethius, but it appears to be the result of rolling words together:

—And Social Security.
—A great consolation.
—And philosophy. Furthermore.
—I read a book. Just the other day. (p. 135)

Simon's question is a phenomenological inquiry that threatens to dismantle the idea of structure at its base, just as Babel destroyed the unifying vision of an Adamic language, since structure is partially formed through repetition and, if "dust" is different every time, only the illusion of repetition is possible. This is not to say that "dust" must necessarily be either different or the same every time (perhaps Simon's lover criticized him for his asking the question); however, to dismiss the inquiry as being naive is perhaps not entirely judicious. Both Simon and Ejxenbaum center on the isolation of one word and the possibility of its subsequent alteration in different clusters of words. When one expands this to include all the words in a phrase, each altering the others and being altered simultaneously, one is nearly in the dimension of subatomic physics. Using this model, one can argue that structure does exist in *Overnight to Many Distant Cities,* but it would seem to be evanescent.

IV

Up to this point I have been treating words as signifiers that possess a multitude of potential significations. Tracing the correspondences between signifier and signified(s) is necessary for the act of reading, but it entails an important omission. The "gap" between signifier and signified has been thoroughly discussed in literary and linguistic studies, but perhaps it needs to be mentioned once again regarding Barthelme's writing—not to repeat that it is there, but to briefly examine what it does. Signification may be utilized so that it seems to deny itself, not necessarily to create new levels of meaning, but to accentuate the distance between meaning and writing.

The final interchapter, one of the more overtly fantastic, "I am, at the moment . . ." (p. 163) is an arabesque that cannot be "read," at least in the ordinary sense of the word. Involving an "alchemy" of signification, which is visionary without being allegorical, it defies logical analysis and wavers on the point of being (as Anna Balakian describes Mallarmé) "so hermetic as to remain in the Closed Book of one man's mind."[13] Parts of the interchapter are vaguely reminiscent of earlier interchapters, specifically "Speaking of the human body . . ." (p. 89), with its "genuine nameless animals" and reversal of ordinary order (people living on the street, having "abandoned" their houses to subway trains), suggesting the exotic "chandeliers" and animals of the final interchapter. There is also a faint outline of external texts. Holding a ladder recalls Babel through Jacob (Genesis 28:12), since both events were occasions of a meeting between heaven and earth, but the image becomes much more diffuse when one recalls Borges's story, "The Library of Babel": "no book can be a ladder, although no doubt there are books which discuss and negate and demonstrate this possibility and others whose structure corresponds to that of a ladder."[14] Although this interchapter resembles one of Borges's fables by being a place that has not yet been mapped, I do not think that it is profitable to read it through Borges or the other interchapters, owing to the hallucinogenic "ornamentation" of the text.[15]

Molesworth cites Barthes's proairetic code to comment on Barthelme's techniques for creating ambiguity: "For Barthes, this code depends on the notion of the 'already-seen, already-read, already done'; in other words, it's a form of describing actions so the reader can readily identify them as stable, known activities without having to break them down into component actions."[16] This particular interchapter would seem to be a repudiation or a complete inversion of this code since, outside of the fairy-tale, there are few stable referents available to the reader. Instead of interpreting this interchapter by recognizing various levels of external signification and then assimilating them into the text, the reader must place himself in the hands of the narrator, as is suggested by the voice addressing an indefinite "you." Interpreting the interchapter becomes less important than listening to the narrator's voice; signification is not denied, but is so internally directed that the gap separating signifier from signified is sealed to such a degree that the reader is unable to enter it. This is not solipsistic in the sense of being isolationist but instead is a use of words that alters the meaning of context: in a sense, the words can have no context other than themselves. Signification in this interchapter, unlike the first interchapter, is precise: "red hams" refers to "red hams" and perhaps "the already-beautiful." If one attempted to remove the quotation marks from the words and shift their meaning to other words, either in an intertextual or intratextual sense, the attempt would fail and the piece would collapse. The reader is not, in this sense, confronted with the post-Babel forms of language, which, as George Steiner describes, necessitate translation; rather, this interchapter borders the "pure" language predicted in Zephaniah. (I say "borders," rather than "enters," because the form of language predicted in Zephaniah is as yet, contradistinguished from the memory of an Adamic language, ineffable.) The interchapter presents a form of language that precludes translation; writing is separate from meaning, which is not to say that this interchapter is meaningless in a perjorative sense; rather, the reader must suspend the desire to determine signification. In a sense then, the final interchapter is the most radical experiment in the text. As a kind of "pure" narration, it exists through itself and defies possession by the reader.

The reader's need to suspend signification in this interchapter extends, in varying degrees, to the other interchapters. As a development in Barthelme's style, the interchapters provide many temptations. The reader is invited, through them, to explore the labyrinth of intertextual and intratextual signification present in *Overnight to Many Distant Cities,* to toy with shape and structure; but *Overnight to Many Distant Cities* resists final imposition. Enigmatic and sometimes obscure, the interchapters investigate the protean nature of narrative, which in turn is an examination of the mechanics of reading.

Notes

1. Carlos Baker, *Ernest Hemingway* (Harmondsworth: Penguin, 1972), 203–4.

2. Charles Molesworth, *Donald Barthelme's Fiction* (Columbia: University of Missouri Press, 1982), 50–51.

3. Donald Barthelme, *Overnight to Many Distant Cities* (New York: G. P. Putnam's Sons, 1983), 9.

4. Maurice Couturier and Regis Durand, *Donald Barthelme* (New York: Methuen, 1982), 64.

5. The following argument has been aided by Foucault's discussion of Borges's " 'certain Chinese encyclopaedia' " where he analyzes the implications of a taxonomy that exceeds Western conceptions. Such a taxonomy, incorporating an impossible structuring of classification, can only be possible, according to Foucault, through discourse. See Michel Foucault, *The Order of Things* (London: Tavistock, 1974), xv.

6. Gwyn Williams, *An Introduction To Welsh Poetry* (London: Faber, 1953), 30. It is interesting to note that in connection to the reference to Corbusier's "radiant city," Taliesin means "radiant brow."

7. Donald Barthelme, *Snow White* (New York: Atheneum, 1967), 120. The connections that *Overnight to Many Distant Cities* has to other parts of Barthelme's writing are complex. For the most part, there are only echoes of texts that were published prior to *Overnight to Many Distant Cities*. Subsequent publications, however, specifically *Forty Stories* (1987), include minor changes, such as the interchapter "Financially, the paper . . ." appearing in prose form under a different title, and major alterations, such as the extensive changes in the story "Wrack," entitled "Rif" in the 1987 collection.

8. Donald Barthelme, *Forty Stories* (New York: Penguin, 1987), 163.

9. Donald Barthelme, *Paradise* (New York: Penguin, 1986), 69.

10. Linda Hutcheon, *A Theory of Parody* (New York: Methuen, 1985), 114.

11. Molesworth, *Donald Barthelme's Ficiton,* 60.

12. B.M. Ejxenbaum, "The Theory of the Formal Method," in *Readings in Russian Poetics,* ed. L. Matejka and K. Pomorska (Ann Arbor: Michigan Slavic Publications, 1978), 26. Recognizing that Ejxenbaum was arguing about poetry rather than prose, I would suggest, along with many others, that generic borders have collapsed in postmodern writing.

13. Anna Balakian, *Surrealism* (Chicago: University of Chicago Press, 1986), 144.

14. Jorge Luis Borges, *Labyrinths,* ed. Donald A. Yates and James E. Irby (New York: New Directions, 1964), 57.

15. Frank Lloyd Wright, as well as a number of other architects, hovers in the background of *Overnight to Many Distant Cities*. It is possible that this interchapter may owe something to the "dendriform" columns of the Johnson Wax administration Building.

16. Molesworth, *Donald Barthelme's Fiction,* 50.

Living Arrangements:
On Donald Barthelme's *Paradise*

PATRICK O'DONNELL

Shall our blood fail? Or shall it come to be
The blood of paradise? And shall the earth
Seem all of paradise that we shall know?
The sky will be much friendlier then than now,
A part of labor and a part of pain,
And next in glory to enduring love,
Not this dividing and indifferent blue.
————Wallace Stevens, "Sunday Morning"

Donald Barthelme's third novel, *Paradise* (1986), is, perhaps, his least-read and most disregarded work. Poorly received by many reviewers, it appears to be Barthelme's failed attempt to write in a more traditional novelistic mode. Even at that, its status as a novel remains questionable, as it is, conceivably, a patchwork of more recognizably Barthelmean short fictions (such as the exchanges between the protagonist, Simon, and his physician scattered throughout *Paradise,* and collated in the story "Basil from Her Garden" previously published in the *New Yorker*) cobbled together to form a series of interrelated vignettes of uneven intensity and quality. In *Paradise,* there is, ostensibly, a more conventional narrative situation than can be found in *Snow White* or *The Dead Father.* Here, those familiar bourgeois subjects of the traditional novel—middle age, adultery, marriage, and domesticity—are at issue, and the autobiographical elements of the novel are foregrounded (Simon is a Philadelphia architect; he has experienced a failed marriage and is recently divorced; he is taking a sabbatical from marriage in Manhattan) while its fabulistic qualities are largely confined to Simon's dreams. And while the major events of *Paradise* may arise from the projection of a male fantasy (three beautiful young women, looking for a temporary residence, move in with Simon for eight months), there is such a lack of causality in this "utopian" vision as to intimate the careless, unmotivated, ironic "realism" we associate with Woody Allen's representations of contemporary heterosexuality. The "paradise" of Simon's *ménage à quatre* is as ordinary as one could

This essay was written specifically for this volume and is published here for the first time by permission of the author.

208

imagine, as the novel consists largely of whimsical, everyday conversations between Simon and the women, scenes of cooking, concerns about housecleaning, and so on. Yet, despite its somewhat unexpected nature, this ignored novel reflects upon certain formal issues that rejoin Barthelme's important, characteristic concern with "living arrangements" in postmodern society—a concern that reveals his profound skepticism regarding the permanence of human relations matched by a desire for order and continuity in an environment where order and repression are equals.

As these preliminary comments indicate, *Paradise* may be regarded as a compilation of Barthelmean forms (the "Q and A" dialogue, the minimally absurdist dream, vignettes of domesticity cast within the fantasy framework of one man living with three beautiful women) that problematizes "form" itself, converting it into one of the novel's primary subjects. Charles Molesworth has commented that the "typical" Barthelme protagonist "values form over substance, but he is also often defeated by his inability to deal properly with form"; this condition, Molesworth argues, arises from a "longing for the fugitive" that signals "an existential ethos, an awareness that all human desire for permanency remains condemned to frustration, and that to institutionalize means to destroy, though *not* to do so is to face the same result."[1]

In *Paradise,* Simon's trade, on the one hand, and his current "lifestyle," on the other—which involves both the extrapolation and undermining of male fantasy—places him solidly in the middle of the dilemma Molesworth describes. As an architect, Simon values structure, repetition, symmetry, yet as "a tattered coat upon a stick," he recognizes that the preservation of form which architecture represents is analogous to the mummification of life, to death. Trapped within an entropic body ("Getting old, Simon. Not so limber, dear friend, time for the bone factory? The little blue van. Your hands are covered with pepperoni. Your knees predict your face. Your back stabs you, on the left side, twice a day. The belly's been discussed. The soul's shrinking to a microdot. We're ordering your rocking chair, size 42"), Simon has "settled for being a competent, sometimes inventive architect with a tragic sense of brick."[2] For him, the resistant medium of his art assumes tragic form because of its permanence—a form that will "stand" (unlike the body) the mock the transitoriness of human corporeality, but one that does not "live."

The paradox of his occupation bespeaks the paradox of his life, where the cyclical and formal features of existence—often perceived as the guarantors of continuance and renewal—have become, in their "institutionalization," the signs of paralysis and advancing death. Marriage, Simon says, is an "architectural problem": "If we could live in separate houses, and visit each other when we felt particularly gay" (p. 97), as if gaiety could be "housed" in any manner. Jazz, his favorite kind of music and, here, as throughout Barthelme's fiction, representing the grafting of improvisation and spontaneity to mercurial form, is important to Simon both because of its rich singularity (in individual musicians) and its historicity or genealogy as a national resource:

> He's listening to one of his three radios, this one a brutish black Proton with an outboard second speaker. The announcer is talking about drummers. "Cozy Cole comes straight out of Chick Webb," he says. Simon nods in agreement. "Big Sid Catlett. Zutty Singleton, Dave Tough. To go even further back, Baby Dodds. All this before we get to Krupa and Buddy Rich." Simon taxes his memory in an attempt to extract from it the names of ten additional drummers. Louis Bellson. Shelly Manne. Panama Francis. Jo Jones, of course. Kenny Clarke. Elvin Jones. Barrett Deems. Mel Lewis. Charlie Persip. Joe Morello. Next, twenty bass players. Our nation is rich in talent, he thinks. (p. 65)

Simon notes that individual architectural styles, when periodized, can be easily incorporated into larger cycles of fashion and design: "[The glass block] had been popular in the 30s, considered a design cliché in the 40s, 50s, 60s, and 70s, and presented itself again in the 80s, fresh as new dung" (p. 42). In each of these instances—marriage, jazz, architecture—Simon maintains an ironic attachment to form or structure—house, genealogy, architectural material. He seems to recognize that the phenomenological "content" of these forms—the gaiety of human relationships; the noise of jazz; the transparency of glass blocks—can only be manifested through some kind of formal arrangement or contextualization, but at the same time, he detests their reduction into mere cliché or formula when they are institutionalized, historicized. In the end, it may be "history" that Simon implicitly fears, or at least that sense of history that reveals itself when one has lived long enough: history as mere repetition where, in the domestic sphere (*the* realm of Barthelme's fiction), routine patterns of habit, form, and convention are all that survive in the long run. Yet, to reassert the paradox, this is a kind of history that Simon also desires, as his avid pursuit of jazz genealogies and naming would suggest—a history of successions, styles, and orders that can be labeled, variously, as "paternal" or "authorial."

In some sense, *Paradise* is the portrayal of a projected alternative to this paradoxical condition: it is fantasy given shape and substance, but the "materials" of the male fantasy that *Paradise* engages suborns its teleology, which includes bringing desire into the realm of domestic order and, thereby, potentially ensuring its continuance and renewal. For Simon and the three women he temporarily lives with (Anne, Dore, and Veronica), there is a kind of rough symmetry to the network of relationships they create as they casually establish the domestic rituals of cooking, conversing, intercourse. In the novel, the trio of women take on a number of stereotyped roles, in a sense, tripling the quantity of the fantasy and "perfecting" it: three mistresses, three graces, three wives. At first, to Simon, it seems (as the women put it to him) like "hog heaven," or the best of both worlds: both guilt-free sexuality and the opportunity to experience the multiplicity of desire, and the calming ordinariness of household order. Indeed, the melding of the libidinous and the symmetrical, desire and domesticity, is so pervasive in Simon's view that his descriptions of his roommates' eroticism often take on, in their variety, the qualities of repetition and banality we usually associate with the quotidian, not the exotic: "White underwear with golden skin. Acres and acres of it. Was it golden? Conventionally described as golden. The color of white birch stained with polyurethane. . . . Dressed women, half-dressed women, quarter-dressed women" (p. 80); or,

> Dore is brusque upon awakening, Anne cheerful as a zinnia. Veronica frequently comes to the breakfast table . . . pale with enthusiasm, for *Lohengrin* or oyster mushrooms or Pierre Trudeau. They're so lovely that his head whips around when one of them enters the room, exactly in the way one notices a strange woman in the crowd and can't avoid, can't physically avoid, loud and outrageous staring. My senses are being systematically dérégled, he thinks, forgive me, Rimbaud. Dore is relatively tall, Anne not so tall (but they are all tall), Veronica again the middle term. Breasts waver and dip and sway from side to side under t-shirts with messages so much of the moment that Simon doesn't understand a tenth of them . . . (p. 43)

In this portrayal of breakfast in paradise, the erotic is made symmetrical and sensuality made routine, banal, as contemporary commonplaces—incomprehensible to Simon because of "the generation gap"—mark for him both the women's voluptuousness and his own advancing age.

This conception of a male utopia, in essence, exists as a recapitulation of those orders and anxieties that, implicitly, and however temporarily, should have been transcended and subsumed in the figuration of paradise. When a major component of this male erotic fantasy—the multiple combinations and exchangeability of female sexual partners—is viewed for its repetitions and symmetries, when sensuality reminds Simon of his own anachronicity, then "paradise" must be regarded as a desire for order *over* desire, even if that architecture has the consequence of "instituting" fantasy. In other terms, the true end of male desire which *Paradise* reveals is not the entropy of libidinous expression but design, pattern, "author"-ity.

The "Q and A" conversations between Simon and his physician—conversations between men largely focused on the female subjects of "paradise"—and Simon's fairly ordinary dreams, reveal most clearly the lineaments of his provisional Eden. Alan Wilde (reading "Basil From Her Garden") has characterized the conversations, where "Q" is the physician and "A" is Simon, in this manner: "For Q transcendence implies an ordering of the world (as well as a removal from it), a ridding it . . . of everything that makes life uneven, unpredictable and recalcitrant, whereas for A it is a matter of coming to terms with guilt, anxiety, and thoughts of inadequacy *in the world,* as it is and as it offers itself to consciousness."³ However true this may be of the positions taken by Q and A at a certain point in the dialogue, as often happens in Barthelme's Socratic conversations, the interlocutors often exchange positions so that the different views exchanged by Simon and the physician, taken together, articulate the paradox of Simon's dilemma, which, again, is the authorial desire to give form to fantasy or to the world "as it offers itself to consciousness."

In their penultimate conversation, Q spins out a fantasy in which he imagines he is "in Pest Control." He visualizes himself in an immaculate outfit meticulously fumigating the house of "a young wife in jeans and a pink flannel shirt worn outside the jeans" (p. 190). In explicit detail, he imagines the orderly furnishings of the house and his role in maintaining its cleanliness. Finally, "the young wife escorts me to the door, and, in parting, pins a silver medal on my chest and kisses me on both cheeks. Pest Control!" (p. 191). If, as is often the case in Barthelme's stories, Q and A can be seen to make up the self-questioning aspects of a single identity—"a central speaking voice or subject, with a weak sense of identity, constantly seeking refuge in fantasy, word-play or self-pity, endlessly playing games of delusion which barely conceal a terror of failure, loss and disintegration"—then Q's Pest Control fantasy can stand as an extreme version of Simon's obsession with domestic order, even in the midst of paradise.⁴ What constitutes this order? Fastidious attention to detail and the arrangement of physical objects in the world ("I do the study, spraying behing the master's heavy desk on which there is an open copy of the *Columbia Encyclopedia,* he's been looking up the Seven Years War, 1756–63, yellow highlighting there, and behind the forty-five inch RCA television"); ritualistic movement through space ("I point the nozzle of the hose at the baseboards and begin to spray. I spray alongside the refrigerator, alongside the gas range, under the sink, and behind the kitchen table. Next, I move to the bathrooms, pumping and spraying"); logical supposition based upon empirical evidence ("Finally I spray the laundry room with its big white washer and dryer, and behind the folding table stacked with sheets and towels already folded. Who folds? I surmise that she folds. Unless one of the older children, pressed into service. In my experience they are unlikely to fold. Maybe the au pair"). Simon longs for the Newtonian world of the eighteenth-century rationalist, but as this vision and his dreams suggest, this is an order which both "includes" a barely repressed version of a clichéd male sexual fantasy ("pumping and spraying"; "a young wife"), along with the implicit forcefulness or violence that seems to inevitably accompany it ("The master bedroom requires just touches, like perfume behind the ears, short bursts in her closet which must avoid the two dozen pair of shoes there and in his closet which contains six to eight long guns in canvas cases").

In his dreams, Simon reiterates the dialectic of control and disorder, cleanliness and pestilence in situations where the "irrationality" of personal assault and the outbreak of violence form continual threats to the installments of dream and dreamer. After the women have left him (the novel is cast in the mode of recollection), Simon begins to dream

> with new intensity. He dreamed that he was a slave on a leper island, required to clean the latrines and pile up dirty-white shell for the roads, wheelbarrow after wheelbarrowful, then rake the shell smooth and jump up and down on it until it was packed solid. The lepers did not allow him to wear shoes, only white athletic socks, and he had a difficult time finding a pair that matched. The leper, a man who seemed to be named Al, embraced him repeatedly and tried repeatedly to spit in his mouth. (p. 9)

In this ironic "nightmare," Simon is a comic Sisyphus condemned to sanitize (make sane?) a world of physical decrepitude, and to be continually confronted with the passion and violence of that world's chief embodiment. Simon confesses to Q that he seems to be suffering from an abnormally distended succession of nightmares, most of which seems to involve his inability to put his clothes on correctly or (as in the dream of the leper island) to find his socks. He often has more than one dream a night and recalls them as seemingly unrelated scenes or vignettes: "In the first dream he was grabbed by three or four cops for firing a chrome .45 randomly in the street. . . . In the second dream he awoke sitting on a lounge in a hotel lobby wearing pants and shoes but bare-chested. . . . He couldn't find a shirt. His mother came out of a closet and asked him to be a little quieter" (176). In such dreams, where maintaining control is the central issue, Simon negotiates the "logic" of the anxieties that beset him, which is also the logic he uses in projecting "paradise." Living in a world where random or planned violence threatens to burst forth, and where Simon fears his bodily erosion, literally, loss of command over bodily functions (intimated by dreams about his inability to clothe himself), the solution—to project a daytime vision where domestic order and eros commingle, the wild energy and gaiety of the latter harnessed to the comforting rituals and institutions of the former—seems self-evident.

Yet what Simon's seemingly casual, unplanned living arrangements exclude or repress, and what his dreams clearly suggest is that the ends of "paradise"—the forestalling of the dissolution of (male) corporeal identity, the maintenance of rational order and control over one's "space," the fantasy of eternal potency—include the means of violence. Like all of Barthelme's fiction, *Paradise* is humorous, ironic, parodic; yet there is a strong undertow of violence in the novel that gives it a more "sociological" dimension, especially in its depictions of violence toward or the abuse of women. Dore bears a scar from a knife wound administered by a former husband who cut her in the act of " 'explaining himself' " (p. 19). For unknown reasons, a complete stranger—a Vietnam veteran—walks up to Veronica in a market and slaps her; moreover, Anne reveals to Simon that Veronica "got knocked around a lot as a kid" (p. 96), a series of events Veronica herself typifies: " 'He used a rolled up newspaper . . . what you'd use on a dog. Only he put his back into it, when I was twelve and thirteen and fourteen' " (p. 111). At one point, Simon witnesses two men beating up a female cop. Simon recounts, or projects, other scenes of violence amidst his recollections of paradise: his wife's Caesarean ("The doctor's name was Zernike and he had a pair of large dull-steel forceps inside the birth canal and was grappling for purchase. The instrument looked to Simon, who knew something of the weight and force of tools, capable of shattering the baby's head in an instant" [p. 32]); his own imagined vulnerability with the women ("Q: These women spread out before you like lotus blossoms. . . . A: More like anthills. Splendid, stinging anthills. . . . Q: The ants are plunging toothpicks into your scrotum, as it were. As they withdraw the toothpicks, little pieces of flesh like shreds of ground beef adhere to the toothpicks. A: Very much like that. How did you know?" [p. 30]). In all of these instances except the last (which is the projection, not the realization of an anxiety) the enforcers or victims of what might be termed "male cultural institutions" are behind the violence: fathers, husbands, ex-soldiers, and doctors seem to be responsible for the inflictions of force upon female subjects in *Paradise*.

Perhaps it might be argued, as Simon implicitly argues to himself, that he offers the three women a safe, if temporary, haven from a violent, hostile "reality"; in return, they offer him erotic renewal and good conversation. But as I have suggested, the very installment of "paradise"—its formation—rests upon the sanitizing or repression of those elements of force, violence, or culturally perceived eroticism that are part of its constitution, and which, fended off, return in dream and recollection. What is forestalled in paradise?

> Simon was a way-station, a bed-and-breakfast, a youth hostel, a staging area, a C-141 with the jumpers of the 82nd Airborne lined up at the door. There was no place in the world for these women that he loved, no good place. They could join the underemployed half-crazed demi-poor, or they could be wives, those were the choices. The universities offered another path but one they were not likely to take. The universities were something Simon believed in (of course! he was a beneficiary) but there was among the women an animus toward the process that would probably never be overcome, not only inpatience but a real loathing, whose source he did not really understand. (p. 168)

These beautiful, tall, "perfect" women are the products of desire, and their choices are limited to marginalization or institutionalization within the very cultural organizations (marriage, the university) that either articulate them as "permanent," domestic objects of desire or, as Simon realizes in the case of the university, are intimately linked to the militarism that is simply the most highly organized form of violence that has threatened them in other male cultural institutions: "Simon had opposed the Vietnam War in all possible ways short of self-immolation but could not deny that it was a war constructed by people who had labored through *Psychology I, II, III,* and *IV* and *Main Currents of Western Thought*" (p. 169). Simon's paradise is no haven at all from this bleak future for, as we have seen, it reproduces the women as the locus of cultural order, on the one hand, and organized eroticism (i.e., prostitution) on the other. Nor is it a haven for Simon himself, however joyful and gay its separate banalized moments, since the events that take place within paradise serve as a constant reminder of his mortality, the artificial (domesticated, structured) and, thus, impermanent form of his own identity. As in the case with architecture, Simon's paradise is ultimately an agonized quest for permanent form using imperfect, time-bound, culture-bound and culturally constrained materials.

In *Paradise,* Barthelme reveals most fully his acknowledgment that the modernist aesthetic quest for form matched with the attempt to maintain the identity of the artist is inflected with certain social and political consequences that comply with prevailing orders. Indeed, much of his fiction is an attempt to break down or break up the connection between form and identity that conservative modernism assumed to be innocent of these consequences. In *Paradise,* we see that he confronts the two dominating impulses of the modern (and, since he is careful to identify it in terms of gender in this novel, male) psyche: rational singularity of form and erotic multiplicity. These impulses can only be "managed" through banalization or force threatening to become violent, specifically in *Paradise,* violence toward women largely promulgated through social agency. Here, the preservation of male identity or the defense against anxieties about its dissolution seems to demand the continuance of the status quo disguised as erotic festival, vacation from marriage. In *Paradise,* what might be nostalgically termed man's individual freedom is played out within the confinements of the institutional orders that dictate both the nature of desire and legitimate its often violent deployments. As Vincent Pecora has argued, the autonomous self in modernist narrative, seeking absolute freedom from all social and cultural orders, ends up reduplicating them as part of "the nature of identity": "the discourse of the autonomous individual . . . is historically made possible by the reifications of consciousness produced in a capitalist market economy; but the unerring tendency of that discourse, even in its self-critical attempts to break through the mystifications circumscribing it, is a reproduction within consciousness of the division and organization of economic life that only increases its susceptibility to manipulation and control by monopolistic or authoritarian administration."[5] Thus Simon, in his recounting, naively reinstitutes domestic order in the household even as he indulges in the fantasy of sexual freedom in a realm dominated, if only numerically, by women. As much as Barthelme's *oeuvre* resists and critiques this state of affairs, it also—in its fascination with material productions, its concern with the breakdown or continuance of identity, and its paradoxically continuous use and deconstruction of received generic forms—partakes of it.

Paradise, then, stands as Barthelme's most extensive reflection on the state of art and the artist in postmodern culture. It is a book about mortality: not one that, as do the lines from Stevens' "Sunday Morning," celebrate the permanent impermanence of life as our only parousia, but one that limns the conditions of our mortal existence as historical beings. The artist seeks to escape these conditions, but his art remakes them, even, and especially, when it comes to utopias. Barthelme's distinctly antiutopian sky is not indifferent—for that would be to attribute to it something beyond ourselves—but it is a dividing blue, in that, for him, what occurs "down here" is of our own doing, the extension of our own desire for order and control. With characteristic irony, he asks in *Paradise,* "but what else could we do, given our models of heaven"?

Notes

1. Charles Molesworth, *Donald Barthelme's Fiction: The Ironist Saved from Drowning* (Columbia: University of Missouri Press, 1982), 24, 21.

2. Donald Barthelme, *Paradise* (New York: Putnam's, 1986), 59, 58; hereafter cited in the text.

3. Alan Wilde, *Middle Grounds: Studies in Contemporary American Fiction* (Philadelphia: University of Pennsylvania Press, 1987), 164.

4. Maurice Couturier and Regis Durand, *Donald Barthelme* (New York: Methuen, 1982), 28–29.

5. Vincent Pecora, *Self and Form in Modern Narrative* (Baltimore: Johns Hopkins University Press, 1989), 15.

Index

♦

DATE DUE

GAYLORD			PRINTED IN U.S.A.